# Critical Studies in Risk and Uncertainty

Palgrave's *Critical Studies in Risk and Uncertainty* series publishes monographs, edited volumes and Palgrave Pivots that capture and analyse how societies, organisations, groups and individuals experience and confront uncertain futures.

This series will provide a multidisciplinary home to consolidate this dynamic and growing academic field, bringing together and representing the state of the art on various topics within the broader domain of critical studies of risk and uncertainty. Moreover, the series is sensitive to the broader political, structural and socio-cultural conditions in which particular approaches to complexity and uncertainty become legitimated ahead of others.

It provides cutting edge theoretical and empirical, as well as established and emerging methodological contributions, and welcomes projects on risk, trust, hope, intuition, emotions and faith. Explorations into the institutionalisation of approaches to uncertainty within regulatory and other governmental regimes are also of interest.

Jens O. Zinn · Manuel Schulz

# A New Phenomenology of Risk and Uncertainty

## Reflexive and Embodied Modes of Reasoning

palgrave
macmillan

Jens O. Zinn
School of Social and Political Sciences
University of Melbourne
Parkville, VIC, Australia

Manuel Schulz
Husserl Archive
University of Cologne
Cologne, Nordrhein-Westfalen, Germany

ISSN 2523-7268 ISSN 2523-7276 (electronic)
Critical Studies in Risk and Uncertainty
ISBN 978-981-95-7404-9 ISBN 978-981-95-7405-6 (eBook)
https://doi.org/10.1007/978-981-95-7405-6



Cover illustration: rhyman007

This Palgrave Macmillan imprint is published by the registered company Springer Nature Singapore Pte Ltd.
The registered company address is: 152 Beach Road, #21-01/04 Gateway East, Singapore 189721, Singapore

If disposing of this product, please recycle the paper.

# Preface I

This book was motivated by my dissatisfaction with the state of risk studies in sociology. Several mainstream theories, such as the cultural symbolic approach and the risk society theory, coexisted alongside Foucauldian scholars' focus on governmentality and biopolitics. A smaller number of functionalists referred to modern systems theory. The edgework perspective on voluntary risk-taking complemented the mix, but it was not meant to serve as a broader approach to risk or risk-taking. These approaches were often described in introductions to risk studies, but there seemed to be little progress beyond these mainstream approaches (Arnoldi, 2009; Boyne, 2003; Lupton, 1999, 2013a; Zinn, 2008b).

More than two decades ago, while working with the Social Contexts and Responses to Risk network (SCARR) at the University of Kent in Canterbury, I wondered whether it was possible to advance the debate about risk within sociology by initiating two research networks: one with the European Sociological Association (2005) and another with the International Sociological Association (2006). At the time, I felt that "Risk Sociology" would be too narrow a name for these groups since the concept of risk remained contested. As a calculative mode for navigating uncertainty, risk was only one among many other ways people rely on when engaging with hazards, threats, or dangers. Therefore, I suggested that the groups have both "risk" and "uncertainty" in their title to maintain a broader perspective. This resulted in the name "Sociology of Risk and Uncertainty" (SoRU).

At the time, I believed there was an urgent need to better understand people's everyday engagement with risk and uncertainty, which is not sufficiently addressed by mainstream, primarily macro-sociological approaches to risk. It would be beneficial to systematize the growing body of small-scale qualitative research that carefully describes how people engage with and manage risk in their everyday lives. Indeed, this research often establishes connections to existing sociological macro theories of risk. Furthermore, other sociological approaches, such as Bourdieu's theory of practice, have been utilized, as patterns of social inequality have been surprisingly underexplored within socio-cultural approaches to risk.

Some central ideas I developed in those early days while working at the University of Kent. I would walk through the corridors to play with ideas and often have chats with Andy Alaszewski to focus my thoughts. He was always open to brainstorming, full of creative insights himself. For him, working in health studies, the clinical and rational approach to risk was very dominant, as it is in risk analysis more broadly. I expressed my understanding of such perspectives, contrasting them with what is often considered "irrational" or at least non-rational approaches, such as hope, faith, and ideology, which remain crucial for many people when facing risk and uncertainty. However, this profoundly modern distinction characterizing occidental rationalization, though dominant in the debate, overlooks the much more common ways of engaging with risk in everyday life. These include trust, which has become a critical topic in risk communication research, as well as intuition and emotion. I spontaneously referred to these as "in-between" since they are, in my view, neither entirely rational nor "irrational" or non-rational, but reasonable. While I was still contemplating how to develop these ideas in detail, Andy encouraged me to put them down on paper. When I succeeded, the article was published in 2008 as "Heading into the unknown—Everyday strategies for managing risk and uncertainty," and it became one of the most cited articles in the international journal Health, Risk, and Society for years to come.

Over the following years, I presented these ideas both nationally and internationally, and I was asked to revisit the original work in a review article. In Between and Other Reasonable Ways to Deal with Risk and Uncertainty (Zinn, 2016) discussed some original concepts and clarified what had remained implicit in the original article, such as the need to understand all modes or strategies as reasonable ways to manage risk and uncertainty successfully. I also believed it was important to adhere to the dominant discourse of rationality in modern societies rather than deconstruct it. This approach enabled us to engage with mainstream worldviews and paradigms in economics and risk analysis, demonstrating that they can be unreasonable under specific conditions (such as excess and complex information). In contrast, other allegedly irrational approaches (e.g., the recognition heuristic, intuition) might sometimes prove superior. In this way, I aimed to connect the available discourses within society to a critical understanding of how people in everyday life (as well as experts) engage with risk and uncertainty. I found substantial support for my framework beyond the growing body of qualitative studies in the social sciences, particularly in economics, psychology, and risk analysis, which are central to interdisciplinary risk studies.

I then began to make the framework useful for the underdeveloped field of risk-taking and used a Friedrich-Wilhelm Bessel award from the Alexander von Humboldt Foundation in 2015 to begin a book manuscript. I was only able to finish it two years later, after I had completed an EU Marie Skłodowska-Curie Fellowship at the Corpus Approaches to Social Sciences (CASS) research center at Lancaster University, during which I turned to another major research interest of mine—the two and a half years of research on the discourse semantic changes of risk in the London Times (1785-2009) allowed me to identify the forces that shaped public understanding and usage of risk in Britain. Consequently, I have dived deeper into the domains of the history of ideas (Koselleck, 1985) and corpus linguistics (McEnery, 2019) and tried to connect these to substantial institutional changes and significant historical events, but was distracted from the framework of the modes of navigating risk and uncertainty for quite a while.

I felt that these modes still required further development to provide them with a better rooting in phenomenology, which I thought would be the place to position them. Alfred Schütz's work (1943, 1972, 2013) on the life-world seemed to have some affinity, but did not fit as good as I had in mind. Inspired by Latour's book *"We Have Never Been Modern"* (1993), I wanted to find a way to better integrate the cognitive, emotional and embodied aspects of people's approaches to risk and uncertainty. This topic has already been extensively discussed in feminist scholarship, notably by Donna Haraway (1991), who strongly opposes modernist binary thinking.

At this point, the COVID-19 crisis created a fortunate coincidence, as most conferences were held remotely during that time. This format enabled me to participate in many more sessions than usual. In one session, Manuel Schulz presented on the New Phenomenology of Hermann Schmitz (2002, 2017a, 2019a; Schmitz, Müllan, & Slaby, 2011), and I sensed that this approach might help fill the conceptual gap. However, it was still not entirely clear to me to what extent New Phenomenology could extend my framework into new domains of theorizing and make sense of empirically observable phenomena.

We began to explore the scope of our collaboration with the first publication project, *Rationales of Risk and Uncertainty and Their Epistemological Foundation in New Phenomenology* (Schulz & Zinn, 2023), which opened up further perspectives for theorizing. As is common with innovative ideas positioned at the intersection of different disciplines, it was initially challenging to find the right venue for publication. Social theory journals considered it too risk-centered, while risk analysis journals deemed it too theoretical. Ultimately, we chose the *Journal of Risk Research*, which is more receptive than others to unconventional and innovative work at the boundaries of disciplines such as sociology and philosophy.

With the foundations clarified, numerous ideas for further conceptual developments emerged from the original article. In particular, the need to better understand the dynamics and institutional shifts across different modes has not yet been adequately addressed. This resulted in another publication: *Rationalization, Enchantment, and Subjectivation—Lessons for Risk communication from a New Phenomenology of Everyday Reasoning* (Zinn & Schulz, 2024). Indeed, the connection to risk communication was a crucial point of origin for further developing conceptual work and highlighting the framework's power. It increasingly moved beyond the relatively narrow perspective on risk communication towards a broader understanding of societal communication of risk and uncertainty as a process involving diverse stakeholders, social institutions, and milieus.

With this book, we have further advanced towards my original project, a phenomenology of risk and uncertainty. Rather than being limited to people's senses and embodied experiences of risk and uncertainty, the conceptual work demonstrated its ability to connect everyday life to broader institutional developments, thereby simultaneously opening new research prospects.

The manuscript benefited from valuable feedback provided by the co-editors of the book series Critical Studies in Risk and Uncertainty-Anna Olofsson and Patrick Brown-as well as from anonymous reviewers, which helped to strengthen the final manuscript. I am also deeply grateful to the Hanse Institute for Advanced Study in Delmenhorst, Germany for awarding me a research fellowship in 2023-24, which enabled me to further develop and complete this book manuscript. I enjoyed the vibrant interdisciplinary research culture and the constructive debates with the other fellows at the HWK and in particular with the Head of Society, Wolfgang Stenzel, and the Director Prof. Kerstin Schill.

Melbourne, Australia Jens O. Zinn
July 2025

# Preface II

The investigation of risk and uncertainty from a neo-phenomenological perspective, substantiated by a wide range of empirical research, is the aim of this book, and it is strongly related to my personal academic development. In the summer of 2008, while studying sociology in Marburg (Germany), I decided to change my minor subject from psychology to economics—a decision which turned out to be highly formative for my later academic interests. In September that year, Lehman Brothers collapsed—an event that marked the initial point of the long-standing global financial crisis that began in 2008 and kept the world on tenterhooks for years. Only four weeks after this economically upsetting event, I was sitting in the lecture hall, listening to the introduction to macroeconomics. There, we were presented with theories of an ideal model world, while outside the auditorium, the worldwide financial markets and the entire global economy moved along the edge of collapse. Contrary to all the theoretical economic modeling with its rational assumptions, a seemingly small event of entrepreneurial mismanagement—the collapse of a single bank—unleashed a highly contagious dynamic that provoked international economic, political, and social turmoil.

For me, as a nascent sociologist, it was impressive to observe how, among other aspects, an overemphasis on "pure" rationality, which had always been reaffirmed, especially regarding financial markets (e.g., Fama 1970), can turn into a devastating disaster. The shift of the crisis from housing assets in the United States to a worldwide banking crisis and, ultimately, a public debt crisis in Europe over the upcoming years has caught my sociological interest. I was overwhelmed not only by the economic dimension of this event, but at least as much by the social and political consequences. Hence, I focused on the credit system and the broader field of monetary policy for a couple of years. Finally, in the process of writing my diploma thesis (Schulz, 2016), I developed (rather unintentionally) a time-theoretical perspective on the power relation between the political field and financial markets. Through this detour, I discovered the entire field of temporality research, which is situated at the intersections of sociology, cultural studies, history, and political economy. The core insight of these studies is that the forms in which societies conceive of the phenomenon of temporality have historically shifted substantially, and so have the institutional frames of societal organization (e.g., Assmann, 2013; Koselleck, 1985; Linder, 1971; Negt, 1988; H. Rosa, 2013). At the same time, I came into contact with the wide range of studies that emphasize the temporal dimension of financial markets (Esposito, 2018; Hope, 2011; e.g., K. Knorr-Cetina & Preda, 2007; Langenohl, 2018; Vogl, 2014).

Motivated by the intention to better understand how a credit-driven monetary system shapes subjective and collective time-apperception, I decided to study the phenomenon of temporality more intensely for several years. Encouragingly, I was able to arouse the interest of Hartmut Rosa for this project and completed a Ph.D. under his supervision from 2017 to 2022 at the Department of Sociology in Jena, Germany (Schulz, 2024). While conducting this research project, I came across the phenomenology of bodiliness, or corporeality ("Leiblichkeit" in German), and a bit later the New Phenomenology of Hermann Schmitz. This approach seemed to me so fascinating that I involuntarily started to dig increasingly deeper into Schmitz's thinking, and finally, I found myself succeeding in changing the focus of my dissertation. Ultimately, it was no longer situated within the context of financial markets and credit theory, but rather at the intersection of social theory and neo-phenomenological epistemology. Finally, this led to my Ph.D. being mentored by Michael Großheim, the holder of the Hermann Schmitz Endowed Chair, who thankfully accompanied my project as a second reviewer.

Considering that my Ph.D. was gratifyingly funded by the German Research Foundation (Studienstiftung des Deutschen Volkes), I not only had the opportunity to undertake a research stay at the London School of Economics in 2018, but also to present my neo-phenomenological insights at various international conferences. At one of these events, I was fortunate to meet Jens O. Zinn in 2021, and we embarked on a highly fruitful academic dialogue, the most recent result of which is this book. Given that I originally came from the field of economic sociology, the aspect of risk and uncertainty, which he is an international expert in, immediately piqued my interest. Due to this, the collaboration with him presented a promising opportunity for me, on the one hand, to bring back my neo-phenomenologically skilled but rather epistemological thinking to more sociological issues. On the other, it aligns with my aim to gradually return to my original interest in economic questions. Motivated by this personal research agenda, I moved to the University of Cologne in March 2024 and have been working on a critical economic phenomenology at the Husserl Archive there ever since. In that sense, this book can be seen as a step towards this research perspective.

Cologne, Germany — Manuel Schulz
June 2025

# Contents

# List of Figures

# 1
# Introduction

There is little doubt that managing risk and uncertainty is an everyday human activity. It is such a fundamental part of human existence that the opposite seems only thinkable as a caricature, like the central character of Ivan Goncharov's book "Oblomov" (1915 [1859]), who is incapable of making important decisions or undertaking significant activities and therefore hardly ever leaves his home or even his bed. Such an attitude contrasts with the worldview characterizing modern societies, which developed through a long period of fundamental social change from approximately the seventeenth century onwards, increasingly replacing the divinely legitimized feudal world order (Giddens, 1990). The contestation of the historically established social order during the upcoming Western Enlightenment was reinforced by the collective experience of the French Revolution at the end of the eighteenth century. As Reinhart Koselleck (1985) argued in his famous study, *Futures Past*, provoked by the French Revolution, a significant shift in time perception occurred. Due to the widening gap between the space of experience and the horizon of expectation, the not-yet-existing, both individually and collectively, became an object of techniques for governing social processes. Although, of course, humankind had been exposed to an unknown



J. O. Zinn and M. Schulz, *A New Phenomenology of Risk and Uncertainty*, Critical Studies in Risk and Uncertainty, https://doi.org/10.1007/978-981-95-7405-6_1

future before, the end of a religiously legitimized eternal social order provoked a shift in the understanding of collective and individual relations to the past, present, and future. In other words, the human capacity to imagine emerging social realities became politically relevant.

Risk management, in this sense of actively engaging with an unknown future, can be seen as a characteristic of modern society—a society "that is future-oriented, which sees the future precisely as a territory to be conquered or colonized" (Giddens, 1999). However, this experience of temporal openness has always been ambivalent. It sparked an emancipatory consciousness of the manageability of the present and future socio-economic path, but coincided with an awareness of one's vulnerability in a historically contingent world.

This shift in collective time perception, along with other aspects, was accompanied by a promising understanding of self-and world relations. As the future was perceived as shapeable, it became an object of human desires and efforts for change. Combined with the growing understanding of natural laws resulting from advances in empirical science, this process reinforced the emerging notion of the human subject as autonomous and capable of harnessing both inner and outer nature. With the increasing desire to control the future, the prevention, control, avoidance, and management of potential harm moved centre stage. Such harm may be caused externally by floods, earthquakes, and epidemics. Alternatively, one might voluntarily expose oneself to harm for personal gain or advantage, as seen among entrepreneurs, speculators, or gamblers. Risk-taking can also stem from a desire to explore the unknown, as demonstrated by modern adventurers and colonizers. Regardless of motivation, two strongly connected aspects are central to the modern worldview: a "rational" approach to the world and the notion of "calculability." Risk, as we will argue, is an expression of the modern approach to addressing potential harm, guided by empirical experience and utilizing numerical abstractions and rational thinking. The two essential aspects, rationality and calculability, have been famously described by Max Weber, who stated that the growing "intellectualization and rationalization" of modernization is fundamentally characterized by "*the knowledge or belief that … there are no mysterious incalculable forces that come into play, but rather that one can, in principle, master all things by calculation.*" Historically, the "quantificational spirit" (Power, 2004, p. 766) can be traced back to the mid-thirteenth century and, driven by new technologies of measurement and the notion of order and system, has become increasingly relevant over the following centuries (Crosby, 1997; Hacking, 1975; Heilbron, 1990). Hence, as Weber emphasized, the world has gradually been disenchanted by quantitative calculation and the forms of rational decision-making that it has offered. "*One need no longer has recourse to magical means in order to master or implore the spirits, as did the savage, for whom such mysterious powers existed. Technical means and calculations perform the service*" (1948, p. 139). Remarkably, Weber already emphasized that rationalization and intellectualization do not mean "*an increased and general knowledge of the conditions under which one lives*" (ibid.) but rather reflect a fundamental change in attitude towards the future.

This is an important insight, as the "modern dream" should become the belief that, through the process of rationalization, unmanageable contingency—due to techniques of calculation—would irresistibly turn into manageable uncertainty and safety. This viewpoint has been held by scholars such as Talcott Parsons (1980), who saw this development as, if not linear, at least unidirectional. The assumption was that with advanced scientific knowledge, social problems would be increasingly managed more effectively, resulting in improved health, wealth, and well-being, ultimately leading to a better life for everyone. However, this dream has only partly been fulfilled (Bonß, 1995). As Weber already mentioned, it is questionable whether an entirely rationalized world leads to a better society or turns into an alienating iron cage. This critique was famously elaborated and sharpened by Horkheimer and Adorno some decades later, with a special focus on the dangers of epistemological reductionism in positivist research (Horkheimer & Adorno, 2002 [1947]).

A crucial aspect of the underlying problem is that rationalization and calculability require a numerical reduction of complexity, an idea that Michael Power (2004, p. 774) terms the "*dream of a final and ultimate commensurability.*" This can be demonstrated by a historical example, such as a deeply private yet no less risky decision: who to marry or with whom to establish a family. Engaging in a long-term commitment with the hope of a fulfilling relationship is a complex, high-risk decision. During a time of growing enthusiasm for modern rationalization, Benjamin Franklin wrote to his nephew, Jonathan Williams, in 1779, offering advice on making a sensible decision about marriage. "*If you doubt, set down all the Reasons, pro & con, in opposite Columns on a Sheet of Paper, and when you have considered them two or three Days, perform an Operation similar to that in some question of Algebra; observe what Reasons or Motives in each Column are equal in weight, one to one, one to two, two to three of the like; and when you have struck out from both Sides all the Equalities, you will see in which Column, remains the Balance. .... This kind of Moral Algebra I have often practiced in important & dubious Concerns; and tho' it cannot be mathematically exact; I have found it extremely useful.— By the Way, if you do not learn it, I apprehend you will never be married* ..." (Zinn, 2020, p. 256). One might wonder whether, nowadays, when intimate relationships are often framed in terms of romantic love, such advice might alienate people. However, such a strategy highlights an important question: when and how to decide about issues when there is very little experience-based knowledge available.

As this problem illustrates, dealing with risk is essentially a challenge that encompasses two dimensions: epistemological and temporal. Epistemologically, any form of calculative rationalization necessitates a transformation of quality into quantity, relying on trustworthy institutions of classification and objectivation (Porter, 1995). In addition to this transformation of the phenomenon being addressed into a calculable format, temporality is crucial when framing the world in terms of risk; this entails viewing it from the perspective of an emerging reality that is not yet known. Although empirically based, from the sixteenth century onwards, science has provided vast knowledge to control the world in general, the uncertainty of the future has remained a problematic issue. Of course, numerically calculated probabilities serve as extremely valuable tools to inform activities at both the individual and collective levels. However, there remains a lack of information about the specific case that a decision concerns. For instance, even when statistics indicate that we can expect a very low rate of unintended side effects or a low probability of harm, such calculations reveal little about the outcomes of a specific action (e.g., a 20-percent likelihood of rain does not tell us whether we will get wet). In other words, the dimension of numeric representation does not achieve a comprehensive depiction of the world's complexity. A persistent epistemological and temporal residue of uncertainty remains. This may relate to the fact that the assumption that Enlightenment inevitably leads to the secularization of the world and a significant decrease in religion and "superstition," as proposed by Max Weber and other thinkers such as Karl Marx and Émile Durkheim, remains a contested notion. Contrary to their expectations, religion remains strong, while religiosity has diversified and taken on new and different forms beyond the large, institutionalized churches (Eller, 2010). Their ongoing relevance may suggest that belief, faith, and (religious and magical) rituals are valuable resources that many people turn to, even in modern societies, to navigate the uncertain and unknowable future and find meaning in their lives. There is a clear connection between religiosity and the lack of existential social security (Stolz, 2020, p. 285). Thus, belief remains an essential resource for navigating uncertainty, providing comprehensive meaning about the world and one's place in it.

Besides the epistemological problem of transforming phenomena into numeric representations and the temporal issue of contingency, another reason for the continued relevance of belief may be that, during modernization, the growth of knowledge, as Matthias Gross (2022) suggested, did not reduce but rather increased non-knowledge and ignorance. Referring to Blaise Pascal (1655), Gross suggested that "growth in knowledge will inevitably bring about a concomitant growth in ignorance… whenever knowledge grows, so too does ignorance." Indeed, some debate persists regarding whether ignorance grows more slowly or faster than knowledge (2022, p. 309). It is worth noting that this ignorance is, on the one hand, a result of the emergence of new questions arising from the knowledge just gained, but on the other hand, as we will argue, it is also the outcome of the transformation of subjective experience into abstract, objectified knowledge, and thus from quality to quantity.

There is also a critical built-in ambivalence in the modern desire to find out and control the future. It includes preventing undesired developments and events, as well as the need to expose oneself to risk and uncertainty to learn about the world and improve social conditions

(Wildavsky, 1988). Not that the early adventurers exposed themselves to high risks carelessly. Instead, they prepared as well as they could to face the unknown. As Fridtjof Nansen (1926), the famous Arctic explorer, once elaborated this attitude:

> The spirit of adventure… "urges mankind forward on the way towards knowledge … For most of us ordinary people, life is a voyage from harbor to harbor, along a fairly safe coast. We run no great risks... But what about the things worth doing, the achievements, the aims to live and die for? You have to take risks and cannot allow yourself to be frightened by them when you are convinced that you are following the right course. Nothing worth having in life is ever attained without taking risks. But they should be in reasonable proportion to the results which you hope to attain by your enterprise, and should not merely depend on luck, giving your ability to overcome the risks no chance of coming into play. … Success can give you no real satisfaction if it depends on mere accident."

Still in the present, risky uncertainties are considered not only necessary but a desired part of one's life, which makes the difference to what Nansen considers a "*voyage from harbor to harbor, along a fairly safe coast.*" The safe, eventless trotting within institutional and physical boundaries, in contrast to a valued life that has meaning and might escape boredom (Heidegger, 1995), was not fully considered in Max Weber's concern about a growing tendency towards instrumental rational living dominated by bureaucratic sovereignty (Weber, 1978). Weber suggested that in modern societies, individuals are often trapped in systems and organizations that operate on the principles of efficiency, rationality, and control, building pressure on us to comply with formal and impersonal rules. With such regulations becoming more substantial and more widespread, people would become increasingly alienated from themselves and others (Weber et al., 1930). As we will argue, this alienation is increasing to the degree that a gap is widening between the subjective experience of daily life and the technologically advanced instruments of self- and world-control. As will be shown, the latter is created through our capacity for reflexive thinking and is institutionalized by practical routines and specialized discourses.

However, something else remains that gives meaning to people's lives and provides them with the feeling that they have a life worth living. Deborah Lupton and John Tulloch titled one of their articles from a research project on people's engagement with risk "*Life would be pretty dull without risk*" (2002), while the French philosopher Anne Dufourmantelle (2011) even suggested that only when life is put at stake from time to time, we would feel "fully alive." In this vein, Stephen Lyng (1990, 2005a) developed the concept of *edgework* to describe individuals who take high risks with the possibility of fatal outcomes, driven by the thrill and adrenaline rush that accompany such behavior. They would experience feelings of self-worth when they successfully took risks and extended their human boundaries. For example, Philippe Petit's 1974 illegal high-wire walk between the Twin Towers of New York's World Trade Center is legendary (Petit, 2003). However, according to Lyng (1990, 2005a), people from all walks of life can engage in edgework through activities such as ice climbing, high-altitude climbing, skydiving, free climbing, BASE jumping, and others. Similar to Lyng, who suggested that people engage in *edgework* in response to experiences of alienation in the modern world, Hartmut Rosa emphasized the human need for positive feelings of connection to the world. In the "*sociology of our relationship to the world*" (Rosa, 2019), he introduced the notion of "resonance" to characterize situations when people feel themselves vibrantly in relation to themselves and the world. For Rosa, alienation occurs when people seeking experiences of resonance do not find circumstances under which this basic need can be satisfied. From this perspective, the phenomenon of voluntarily engaging in life-threatening risks emerges as a symptom of a widely alienated society, one that does not allow people to find these resonant experiences in their everyday lives. In sum, one should be cautious about assuming that the voluntary exposure to life-threatening situations, as observed in some individual cases, constitutes an anthropological feature.

The social engagement with risk, whether at the individual or institutional level, is an ambivalent enterprise in which neither complete control nor unmanageable uncertainty seems desirable. However, as Aaron Wildavsky proposed, social advancement requires a level of uncertainty that allows one to learn through trial and error (Wildavsky, 1989).

Moreover, as emphasized in economic sociology, capitalist and, in particular, financialized societies require an open future that can serve as a cumulative resource for commodification, enabled by imaginative power (Beckert, 2016; Hope, 2020; Leyshon & Thrift, 2007). For instance, large insurance companies, such as *Bayerische Rückversicherung* (1987, p. 7), have suggested that a guarantee of permanent and continuing security leads to stagnation (Bonß, 1995, p. 39).

Specifically, on the individual level, the conditions for learning under risk and uncertainty vary systematically. There are structural differences among the people who are exposed to and take risks. In contrast to celebrated risk-taking, for many people, everyday life is a struggle, a balancing act among various risks and uncertainties. Taking risks mainly means taking risks that seem less dangerous than others. Adverse outcomes are subjectively less likely when taking a risk, or there is little choice other than to expose oneself to the possibility of harm (Zinn, 2020). Such "*center work*" (Parker & Stanworth, 2005) is characterized by people trying to conform to social expectations. It aims to achieve a life similar to the imagined "*safe voyage*" described by Fridtjof Nansen. Coping with the risks and uncertainties of everyday life, as well as managing recurring disasters, is a common experience. The need to take risks as part of everyday risk mitigation strategies indeed falls disproportionately on particular strata of society. A good example are the poor family members looking for work during the COVID-19 pandemic, not because they are misinformed or negligent of the dangers of the virus, but because they did not see an alternative to secure their family's survival other than taking the risk of infection (Egger et al., 2023; Wright et al., 2020).

Early poverty studies (Mayhew, 1861) from the nineteenth century have already argued that the living conditions of the working class would lead to an attitude and behavior characterized as "moral degeneration," involving desperate and frivolous behaviors such as gambling and betting. In this perspective, it was less the low income but the moral impact on the population that raised concerns. Social political efforts aimed at improving living conditions by introducing poverty legislation and social insurance (e.g., Bismarck in Germany and Beveridge in the UK, Evers & Nowotny, 1987), while gambling became a profitable industry and the lottery an invitation to dream about a better life after winning the jackpot (Beckert & Lutter, 2012; Lutter, 2010). Interestingly, in this context, Urs Stäheli (2007, pp. 37 ff.) points out that, from the nineteenth century onward, it was a discursive achievement to distinguish gambling from financial speculation. Following Stäheli, it required significant semantic work to develop the imagination—that we will later characterize as enchantment—that there are not simply negligent and self-interested gamblers at work in financial markets, but highly professionalized actors who handle risks that are supposedly economically meaningful.

In summary, one might respond to external threats or take risks deliberately to achieve what one desires. Being human is closely connected to engaging in risky uncertainties in one way or another. This seems too obvious to mention, but how this experience of engagement with risk and uncertainty is understood, as well as the preferred ways of engaging with it, differ historically and vary depending on the social domain and individual resources. Considering the perspective offered, risk itself is a specific modern form of dealing with the unknown, grounded in notions of calculability and rationalization. It is moreover deeply connected with the human capacity for imagination.

When considering risk, it becomes clear that risks are pervasive, and how we manage them is both a routine practice and an exceptional, reflexive activity. However, our attitudes towards risk and uncertainty can vary significantly depending on factors such as whether we are taking risks voluntarily, are exposed to risks imposed by others, or respond to our living conditions (Starr, 1969). As we will show, the concept of risk refers phenomenologically to the subjective experience of various forms of threat, and it is a more or less elaborated and quantified activity due to reflexive thinking.

Moreover, modern societies have differentiated systems of knowledge production, which provide expert advice and guidance on how to navigate risks rationally. There is expertise in minimizing risks (e.g., eating more vegetables and exercising regularly to prevent becoming overweight and developing high blood pressure) and determining which risks are worth taking (e.g., investing in stock market portfolios). Such information or social marketing strategies are often underpinned by scientific knowledge and professional experience, guiding us through everyday life and informing our decisions. Specific institutions, such as insurance, have developed to compensate financially for experienced loss or harm, but also exploit our worries to generate profit. Indeed, the healthcare system provides means for healing and thereby follows medical knowledge. Still, we might be concerned about going to the best hospital and being treated by the best doctors if we have the opportunity. There are also legal regulations that govern the social management of risk, such as the social evaluation and management of technological and security risks.

Institutional guidance, however, is only one of the sources people refer to when managing risks. In a world of increasingly complex knowledge, there might also be competing expert advice or varying quality of expertise provided by institutions (e.g., hospitals, research institutions, ministers, consumer organizations). Thus, one must decide which or whose expertise to follow. Ultimately, it is personal experiences and convictions that are crucial for engaging with risk in everyday life.

During the COVID-19 crisis, a vaccine became available to help curb the spread of the virus. However, to the astonishment of health experts in many countries, it proved difficult to motivate a large proportion of the population to vaccinate, which was considered necessary to protect the population (reaching herd immunity and reducing the proportion of people developing severe symptoms). Neither large-scale campaigns nor epidemiological arguments helped. Instead, many of the refusers turned to conspiracy theories. They questioned the scientific advice of experts and the institutions they represent (for example, the followers of the then-President Donald Trump in the US or the "Querdenker" movement in Germany[1]). Nevertheless, not only were populists and coronavirus deniers critical of vaccination. People prioritizing liberal values also campaigned against (compulsory) vaccination. They emphasized citizens' free will in democratic societies and valued this principle above potential harm to others (Denu et al., 2022). Indeed, the new method of vaccine production and the accelerated approval procedures

---

[1] *Querdenker* or literally "lateral thinkers" refers in contemporary Germany to a protest movement that arose during the COVID-19 pandemic. While the word once had a positive meaning of unconventional or creative thinking, it is now widely associated with opponents of public health measures, conspiracy theorists, and far-right actors.

have provoked skepticism and concern, which seem, at least to some people, justified.

Many would consider vaccine resistance unreasonable or irrational. In contrast, they might consider aid workers or doctors who risk their lives in the service of good to be more laudable, even when it might be an open question whether they are more rational in their judgments about the risks they expose themselves to. For example, with aid work having become much more dangerous with growing numbers of aid workers being killed, kidnapped, or wounded from the 1990s onwards (AWSD, 2023), volunteers had to consider the reality of the risks and uncertainties they expose themselves to during a mission. There is a tendency to overestimate their employer's ability to rescue them in case of an imminent emergency (Roth, 2015a). Besides trusting their employer, some are hoping or praying that they will be fine. Another important aspect is the commitment they feel towards their work. Similar patterns have been observed among healthcare workers who volunteered during the 2014–16 Ebola outbreak in West Africa. High professionalism is a key element, but is often accompanied by trust, hope, or faith to manage cognitively and emotionally the dangers of a mission such as fighting Ebola in Africa, a disease that repeatedly claims the lives of volunteers (Gee & Skovdal, 2017).

There are endless examples of how people engage with risk and uncertainty for various reasons. Such examples indicate crucial dimensions and ways in which risks and uncertainties are managed and transformed in everyday life. These include personal experiences, expert advice, and a systematic weighing of pros and cons according to people's preferences. However, these elements of what is typically considered rational in economics and decision-making theory overlook aspects commonly found in people's everyday sense-making.

As the above example illustrates, people regularly turn to hope, faith, and ideologies when engaging with risk and uncertainty. While often considered coping mechanisms, these are crucial elements of decision-making in everyday life. They do not only help to cope with situations where little agency is left in face of risk (e.g., when terminally ill or dependent on external forces considered out of control) they are also enabling people to enter uncharted waters where control or knowledge about outcomes are limited such as soldiers facing a confrontation with enemy forces during World War Two (Stouffer et al., 1949). Such *non-rational* modes are typically not causally connected, but a way of seeing the world. People can turn to different religions or mobilize hope alongside their efforts to change their lives. A positive attitude towards the future can, in many ways, positively influence people's performance and well-being in the present. This means even though they seem "irrational" or "non-rational"[2] from the perspective of experts, they are indeed reasonable. They are beneficial when no other resources are available to manage uncertainty, but this does not mean they are used only when proven knowledge is lacking.

In summary, our discussion of risk and uncertainty is structured around three critical aspects. Firstly, risk, due to its close relation to the human capacity for imagination and the possibility of reflection and planning, inherently contains an anthropological component (compare the concept of the eccentric positionality of Helmuth Plessner, 2019). This, nevertheless, is an aspect that will remain in the subtext of our book. Secondly, and more prominently examined in the following sections, investigating subjective action under risk concerns the epistemologically problematic transformation of subjective, non-reflexive experience into objectified knowledge. And, thirdly, the study of risk requires a consequential historical approach, insofar as risk is deeply linked to the processes of modernization and rationalization.

Regarding the field of this research, we argue that a growing number of qualitative studies have shown that people navigate risk and uncertainty in several ways, which have not yet been sufficiently explored. These are not "rational" nor "irrational," but rather "in-between," relying on experience but not entirely determined by positive knowledge. They are connected to practical wisdom or embodied, tacit knowledge.

Already, the Greek philosopher Aristotle (1926) recognized the specific skills needed for responsible decision-making in real life. In contrast

---

[2] Since the phrase "irrational" is a normatively loaded concept which follows a modernist perspective, we prefer the more neutral phrase "non-rational." In this way, we keep the connection to the modern notion of rationality but indicate that there might be other forms of reasoning which might not follow the strict demands of rational choice theory but are still reasonable.

to episteme, which denotes analytical rationality, and techne, which signifies instrumental rationality, he highlights the vital importance of phronesis, characterized by practical rationality. It is a type of expertise that develops with experience rather than through formalized education and includes values and interests. Phronesis, therefore, describes practical judgment and wisdom, as well as common sense (prudence), and is mainly based on experience (Burch & Furman, 2019).

The art of *phronesis* is also significantly shaping expert decision-making. Even though Horlick-Jones (2005) did not refer to the old philosophers, he demonstrated through several qualitative studies that experts, such as policemen, do not merely apply and enforce laws and regulations, but also balance different values and risks to ensure reasonable outcomes. That includes not provoking conflict and enforcing compliance with legislation when doing so might produce more harm than good, and courtesy could prevent escalation instead. For example, he documented the balancing of risks by policemen at a large festival, which considered not only the formalized security measures but the secondary risks of enforcing them, such as confronting a group of emotionally agitated and drunken participants who did not comply with the set end time of the celebrations (Horlick-Jones, 2005). He called this "informal logics of risk," "practical reasoning," and "bricolage," and what philosophers would consider "phronesis." However, this logic of reasoning cannot be reduced to the formal application of rules or the arbitrary application of legislation but instead involves practical wisdom.

This practical wisdom pertains to modes of reasonable conduct in-between, such as trusting others, a more intuitive approach to decision-making, and the emotional assessment and framing of a situation, including issues related to shame and desire. These have all been intensively researched and considered across disciplines and are therefore discussed in more detail in Chapters 3 and 4.

While there is strong empirical evidence for these different modes of engaging with risk and uncertainty, it seems conceptually beneficial to systematize their epistemological foundations to enhance understanding of how they relate to one another. For this purpose, we are turning in Chapters 5, 6, and 7 to the *New Phenomenology* introduced by Hermann Schmitz (2019), since his approach seems to be better capable of acknowledging the relevance of embodied forms of knowledge and experience for the management of risk and uncertainty than, for example, the phenomenology of Alfred Schütz. Although Schütz, in his late work (1970), refers to the philosophy of bodiliness as well, we decided to focus on New Phenomenology, which is more rigorously grounded in the sphere of embodied experience and takes the whole dimension of the involuntary[3] as the epistemological ground of knowledge. Nevertheless, we will discuss some selected aspects of Schütz's late work, especially his study of the problem of relevance.

The advantage of New Phenomenology is that it allows us to distinguish between the sphere of involuntary and non-reflexive (embodied) experience on the subjective level and its objectivation due to our capability of reflexive thinking. At least three beneficial aspects of a neo-phenomenological perspective on risk and uncertainty can be mentioned initially: Firstly, the underlying epistemology allows us to develop an understanding of the deep structure of sense-making in general. By distinguishing the subjective and involuntary embodied experience on the one hand and its systematization by reflexive thinking on the other, it becomes possible to methodologically reconstruct the aforementioned transformation of qualitative experience into quantifiable and calculable items. Secondly, this allows an insight into the relationship between the affected self and abstract forms of knowledge, which appears to be a crucial aspect in decision-making situations involving risk and uncertainty. Hence, the widening gap between people's everyday lives and the growing volume of abstract knowledge characterizing modern, technologically advanced societies can be adequately considered. And thirdly, this approach opens a fruitful perspective to fathom the tension between formal rationality and the concept of reason, as it was famously problematized by critical theory.

In general, Schmitz's approach leads to a perspective that suggests phenomenologically tracing back the individual and institutionalized

[3] Following New Phenomenology, the "involuntary" denotes all phenomena that evidently occur to the self without being the result of our free will. It arises to the subject as a kind of embodied factuality. We will elaborate on this aspect in Chapter 4.

forms of dealing with risk to the subjective sphere of bodily perceptible[4] threat. Though this epistemological anchor is in subjective experience, it is essential not to see the modes of dealing with risk and uncertainty only on the level of individual judgments but to position them in their relationship to institutional contexts. Therefore, in Chapters 6 and 7, we turn to the connection between people's life-world[5] experiences and abstract institutionalized knowledge systems. For this purpose, among other aspects of New Phenomenology, we introduce its specific understanding of situations, characterized by a balanced emphasis on constructivist and determinist aspects of human action—an approach that Schmitz (1994, pp. 215 ff.) calls "epistemological explicationism." The analytical view is then elaborated with the concept of interpretative relevance, as Alfred Schütz (1970) developed it. This perspective helps to reconstruct decision-making as it is experienced individually. A person who has to act under risk, neo-phenomenologically, finds themselves confronted with a tense relationship of two forms of knowledge: on the one hand, there is the involuntary and non-reflexive knowledge, like trust or intuition, and on the other hand, a range of institutionalized knowledge that is provided by the respective social environment. From this perspective, to make abstract knowledge, such as that from science, subjectively relevant to people's lives, it must be translated in a way that it gains relevance in the subjectively experienced situation of decision-making. Indeed, that may not be successful. Abstract systems and their representatives might lose contact with people's life-world; in Schütz's words, they lose interpretative relevance. Or people might not be able to

[4] While the "body," neo-phenomenologically, is an object, the whole sphere of the "bodily perceptible" is an experience that is characterized by a dimension of subjective affectedness. In this sense, we also use the noun "bodiliness" to denote the sphere of subjective and embodied factuality, in distinction to the "body" as a phenomenon that is empirically attainable by other persons than the affected one as well.

[5] Strictly speaking, it is not appropriate to use the classical term "life-world" in a book that applies the New Phenomenology. Hermann Schmitz (1980, pp. 24 f.) rejects this term explicitly and stresses "that even for the phenomenologist there can be no return to pure nature in simple unbiasedness beyond all artificial idealizations. Husserl promised himself something like this from the regression of phenomenology to the life-world. The life-world does not exist, any more than a natural language." As an alternative epistemological approach, Schmitz developed the concept of being embedded in situations (compare Chapter 6). Nevertheless, we use the term life-world from time to time, but it should always be understood in the neo-phenomenological sense of a subjectively experienced, situationally embedded world.

distance themselves and reflect on their embodied, routinized, and practical but limited experiences. Altogether, we argue that embodied forms of knowledge evoke a more immediate sense of truth, in contrast to the reflexive and abstract forms of knowledge provided by expert systems, which necessitate reconnection to sensed truths to be convincing and subjectively relevant. This does not say anything about the accuracy of the connection of the reflexive to the subjectively embodied. People might—even under the guidance of experts—well overestimate, idealize, and wrongly judge a situation.

Institutions can offer interpretations of social realities that favor specific methods to serve their purposes or functions. For example, when scientific organizations express their hope or belief that scientific progress can effectively solve particular social problems, or when representatives of faith systems or ideologies attempt to justify their viewpoints scientifically (e.g., the scientific proof of God's existence), these institutions try to expand their influence to manage the uncertainties of the world. This framework can be used to describe how institutional dynamics and shifts serve to increase their persuasive power by integrating or exploiting different reasoning modes. In Chapter 8, we describe these dynamics as *rationalization*, *enchantment*, and *subjectivation*, exploring how they connect various ideal-type modes of reasoning and what happens when they become detached from each other in managing risk and uncertainty.

# 2

# Occidental Rationalization

The understanding of risk as a social concept is deeply rooted in the transition to modernity, which, until today, shapes the way we see and make sense of the world (Bonß, 1995; Giddens, 2000; Luhmann, 1993). Therefore, we begin by reconstructing how the current understanding of risk in the context of risk studies relates to societal modernization. We suggest that there is a systematic tension between the development of rational ways of approaching the world (or modern rationalization) and the more comprehensive forms of sense-making of risk in everyday life, to be examined in more detail in Chapters 3 and 4. We assume that this tension shapes today's understanding of risk and provides the foundation for our phenomenological outline of the different forms and dynamics of the social engagement with risk in present-day societies (Chapters 5–8). Before we discuss the broader social process of modernization transforming the social world, its limits and contradictions, we first outline the *measuring and control orthodoxy*, which is central for the management and communication of risk and uncertainty in modern societies.



J. O. Zinn and M. Schulz, *A New Phenomenology of Risk and Uncertainty*, Critical Studies in Risk and Uncertainty, https://doi.org/10.1007/978-981-95-7405-6_2

## 2.1 The Measuring and Control Orthodoxy

In modern societies, the analysis and management of risk have become a professional enterprise driven by high standards of expertise and scientific knowledge. Its purpose is not merely to analyze and manage risks but to provide the knowledge for societal decision-makers and the public, allowing them to make reasonable decisions (Árvai & Rivers III, 2014; Atman et al., 1994; Covello et al., 1988; Kasperson, 2014; Krimsky, 2007). This is the standard position in scholarship on risk communication and includes deliberative and participative approaches, which later developed to give greater weight to public opinion and stakeholder involvement (Fischhoff, 1995; Renn, 2008; Rosa et al., 2014). In so doing, *risk communication* is a normative social project that is connected to the modern roots of democratic societies in the Global North. It rests on the assumption that (social) decisions should be evidence-based and supported by a majority of the public.

This approach could be called the modern *measuring and control orthodoxy* of risk studies, which aims to calculate, control, and reduce risks (Fischhoff & Kadvany, 2011). It is characterized by overcoming laypeople's misperception of risk. For example, the *mental models* approach aims to identify the cognitive models that underpin laypeople's misjudgments of risk to correct them (Atman et al., 1994; Breakwell, 2001; Morgan et al., 2002). Wolfgang Krohn and Georg Krücken (1993, p. 12) suggest that the distinction between true and subjectively distorted knowledge, or between real and perceived risk, is one of the fundamental distinctions that every society relies upon. It underpins the modern distinction between a world in which actions are either rational, based on *empirically proven knowledge*, or *irrational*, based on *hope*, *faith*, *magic*, or *ideology*.

There is good evidence that laypeople sometimes lack a thorough understanding of the risks they voluntarily engage with or are exposed to. They might worry about very low risks, such as being involved in a plane crash or being killed by lightning, and worry far too little about more likely issues, such as health risks related to smoking, drinking alcohol, lack of exercise, and bad eating habits (Slovic, 2000). Therefore, the lay-expert distinction has supported a generalized view that laypeople have access only to folk wisdom, everyday myths, beliefs, and ideologies. In contrast, experts have access to or a good command of superior (scientific) knowledge. It would thus be rational for laypeople to trust experts (Fischhoff & Kadvany, 2011; Slovic, 1999).

In practice, however, this perspective has contributed to a stalemate in the communication and management of risk, reflecting experts' powerful position relative to laypeople. The distinction between inferior lay knowledge and superior expert knowledge, however, was challenged in the 1980s (Pidgeon et al., 1992; Wynne, 1982a, 1989). In particular, Brian Wynne (1989, 1996) became known for research that argues that experts also rely on specific *belief systems* or *epistemic cultures* (Knorr-Cetina, 1999). Thus, not only laypeople's knowledge but also experts' knowledge is subject to systematic limitations and biases and sometimes fails (Wynne, 1992). Over decades, Wynne contributed a growing body of empirical research supporting this assumption. According to Wynne, so-called *laypeople* possess significant local and practical knowledge, often superior to researchers' abstract laboratory knowledge, which can lack ecological validity.

Despite such observations about the different forms of knowledge experts and lay-people command, the dichotomy between the ideal types of *rational knowledge* and *non-rational knowledge* persists and may represent a continuation of the expert/lay-people distinction. We suggest that there are historical and systematic reasons why this is the case. To further elaborate this point, we argue in the following that the distinction between expert and lay knowledge goes back to the differentiation of expert systems and scientific knowledge on the one hand, which contrasts with people's holistic experience of their respective life-world on the other (compare for a similar distinction Brown, 2022, pp. 93–94). The latter one is founded in embodied perception of everyday life and is "merely" subjective, whereas expert knowledge is abstract and supposedly impersonal. The growing abstraction of knowledge and social practices is connected to the systematic differentiation and increasing specialization of societal domains (e.g., economy, science, politics) that goes back to the modernization of Western societies.

## 2.2 Modernization

Modernization is a concept used to describe a complex process of social transformation that involves a range of ideas, political forms, economic structures, and cultural patterns that emerged as Western societies shifted from an agricultural to an industrial foundation (the Industrial Revolution) and from a feudal to a capitalist economic framework. It also includes the differentiation of relatively autonomous social spheres characterized by their own rationalities. As is often the case with such long-term societal changes, there is little agreement on when exactly they started and became dominant. The origins of modernity are commonly located around seventeenth-century Europe before becoming the primary form of social organization in the twentieth century (Krieken, 2014).

Some of the key characteristics of modernity, among others, are its industrial and capitalist economic structure, the form of nation-states in its political organization, and a growing adherence to the principles of rationality rather than religion, magic, and tradition. This was accompanied by a growing belief in social progress and an exploitative relationship with nature. Modernization came with an increasing focus on the individual as bearer of rights and freedoms, and the development of bureaucracy and the growing intrusion of the state and other organizations into people's daily lives. To provide an overview of central assumptions and debates in sociology about the modernization process, we first turn to Max Weber's work before highlighting a range of additional important authors.

The German sociologist Max Weber (1864–1920) is famous for his studies of modernization and the *rationalization*, *secularization*, and *disenchantment* of the social world. He suggested that ascetic Protestantism played a key role in the socio-cultural changes that paved the way for the unfolding of market-driven in the Western world. Weber characterized the shift in people's outlooks, the systematized and formalized organizational forms, and the growing dominance of purpose-based decision-making (*zweckrational*) as the conditions of a rationalized lifestyle to emerge and a broader societal transformation towards modern society—a process that was accompanied and enforced by the aforementioned measuring and control orthodoxy.

Weber was open to the question of where these developments are heading. He suggested that "*Nobody knows yet, who will live in this cage [of a purpose based rationality] and whether at the end of this tremendous development [of rationalization and intellectualization] new prophets or a mighty rebirth of old thoughts and ideals will stand, or—if none of these—mechanical petrification, with a kind of obsessive aggrandizing oneself embellished.*"[1] But he was indeed worried that such conditions could finally result in "*Experts without spirit, pleasure-seekers without heart: this nothingness imagines that it has reached a level of humanity that has never been reached before.*"[2] Possibly more conciliatory, he also suggested that at a time of rationalization and intellectualization the last and most sublime values are removed from the public realm and have to find other places, such as the realm of backdoor mysticism or fraternalism of personal relationships. The grand monumental narratives were gone and are increasingly replaced by smaller expressions of community-based forces.[3]

Weber was not the only scholar who was critical of the side effects of modern rationalization. There were indeed already before and long after Weber all kinds of criticism of the rationalization process, often in tandem with the development of technology, which was considered a pure expression of a rational, purpose-based approach to the world. Like Weber, there was widespread concern that an important, if not crucial, aspect of what it means to be human would be neglected or lost as rationalization, purpose-based reasoning, and technological rationality advanced. These scholars' views vary in scope and perspective, with many

---

[1] "Niemand weiß noch, wer künftig in jenem Gehäuse wohnen wird und ob am Ende dieser ungeheuren Entwicklung ganz neue Propheten oder eine mächtige Wiedergeburt alter Gedanken und Ideale stehen werden, oder aber—Wenn keins von beiden—Mechanisierte Versteinerung, mit einer Art von krampfhaftem Sich-wichtig-nehmen verbrämt." (Weber Weber-RS, Volume 1, p. 204)

[2] "Fachmenschen ohne Geist, Genußmenschen ohne Herz: dies Nichts bildet sich ein, eine nie vorher erreichte Stufe des Menschentums erstiegen zu haben" (Weber Weber-RS, Volume 1, p. 204).

[3] Weber Wissenschaft als Beruf, Weber-WL, p. 612. Compare also the later claim of postmodernists such as Jean-François Lyotard who proclaimed "the end of social metanarratives" (Lyotard, 1979, 1984).

focusing on the influence of technological development and the effects of industrialization, while others take a broader view of social change in humanity and its connection to inner and outer nature.

Famously, Karl Marx (1818–1883) had described the shift of the economic production process and how it fundamentally reshaped industrializing societies, producing new social groups and the modern class society. The rationalization of mass production has not only raised the production of goods to a new level. It had also alienated workers from their work and the goods they produced. Beyond such a strong emphasis on political economy, Henri Bergson (1859–1941) criticized the notion of the human being as *homo faber*—the tool-making animal—that controls its own fate. Bergson rejected the reification of the human being, which would miss the importance of immediate experience and intuition, in contrast to abstract rationalism and science for understanding the world (Bergson, 1907). The famous German philosopher Martin Heidegger (1889–1976) suggested that modern technological society is nihilistic. Technology was not merely instrumental. It was a specific way of seeing the world. But technology thinking would deny other essential qualities of humans beyond technology (Heidegger, 1977 [orig. 1954]).

A partially similar but in its consequences significantly different critique was formulated by Theodor W. Adorno (1903–1969) and Max Horkheimer (1895–1973) (Adorno, 1966; Horkheimer & Adorno, 1947). They suggested that modern societies conceive the value of nature primarily in instrumental terms (purpose-based rationality). This would mean nature is an object for and an instrument of human will. Thus, with the increasing rationalization and control of inner and outer nature, we would become alienated from and lose control over the deeper qualities of nature. Famously, they stressed that this process of alienation goes back to the inner logic of Enlightenment itself; that it turns into mythology due to its epistemological reductionism, which merely acknowledges what is expressible in numbers. In this way, the program of Enlightenment leads to human alienation from its natural basis.

In the tradition of the Frankfurt School of Critical Theory and influenced by Martin Heidegger, Herbert Marcuse (1898–1979), in his "One-Dimensional Man" (1964), developed the concept of technological rationality, which would, in advancing industrial societies, increasingly replace earlier, substantial forms of (political) rationality. Technology and industry would shape not only the structure of the economy but also intellectual pursuits and leisure activities. Human needs would increasingly become inseparable from artificial needs produced by technological rationality (for example, the need for a car, a widescreen television, and keeping up with the latest fashion trends). People would become content with the improved quality of life offered by new technology and, therefore, have a bias towards the status quo (in this perspective, it would be unlikely that societies restrict consumption patterns to save the climate). Consequently, it becomes increasingly difficult to oppose technological rationality. Instead, technological rationality becomes totalitarian.

The French philosopher, Jean-François Lyotard (1924–1998), outlines in *The Postmodern Condition* a slightly different but not less daunting perspective. The loss of grand legitimizing narratives would be replaced by a diversity of language games, which would follow a logic that supports the growth of power, which is legitimized "by optimizing the system's *performance-efficiency. The application of this criterion ... necessarily entails a certain level of terror, whether soft or hard: be operational (that is, commensurable) or disappear*" (Lyotard, 1984, p. xxiv).

Also, the recent work of Hartmut Rosa on Social Acceleration (2013) and his attempts to systematize a *sociology of good life* can be considered a new approach to understanding how, in a modern world, positive meaning can be generated and a sense of a *good life* experienced. At the center of his considerations is the concept of *resonance,* which would characterize a vibrantly meaningful and positive relation to one's world and might be difficult to experience under the current circumstances of an accelerated society (Rosa, 2019).

Ongoing critique of the modern dream of growing rationalization, social advancement, and the disenchantment of the social world has raised interesting questions about how rationality, as represented ideal-typically by science, technology, and economy, relates to other social rationales such as hope, faith, or ideology. We will return to this point later to systematize our scheme for understanding how people and social institutions make sense of and respond to risk and uncertainty. With the differentiation of specialized social systems such as the economic, legal, and scientific systems (Luhmann, 1984), there emerged at the same time the question of how such systems relate to people's everyday life, which includes whether these can be meaningfully integrated or do colonize the life-world as suggested by Jürgen Habermas (1984). How do the highly rationalized and autonomous societal domains and their specialized knowledge affect people's everyday experiences? This question is best understood by conceptualizing rationalization as a multilevel process, as in the work of Max Weber.

## 2.3 Rationality, Rationalization, and Rationalism

The value of Max Weber's analysis for the following considerations lies in its differentiated systematization of the modern rationalization process. He approaches societal rationalization on the level of social institutions and organizations as well as on the level of people's experiences. Although many commentators suggested that Weber is inconsistent in his use of the concept of rationality, most agree that it is possible to distinguish three different usages related to the micro-, meso-, and macro-levels of analysis (Habermas, 1984). These can be distinguished as *rationality* on the micro-level, *rationalization* of the meso-level, and *rationalism* on the macro-level (e.g., Müller, 2011).

In Weber's analysis, *Rationalism on the macro-level stands for the broader worldviews dominating the zeitgeist at a time,* such as the view that everything is explainable by rational, experience-based means or calculation. Such a broader worldview would underpin rational action on the meso-and micro-level.

*Rationalization* at the meso-level of organizations and social order refers to the organized forms of social activities, such as the systematization of tasks in bureaucracies, universities, the church, and similar institutions. This involves making social processes rule-based and more defined through membership roles, which are mostly documented in written form and often include options for sanctions.

*Rationality* as a form of action on the micro-level is most important for our debate on individual modes of engaging with risk and uncertainty. Weber distinguishes between *purpose-based rationality* (typical for the rational choice model of economics) and *value rationality* (when action is justified by values independent of outcomes) in contrast to *tradition*-based activities, driven by customs and social convention, and *affectual* modes driven by emotional states (Weber, 1980, p. 12). Value rationality appears less rational than purpose-based rationality, as it is relatively independent of outcomes. The value rational perspective he does not consider for the rationalization processes on the meso-and macro-level. However, it is crucial to differentiate between evidence-based, instrumental rationality in decision-making, which is closely tied to science and economy, and the faith-based and ethical forms of decision-making associated with, for instance, religion and ideology. What makes this relation of the value rational and the purpose-rational so complex is that most purpose-rational decisions in the last consequence refer to a set of value-founded definitions. A good example of this might be the implementation of a constitutional law. It establishes a value rational framework for all forms of legal action—even those that consider themselves purely purpose-oriented. In that sense, it might be purpose-rational to define a set of values that are obligatory for all members of society.

Due to Weber, the social process of rationalization took place on all these levels, which complement each other to allow a rational way of life (*rationale Lebensführung*). A rationalized worldview towards the future would manifest in the type of formalized bureaucracy characterizing the state, but would also become influential in other social domains such as institutionalized religion, science, and the economy, and requires rule-based formal membership roles and purpose-based behavior. But this form of means-to-ends rationality would also increasingly dominate one's way of life. Differentiated social domains would not only rationalize the social management of specific social functions invading people's everyday life but also serve other expert systems.

An example would be the legal system providing contract law for the economic system to flourish. Similarly, science provides evidence for political decision-making and the knowledge for advancing technological production of goods. In this way, rationalization in all its forms would pervade society on all levels and in all domains.

However, many modern thinkers did not imagine the degree of reluctance of people to give up on "enchanted" forms of reasoning. Already,

Max Weber, who was worried about the effects of advanced rationalization processes, saw clear limits since advanced rationalization would lack values and meaning to give purpose-rationality direction. In his work on charismatic authority, Weber opens his work to other dimensions than rationality. Specifically, when rational systems do not work well or break down, and people experience "psychic, physical, economic, ethical, religious, or political distress" charismatic authority gains influence (Weber, Economy and Society, §10, "Charismatic Authority"). As Iain Wilkinson (2005, 57) argues, referring to Weber, "charisma responds to suffering not by eliminating it in technical terms, but by offering an interpretative frame that gives it meaning and value." Charismatic authority is one of the cases Weber offers, outlining how values and emotions can be systematized in relation to rationality and enchantment. However, he mainly conceptualizes rationality in opposition to values and affects. Thus, it may require further explanation and systematization of arguments as to why people still engage with ideologies, religion, or secularized hope. As we will argue later (Chapter 8), institutions not only rationalize their practices but also enchant the social world, sometimes even both at the same time, as George Ritzer (2005) has pointed out. In the following, we trace the argument of modern rationalization by the example of the development of insurance, which is considered one of the earliest examples for a modern risk approach—a calculative way of engaging with the future (Bonß, 1995; Giddens, 2000; Luhmann, 1993)—before turning to the complexities of rationalization (disenchantment) and enchantment (or re-enchantment).

## 2.4 Individual Rationality Versus Institutional Rationalization

Max Weber and other authors have highlighted rationalization processes in many social domains even when not all of these were in the center of Weber's analysis: the economy including the production process and the monetary system (Marx, 1867; Simmel, 1900); a legal system becoming more independent from external moral justification but legitimized through procedures (positivization of law) (Habermas, 1984;

Luhmann, 1985); the development of a scientific domain that moves questions about a comprehensive meaning of human existence to the formalized procedures of knowledge generation (Weber, 1948). Rather than reconstructing all these and how they relate to individual rationality, we highlight the connection between individual *rationality* and institutional *rationalization* by the example of the development of the insurance industry, which has been a key example for the rational calculation and management of the future in risk studies and the sociology of risk and uncertainty. Others would be the development of *epidemiology* (health studies) and case *management* (social work) (Dean, 1999, pp. 183–190).

The insurance principle is emblematic of the spread of a rationalized engagement with the social and natural world. It is a way of making an uncertain and risky future accessible to human planning and decision-making. The central rationale is the transformation of a material problem, such as the possible loss of goods, health, or life, into a monetary problem, which then can be compensated for financially. It is important to keep in mind that insurance does not prevent an undesired event from happening, but rather manages the assumed, defined, or agreed financial implications of such an event (Dean, 1999, pp. 183ff.). With formalization, advancement, and spread of insurance, a powerful industry emerged from the seventeenth and eighteenth centuries and is still crucial for the societal management of an uncertain future.

There is good historical evidence for arrangements spreading "risks" of far-distance-trading or economic adventures using strategies similar to modern insurance. Pietro Masci (2011), in his history of insurance, traced the roots of insurance back several thousand years before the Christian era to Chinese merchants spreading their risks by dividing their precious load on several boats, so that the loss would be limited if some of them were lost on long and dangerous journeys. Also, Babylonian caravan traders shared their risks, investment, and profit by settling individual losses and jointly caring for the safety of the caravan (Masci, 2011, p. 28). In the long transition to the modern era similar developments are connected to the emergence and spread of the risk semantic even though it is difficult to pin down a specific source of origin (Bonß, 1995; Luhmann, 1993). While there were early forms of insurance already before the fourteenth and fifteenth centuries, Niklas Luhmann

(1993, p. 9) suggested that a fully developed decision consciousness, in contrast to divine understandings of the future, developed during the long transition from the Middle Ages to Early Modernity.

During the Middle Ages, Italy was at the center of several developments in insurance starting as early as the fourteenth century. By the middle of the fourteenth century, "marine insurance was practically universal among the maritime nations of Europe (Winter 2010)," and it laid the groundwork for the expansion of the insurance principle across different social areas and internationally. It is important to note that "many insurance contracts have been introduced without the full backing of statistics, probabilities, policy research, and a full quantitative understanding of the risks, but instead relying on the intuitive and practical assessment of risk and the operational capability of introducing, adopting, and implementing workable and effective instruments—such as insurance policies" (Masci, 2011, p. 31). However, during the seventeenth and eighteenth centuries, insurance became more professional and institutionalized, with large insurance companies emerging alongside the growth of commerce. For example, in 1688, the famous Lloyd's insurance company, which primarily focused on shipping, was founded and became one of the first modern insurance companies in Europe.

The nineteenth century saw the expansion of new types of insurance, such as coverage against house fires and early death (Evers & Nowotny, 1987, p. 36). By the late nineteenth century, the insurance principle had finally reached the working class. For example, to increase loyalty among ordinary Germans to the throne and empire, German Chancellor Otto von Bismarck introduced several laws mainly focused on sickness insurance (1883), accident insurance (1884), and old age and disability insurance (1889). These initially limited programs gradually evolved into a more comprehensive social insurance system. Similar efforts took place in France (Ewald, 1986) and Britain (Fraser, 1981), primarily aimed at offsetting the adverse effects of industrialization and stabilizing society—particularly in Bismarck's case, against the political influence of liberalism and socialism. The new system helped weaken the established mutual aid organizations, known as friendly societies, which played a vital role in developing working-class identity and solidarity (Thompson, 1963).

However, friendly societies gradually became less prominent as they were replaced by state social insurance.

Insurance, more generally, developed from a tool to help businesses flourish and a lucrative investment to a strategy for stabilizing nation-states by compensating the public for the negative side effects of industrialization, and finally to manage various side effects of the modernization process. But how do individuals in rationalized modern societies respond to the institutional offers? Is the rationalization through insurance in a similar way reflected in the rationality of people's insurance decisions? To answer such questions, it is important to note that the formal technological logic of the insurance principle focuses mainly on the financial implications of future harm. At the same time, it remains contested to what extent the "real costs" can be covered, or the financial burden is sufficiently lightened (e.g., health insurance often does not cover all the costs of an illness and life insurance is more of a financial transfer). Compared with the *friendly societies*, which depended on small community support, the state systems of social insurance are much more abstract and detached from people's lives. While the financial issues might be sorted by insurance, as long as one can afford them, the general uncertainties of the future cannot be managed based on insurance alone. Since money cannot fully compensate for potential losses, other forms of solidarity by family, friends, and the local community are still necessary to manage unforeseen harm of the future emotionally and socially. This might become even more crucial when resources are limited and must be balanced against each other. Under such conditions, it might be more rational not to "overanticipate" and focus on more immediate and subjectively more likely risks rather than possible issues of a distant future, as Sarah Vickerstaff and colleagues (2008) found in their study of old age insurance. The extent to which an individual invests in personal protection through insurance or other means, or relies on group solidarity, is shaped more by personal preference and experience across the life course than instrumental rationality (Brown & Vickerstaff, 2011).

Research indicates that it is challenging to base personal decisions on abstract knowledge or formalized rationality. Probabilistic knowledge provided by epidemiologists about the likelihood of smokers developing cancer does not tell one anything about whether they would be personally affected. Therefore, one might rather rely on personal experience in one's personal networks. One can also mobilize everyday theories to exploit the uncertainty, as Annmarie Ruston and Julie Clayton (2002) reported in a study on women who are being treated for heart disease. Informants denied being at risk by referring to being a "careful person," having "good genes," or "living a balanced life." A study on smoking and drinking during pregnancy showed similar patterns. Even though women were aware that smoking and drinking during pregnancy would threaten their baby's well-being, they shifted responsibility by strategies such as suggesting that the baby's health is rather a lottery game, or that smoking a little is better than quitting altogether, and getting "stressed out" (Wigginton & Lafrance, 2014). There is a growing body of research that documents such strategies to manage risk and uncertainty of the future, deflecting the need to change valued lifestyles. Such explanations seem to be experienced as "more real" and relevant to people's everyday lives than abstract calculations provided by experts.

So, how do people decide whether to buy insurance or not?[4] In a study of Australians purchasing health insurance conducted by Natalier and Willis (2008), there is very little evidence for a rational weighing and calculating process of possible options and costs. Instead, the decisions seem to be dominated by questions of social solidarity and trust.

This research already shows that even when rational technologies such as insurance are institutionalized to make accessible and rationally manage the risky uncertainty of the future, this does not mean that people engage in a highly rational and reflexive way of decision-making when buying insurance. Such reality of people's decision-making practices beyond the rationality paradigm has been a topic in economics, where the rational action paradigm is the central theory, which has become modified over time and complemented by other frameworks,

[4] Such forms of intertemporal decision-making, especially with regards to financial investment decisions, are of great interest in economic theory too. The willingness of reducing the present budget in order to (potentially) achieve a higher utility level in the future is economically termed as a result of the subjective "time preference." This phenomenon was prominently investigated by Irving Fisher (Fisher, 1930) and, up from the first half of the twentieth century, has become an important aspect of monetary theory.

as we will argue in the following section. Even though the limits of the rational actor paradigm and its continuation in research and policy cannot be reconstructed in large detail, we are highlighting some of the concerns that are also relevant for a phenomenological understanding of people's engagement with risk and uncertainty.

## 2.5 Limits of the Rational

According to Max Weber, the modernization of the West has resulted in a comprehensive rationalization process that is affecting the available worldviews or *zeitgeist* on a societal level, the formalized procedures and systematization of knowledge on an institutional level, and the individual engagement with the social and natural world. As we have argued in Sect. 2.2, from the beginning onwards, there have been scholarly concerns that rationalization of the social world might go too far, driving humanity away from its "nature" or what it means to be human. At the same time, there are clear indications of epistemological limits of the rationalization process. As we will argue and illustrate in the following, modern rationalization is a modern *imaginary*, *myth*, or *idealized motif*, which meets its limits in societal practice (Latour, 1993). But still, it has been informing societal practice ever since, even when facing challenges over time (Beck, 1992, 2016; Giddens, 2000).

A good example of the pervasiveness and challenges of the rational orthodoxy is the model of the *homo economicus*, the idealized decision-maker in economic theory, who maximizes utility, has stable preferences, and complete knowledge to calculate his/her options and makes well-informed decisions. These ideal-type assumptions, in one way or another, also underpin risk communication approaches, for example, by assuming that individuals in everyday life mainly lack the knowledge to make well-informed decisions (e.g., Covello et al., 1988). However, even within economics, the original orthodoxy of *homo economicus* has increasingly been challenged and refined. The neoclassical assumption of actors calculating *objective* utilities has given way to models that recognize the *subjective* nature of utility: what counts as beneficial or desirable varies across individuals and situations. Moreover, research has demonstrated that people do not necessarily maximize utility in every choice. Instead, they often follow a principle of *bounded rationality*—settling for an option that is *good enough* once a satisfactory level of utility is reached rather than pursuing an optimal one (March, 1988; Simon, 1982). A growing body of decision-making research further challenged the normative model. Aaron Tversky and Daniel Kahneman (1974), in laboratory experiments, and others in natural environments (Gigerenzer & Todd, 2001), showed that people often do not follow the normative model. They argued that people's brains do use heuristics when making decisions, which do not rely on rational balancing or maximizing utility. Tversky and Kahneman (1974) concluded from their research that

> The deviations of actual behavior from the normative model are too widespread to be ignored, too systematic to be dismissed as random error, and to fundamental to be accommodated by relaxing the normative system… We conclude from these finding that the normative and descriptive analyses cannot be reconciled. (Tversky & Kahneman, 1988, p. 167)

Such heuristics include *availability*, *adjustment*, and *representativeness*. For example, they showed that people judge the probability or frequency of an event by the ease with which this event can be recalled (*availability heuristic*). For example, aviation accidents with many fatalities are well and repeatedly communicated in the media and might therefore give the impression that flying by plane is unsafe. However, the ease of remembering is influenced by factors other than the likelihood of occurrence or the seriousness of an event. Therefore, the normative model cannot provide reasonable predictions of people's behavior and can only evaluate people's responses as irrational.

These heuristics indicate that decisions are influenced by factors other than those assumed in the normative model. Such insights supported the development of descriptive decision-making research with a stronger focus on reconstructing and modeling how people make decisions, rather than abstract assumptions about how they should decide, and the modeling of observable deviations. In so doing, Gerd Gigerenzer and colleagues showed that *fast and frugal heuristics* are in many ways superior to rational decision-making (Gigerenzer & Todd, 2001), for example, in situations when knowledge is limited or too complex for processing available information. There is good evidence that other approaches to processing risk might be even more reasonable than formal or subjective rationality (Gigerenzer, 2007; Gigerenzer & Todd, 2001).

These developments reflect early, more systematic insights into the limited knowledge available for decision-making situations. Economic scholars acknowledged that risks, as calculable uncertainty, are rare and have to be separated from uncertain uncertainties, which cannot be calculated similarly. Namely, Frank H. Knight suggested that risk is rather the exception and uncertainty the rule. Therefore, a significant degree of uncertainty has to be included in most models of decision-making (Knight, 1921).

This lack of knowledge is not a surprising observation for economists but rather illustrates a significant tension in entrepreneurial activity. A famous quote highlighting the limits of knowledge is from the economist John Maynard Keynes, who suggested in the *General Theory of Employment, Interest and Market* (Keynes, 1936):

> We are merely reminding ourselves that human decisions affecting the future, whether personal or political or economic, cannot depend on strict mathematical expectation, since the basis for making such calculation does not exist; and that it is our innate urge to activity [animal spirits] which makes the wheels go round, our rational selves choosing between the alternatives as best we are able, calculating where we can, but often falling back for our motive on whim or sentiment or chance. (Keynes, 1936, pp. 161–163)

This argument contradicts Max Weber's suggestion that the modern rationalization process is characterized by the knowledge and belief that any issue can be calculated in principle. It is of interest insofar as it acknowledges a part of reality outside of economic theory and its rationality assumption. The driving force for entrepreneurial action is not based merely on calculating and balancing the opportunities. It requires something else, which Keynes identified as part of the nature of humans, their "animal spirits." This other element of decision-making cannot be fully separated from the calculative sphere but is always involved and mixed up with it. As we will argue later, based on New Phenomenology, the embodied affectedness is always part and parcel of the decision-making. It demonstrates that there is something else that is crucial for understanding people's activities and constitutes a systematic ambivalence that cannot be overcome.

Furthermore, limitations of rational control over uncertainty are unavoidable due to the indeterminacy of the future, which is at the same time a prerequisite for all autonomous and innovative (rational) activities. It is this uncertainty that makes entrepreneurial activity possible. At the same time, it is the uncertainty about others' behavior in the market that allows innovation and success as much as failure. Following a perspective of social interaction theory, this has been termed a "double contingency" that plays a crucial role in economic action in general:

> "Double contingency" refers to "a constellation in which two actors not only think of themselves as being free to choose their actions, so that what they do is contingent, but that they also (have to) attribute the same freedom of choice to their counterpart, so that both are aware of this double openness of possible actions. [...] Each actor tries to see not only themselves and their environment, but also themselves through the eyes of the other person who appears in this environment. (Ganßmann, 2007, p. 63)

Given the impossibility of dissolving uncertainty, in his history of risk, the financial historian and economist Peter L. Bernstein (1996) emphasized its central importance. It was not merely a danger or threat but a fundamental basis of any attempts to change or improve the future: "uncertainty makes us free."

Nevertheless, in a relatively stable economic environment, the degree of uncertainty might still be relatively calculable and expectable. In the 1980s, approaches to uncertainty slightly radicalized. Authors such as Tom Peters (1987) emphasized the need for successful management, as outlined in *Thriving on Chaos* (1987). This perspective is of interest for our discussion since it comes not only with an acknowledgment of the remaining and increasing uncertainty, but also the acknowledgment of the need for exploiting uncertainty successfully rather than dissolving it. This suggestion also connects well to a strengthening debate on resilience in disaster studies, which has started to focus on how to prepare for the unforeseen and unpreventable disasters. Thereby, the focus turned to communities' and individuals' ability to cope and respond successfully to risk and disaster (Bonß, 2015).

Further issues are relevant when people face an unknown future that challenges the rational model of decision-making. Where lacking knowledge cannot be overcome by more knowledge, people often turn to others, who might have better knowledge and are considered trustworthy. There is good evidence for people turning to experts when a crisis or a disaster is imminent (Balog-Way & McComas, 2020). In economics, the reality that people trust others has been integrated into economic theory. On the one hand, for example, Robert D. Putnam (1993) conceptualized trust as a form of social capital that might be of great importance for economic and political development in general. On the other hand, *trust* has been reconceptualized in a way that it can be subordinated to the realm of rationality (Coleman, 1990) but there is also reasonable doubt that these suggestions are conceptually consistent (Frederiksen, 2016; Luhmann, 1988) and there is good evidence for other-than-rational dimensions being involved in trusting such as emotions, familiarity, sympathy (Barbalet, 2009; Renn & Levine, 1991; Siegrist, 2021). Even emotions have been considered as having to play a role. Consequently, ways of integrating them into the economic models have been considered (Damasio, 1996; Elster, 1998; Hirschman, 1977).

There was already a contemporary of Max Weber, the Italian civil engineer, economist, sociologist, political scientist, and philosopher, Vilfredo Pareto (1848–1923), who challenged the dominant rational orthodoxy and developed a social action model quite different from that of Weber (Pareto, 1916). Pareto was rather critical regarding a historical trend towards increasing rationality. Rather than rationality supplanting other forms of reasoning, such as magical and religious sense-making, these would still be prevalent and influential, competing with, challenging, or even outperforming rationality. Instead of highlighting a growing rationalization and emphasizing purposeful rationality, Pareto fundamentally questioned the idea that rationality would guide most people's activities

(Bach, 2004; Pareto, 1916). Instead, what is often considered a residual category, the emotional dimension, deserves, in Pareto's view, to play a central role in explaining human activities (Pareto, 1916). For Pareto, *rational*, or as he calls it, *logical action* is less common. It is typically observable in science and scientific reasoning, where there is a discernible relationship between action explanations and action outcomes. In most cases, however, the reasons individuals give to explain their activities and outcomes often do not connect logically. In Pareto's view such *non-logical* activities would also be the most common within society. For Pareto, non-logical action is the most frequent form of action; sociology has to explain rather than seeing it as a not-yet-rationality (Weber, 1948) or a "residual category" (Keynes, 1936), which will increasingly be sidelined by rationality. This approach, therefore, tries to examine and explore in more detail the sources of *non-logical* action and how it is justified. A full acknowledgment of Pareto's work is not possible here (but compare, for example, Bach, 2004). What is, in our view, most important, however, is the acknowledgment of the more common other-than-rational basis of human activity. A basis, which Pareto called *residuals*, has an embodied and emotional existence in contrast to derivations, which are the manifold explanations given to make sense of or justify activities rooted in emotional and embodied states. Interestingly, for Pareto, science as well as people in everyday life refer to derivations for sense-making. Science uses them to make sense of empirical observations, and people in everyday life to make sense of embodied, tacit, or subjective forms of knowledge and reasoning.

We do not aim to create a universal action model like Pareto or Weber, but rather to develop a more modest typology of the different ways people engage with risk and uncertainty. This typology can help interpret the results of the growing body of qualitative research, which shows a variety of engagement modes that differ greatly from the orthodox idea of rationality. Although science may have become the rational foundation for decision-making about risk, people in everyday life, as well as organizations and societies, still rely on other modes of reasoning. Magic, faith, hope, and ideologies have not disappeared; instead, they remain powerful ways of managing risk and uncertainty, as we will see. One reason for this might be that all probabilistic predictions do not tell us much about whether we will personally be affected by a risk. However, when risks are potentially disastrous, such as in cases of personal loss, no perceived likelihood of occurrence seems acceptable (Luhmann, 1993, pp. 2–3), and other modes of reasoning may come into play.

As we will argue in the following, these other-than-rational modes also provide guidance when knowledge is lacking or when overwhelming complexity prevents or makes rational decision-making impossible. In such cases, people may turn to magic, faith, hope, or ideologies when engaging in high-risk, low-likelihood-of-success activities/or try to avoid decisions altogether. As we will argue, this has not to be a reflexive choice but an intuitive, learned, or routinized tendency. Research has also documented that people turn to various modes that seem to have different characteristics. Zinn called them *in-between* modes, and subscribed trust, intuition, and emotions or gut feelings to this category. These were experience-based but not formalized or scientifically testable, and are connected to other values than facts, such as qualitative evaluations of ethical standards and emotions, and are much more common in everyday life reasoning. As we will argue later, highly specialized forms of knowledge, such as in science, are often difficult to comprehend and connect to everyday life. Similarly, to convince, complex ideologies and faith need to connect to everyday life reasoning. These empirically observable modes of engaging with risk and uncertainty seem to parallel the broader processes of rationalization, enchantment, and their *subjectivation* in people's everyday life. But how do these relate within available theorizing?

## 2.6 First Steps Towards Rationalization, Enchantment, and Subjectivation

We started this chapter with the assumption that the sense-making of risk as a social concept is deeply rooted in modern *rationalization*, which, until today, shapes the way we see the world. We suggest that the tensions and shortcomings observed in risk management and communication are rooted in these modern imaginaries, which have driven the *rationalization* process but face systematic limits we have outlined in this chapter so far. We highlighted that not only were various scholars critical of the "modern dream," but its shortcomings are also evident in the micro-level practices of people's and experts' engagement with risk. We take these as initial indications for the need to conceptualize rationalization and enchantment not only as historical processes, but also as mutually entangled processes in the management of an uncertain and risky future. Guided by the differentiated understanding of the *rationalization* process in Weber's work, we revisited empirical studies to argue for the need to reconstruct the connection between the subjective and institutional levels. People engage with and make sense of risk and uncertainty in different ways. Not all refer to rational, but non-rational modes such as hope and faith, or in-between modes such as trust, or intuition, as indicated above. There is no doubt that the rationalization process has not transformed and cannot transform all people's experiences into rational ones. Social institutions do not produce only rationalized forms of knowledge, but also myths, imaginaries, or ideologies. As we will argue below, available literature, which engages with rationalization and disenchantment processes on the one hand and enchantment or re-enchantment on the other, distinguishes more or less clearly between *rationalization* and *enchantment* on the institutional level and *subjective* experience on the individual level. Such distinctions are, in our view, important since micro-level sense-making can vary and even include the possibility of alienation. These conceptual distinctions will become a key issue when we systematize in later chapters how individuals experience and make sense of the world (Chapter 6) and are exposed to both institutionalized as well as embodied forms of knowledge when engaging with risk and uncertainty (Chapter 8). As a first step, we are now turning to conceptual work that is sensitive to the different analytical dimensions. In particular, we consult George Ritzer's work, which started to address more complex relationships between rationalization and enchantment and their connection to the *subjective* level. These are preliminary observations, which will be taken up again in Chapter 8, after everyday life rationales of managing risk and uncertainty have been further explored (Chapters 3 and 4) and their epistemological basis clarified (Chapters 5, 6, and 7).

The work of George Ritzer is a good example of the different ways in which rationality, enchantment, and *subjective* experience can relate. Even though he focuses on the economic domain of production and consumption rather than knowledge, he provides several vital insights relevant to our conceptual considerations. Firstly, enchantment and rationalization are not necessarily exclusive but might mutually intensify. Second, enchantment does not have to take place outside or in opposition to institutional rationalization, for example, as resistance or a lack of rationalization. Still, enchantment can also be rationally encouraged or even produced. Third, enchantment might not only be produced institutionally. Consumers might also actively demand enchantment and seek it through social institutions. In this way, we will gain a differentiated perspective on social tendencies of rationalization and enchantment, and the connection between institutional and individual dynamics.

In his work on *Enchanting a Disenchanted World*, George Ritzer (2005) examines consumption in advanced modernized societies. He highlights that the modern rationalization process does not overcome enchantment as one might expect based on Max Weber's work. Instead, *Cathedrals of Consumption* enchant consumers. Here, the enchantment of consumers is a rationalized process fostered by companies to increase consumer consumption. The driving force behind this process, in Herbert Marcuse's words, is the artificial needs produced by capitalist society. However, when these processes of strategic enchantment become too rational, companies might jeopardize the success of their efforts. In this way, Ritzer systematically connects rationalization and enchantment, where heightened rationalization encourages heightened enchantment, but might also over-rationalize. However, he suggests that this does not have to be a one-directional process. In contrast, consumers also pressure companies to increase their efforts to enchant consumption when securing profit (2005, p. 69).

Ritzer acknowledges that both rationalization and enchantment have an institutional form, such as in the Cathedrals of Consumption, which produce an enchanting environment as well as alluring imaginaries to attract consumers (compare in this context also Böhme's work on aesthetic, 2013, 2016). Or in Ritzer's words: "*Enchanted settings would seem to be well-suited to controlling consumers by luring them into a dream-like state so that it is easier to part them from their money*" (Ritzer, 2005, p. 66). Enchantment then refers to the subjective sense-making of consumers fostered by the rational efforts of economic enterprises. In this way, there is the notion of an independent experience on the subjective level, which can experience desired enchantment, feel alienated by the over-rationalization of institutional enchantment practices, or even demand institutional opportunities for enchantment (2005, p. 69). One might think about the Romans' public spectacles, such as Roman chariot races or, more generally, the policy of *bread and circuses* (panem and circenses), which Roman Emperors organized to please the public. Also, the modern experience in a football stadium or modern adventure tourism might from time to time become sources of enchantment (compare, e.g., Gugutzer, 2020; Gugutzer & Böttcher, 2012). This contrasts with assumptions of enchantment happening as a personal experience beyond the social sphere, as a purely embodied, even a-social experience. In high-risk leisure sports such as free climbing, BASE jumping, or skydiving, described by Stephen Lyng (1990) as *edgework*, the feeling of a hyperreality results from a disruption of the bond between the subjective experience and the social expectations. For Lyng people's alluring experience of edgework produces a kind of hyperreality grounded in heightened control and, active engagement with the world. In contrast, the political theorist and philosopher Jane Bennett (2001) emphasizes a more receptive mode of enchantment. Similarly to Lyng, she describes a suspension of chronological time and bodily movement as a "moment of pure presence," but for her, enchantment is a state of wonder characterised by being "transfixed, spellbound," and "caught up" or "carried way" (Bennett, 2001, p. 5).

To further specify the different examples of enchanting experiences, it could also be helpful to distinguish between an individual and a subjective sense-making. For example, an enchanting atmosphere of a shopping mall, a football stadium, or the aura of a symbolically charged product are perceived subjectively. But these experiences are not necessarily individual, since many people can sense them, and they might even constitute a collective event.

Ritzer (2005, p. 66) provides some more insights regarding the connection between enchantment and disenchantment and even suggests that Weber's metaphor of an iron cage-like realm of rationalization can also be used for the modern experience of enchantment: "*enchantment and disenchantment are not easily distinguished from one another; one does not necessarily preclude the other. There is a reciprocal relationship. Fantasies draw people into the new means of consumption, and those fantasies can be rationalized to further draw people in and to reinforce the cage. The cage-like quality of the new means of consumption can itself be a fantasy—the fantasy of being locked into one of these cages with ready access to all of its goods and services. In fact, Campbell concluded his work with just such an image: "Modern individuals inhabit not just an 'iron cage' of economic necessity, but a castle of romantic dreams, striving through their conduct to turn the one into the other.*"

In this way, Ritzer's suggestion contrasts with postmodern thinkers, who emphasize that the postmodern society might have some rational elements (e.g., Rosenau, 1992, p. 6), while there is a continuation of "*emotions, feelings, intuition, reflection, speculation, personal experience, custom, violence, metaphysics, traditional, cosmology, magic, myth, religious sentiment, and mystical experience*" (cit. in Ritzer, 2005, p. 67) that would resist rationalization. Such a position would rather align with Vilfredo Pareto's observation, and also with the large body of risk studies documenting how other-than-rational modes of reasoning are pervasive in modern societies.

In this vein, but closer to the growing significance of uncertainty and non-knowledge in risk studies, is Zygmunt Bauman's (1993) suggestion of an ever increasing positive recognition of re-enchantment in late modern societies: "*Postmodernity … brings 're-enchantment' of the world after the protracted and earnest, thought in the end inconclusive, modern struggle to dis-enchant it (or, more exactly, the resistance to dis-enchantment, hardly ever put to sleep, was all along the 'post-modern thorn' in the body of modernity). The mistrust of human spontaneity, of drives, impulses, and inclinations resistant to prediction and rational justification, has been all but replaced by the mistrust of unemotional, calculating reason. Dignity has been returned to emotions; legitimacy to the 'inexplicable,' nay irrational … The postmodern world is one in which mystery is no more a barely tolerated alien awaiting a deportation order … We learn to live with events and acts that are not only not-yet explained, but (for all we know about what we will ever know) inexplicable. We learn again to respect ambiguity, to feel regard for human emotions, to appreciate actions without purpose and calculable rewards*" (cit. in Ritzer, 2005, p. 68).

In this way, the non-modern and non-rationalized spheres of life would, according to Bauman, increasingly gain ground against trends of rationalization again. A form of heightened rationalization, Ritzer has described in another book, where he emphasizes new, intensified forms of rationalization.

With his hypothesis of the *McDonaldization* of society, Ritzer (2013) re-engages and extends Weber's analysis of the rationalization process. He suggests that changes within science, economy, and culture have shifted away from Weber's bureaucracy and have led to a new mode of hyper-rationalization expressed in the business of McDonald's, and are characterized by efficiency, calculability, predictability, and control:

1. *Efficiency* refers to the managerial efforts to minimize the time required to conduct individual tasks as well as the whole process of production and distribution of means and goods.
2. The notion of *Calculability* is still close to Weber's claim of a systematic manageability of the world, but here with a very clear focus on quantifiable numbers rather than subjective evaluation of the quality of things.
3. *Predictability* refers to both the production process and the consumption process. Consumers can expect the same product (e.g., McDonald's products) and consumption processes everywhere in the world.
4. The notion of *control* refers to strict control of the production process. It might also include the use of robots and automation technology to secure the smooth process of production and consumption of services.

These tendencies would also ripple through further domains of society other than the economic production process and thereby more generally change people's life-worlds as much as identities and social relationships. Here, Ritzer emphasizes again that the narrow focus on rationalizing the production process results in producing irrationality and explains:

"*By that, I mean that they [irrational systems] deny the basic humanity, the human reason, of the people who work within or are served by them.*" In this way, he seems to go back to the Marxist argument of intensified rationalization during industrialization, leading to alienating work experiences.

Interestingly, more recent studies have also shown other developments, indicating attempts to re-enchant work experiences (Endrissat et al., 2015), such as in a study on service work in an Organic Supermarket in the US, which not only focused on enchanting consumers but also their employees by the creation of a positive and aesthetically appealing shopping experience.

Such examples indicate that the boundaries between the concepts of rationalization and (re-/dis-) enchantment might become blurry and gradual rather than dichotomous. This also supports the view that there are different spheres of enchantment and re-/disenchantment running parallel within society. Instead of suggesting general social tendencies based on a limited number of case studies, we prefer to develop a framework that allows us to characterize the complexity of empirically observable tendencies of *rationalization*, *enchantment*, *subjectivation*, or even *alienation*. This will also enable us to pose critical questions about the unequal allocation and socially differentiated experiences of such dynamics of sense-making within society.

To prevent confusion, we also suggest clearly distinguishing between enchanting and disenchanting tendencies of reflexive knowledge, which is culturally and organizationally institutionalized, and to distinguish these from the embodied subjective experiences that provide us with evident sensations such as feelings of excitement, joy, desire, trustworthiness, rage, or fear (compare in more detail Chapter 8). We assume that *rational* and *enchanted* engagement with the world requires some embodiment if we do not want to fall back on the dichotomous thinking of modernity and Descartes' mind-body division (1644). Both rational and enchanted forms of engagement, which rely on reflexive knowledge, require a connection to people's subjective experiences. In this way, as we will discuss in more detail in Chapter 8, we can analytically distinguish institutional forms of enchantment and disenchantment and subjective experiences, which relate to one or the other. We can also consider forms of *alienation* when reflexive knowledge and embodied experience do not well connect, as in the case of alienating working conditions.

Before outlining this conceptual framework using epistemological insights from New Phenomenology, we explore in more detail the "irrational" modes of engaging with risk and uncertainty, which Zinn (2008, 2016) describes as non-rational and in-between modes.

## 2.7 Summary and Perspectives

Debates in (social) science, politics, and the public sphere often emphasize the need for rational consumer decisions or sound science and warn against empirically unsupported "scaremongering," which could obstruct necessary economic choices or scientific progress (Füredi, 1997). From this viewpoint, the world is divided into ideal types of *rationality* and *irrationality*. However, as we have argued, the realm of rationality comes with flaws and challenges that must be addressed. The historical processes of modern rationalization have significantly reshaped the social sphere but are still incomplete. We, therefore, share Jane Bennett's (2001, p. 3) concern with narratives of rationalization that overlook ongoing processes of *enchantment*, *disenchantment*, and *re-enchantment* associated with modernization. We also concur with George Ritzer (2005, 2013) that there appears to be a systematic place for the *non-rational* or *enchanted* spheres of life within institutions. The *enchanted* and the *rational* may even be interconnected in more systematic ways. Thus, we aim to keep different institutional dynamics and subjective experiences analytically distinct to develop a nuanced framework for understanding the various ways people engage with the uncertain risks of the future. In Chapters 3 and 4, we further differentiate between *non-rational* and *in-between* modes of reasoning to enable a more detailed analysis of these alternative ways of engaging with risk and uncertainty. Additionally, we underpin these modes epistemologically (Chapters 5, 6, and 7) to establish a solid foundation for an analytical framework that explains the social dynamics of *rationalization* and *enchantment*, and how these may or may not connect to subjective experiences (Chapter 8).

# 3

# Counter-Modernity: Hope, Faith, and Ideology

What are the other-than-rational modes people turn to when engaging with risk and uncertainty? Referring to earlier work (Zinn, 2008, 2016), we suggest first distinguishing *non-rational* modes from *rational* ones before turning to *in-between* modes later (compare Chapter 4). From the perspective of modern orthodoxy, such as in the work of Max Weber or the normative model of homo economicus, *non-rational* modes might be interpreted as "irrational" because they are not based on empirical evidence and do not establish valid links between means and ends. We hesitate to blur the boundaries of rationality by considering *non-rational* modes as being *rational* too, even when people believe in their effectiveness. Instead, we consider them reasonable when they improve either subjective or objective outcomes, such as feeling better when managing anxieties or staying focused under risk. They may also serve as motivation "to keep going" when there is insufficient knowledge or time to process *rationality*. In this way, one might see a parallel here to Pareto's notion of non-logical action (1916). This is not intended to support a dichotomy between rational and other-than-rational modes. Considering the limits of formalized rationality as outlined in Chapter 2, we view rational modes in a social sense as a relatively narrow way of engaging



J. O. Zinn and M. Schulz, *A New Phenomenology of Risk and Uncertainty*, Critical Studies in Risk and Uncertainty, https://doi.org/10.1007/978-981-95-7405-6_3

with risk and uncertainty. With the focus on abstract forms of knowledge and individualized utility functions, such rationality lacks social meaning and ecological validity. Our distinction is therefore closer to the view that all modes have their value and are consequently reasonable under specific circumstances. Still, to achieve subjectively satisfying and objectively measurable outcomes with risk and uncertainty, these modes must be combined. We suggested in the introduction of this book the concept of *phronesis* (Aristotle, 1926), which has been introduced by Greek philosophers such as Plato and Aristotle and might come closer to the "wisdom" we are thinking about for this socially "rational" or better *reasonable* engagement with risk and uncertainty since it combines forms of practical and implicit knowledge with values and other important social factors. This concept has already been proven productive in the sociology of professions such as in education, healthcare, nursing, and social work (e.g., Banks, 2008; Gadamer, 1996; Kinsela & Pitman, 2012; Montgomery, 2006; Pellegrino & Thomasma, 1993). Indeed, *rational*, calculative technologies, as well as *non-rational* resources, must also be considered.

What we refer to here as *non-rational modes* are less empirically informed but *imaginative extensions of one's horizon* (Schulz & Zinn, 2023, p. 226). They rely on *hope* and different institutionalized forms of reasoning, such as faith and ideology, which offer broader frameworks for fostering hope in the face of uncertain and risky futures. We also incorporate magical beliefs and rituals, which remain pervasive in modern societies (Brown, 2022; Vyse, 2020). As we will see, all these *non-rational* modes are quite common in the everyday life of many people and are a crucial resource learned as part of growing up in a social milieu or as part of a chosen lifestyle. In Chapter 4, we will also introduce several *other-than-rational* modes called *in-between* (Zinn, 2008, 2016), such as trust, intuition, and emotions, which we consider as neither following the modern orthodoxy of rationality nor the counter-modern modes we are discussing in this section. As we have already indicated and we will outline in much more detail in Chapters 5, 6, and 7, distinguishing modes by the kind of knowledge they are resting on is helpful to develop a better epistemological understanding of the systematic differences of reasoning we have provisionally grouped into *rational*, *non-rational* and

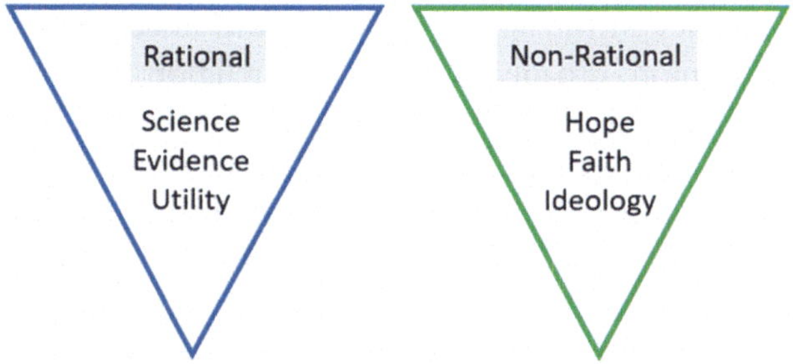


**Fig. 3.1** Modern dichotomy of rational and non-rational modes

*in-between* modes (Schulz & Zinn, 2023). Turning to knowledge has also proven fruitful in the work of Patrick Brown (2022), who used the three concepts of embrained/encoded, tacit, and postformal knowledge to connect the typology to his empirical work in health studies.

Many researchers have identified *non-rational* modes such as *hope*, together with *faith* and *ideology*, as essential resources for dealing with risk and uncertainty in many social contexts and situations. Indeed, such modes of engaging with risk and uncertainty, whether voluntarily taken or in response to an external threat or hazard, are not entirely freely chosen from a set of equally available tools. Even when there is some freedom to which mode one turns, there is a clear indication that such modes are more often observable when there is little knowledge available or resources are scarce to engage in a narrative of rationality (Peltzer & Renner, 2003; Peou & Zinn, 2015). There is also little doubt, as we will argue, that people's responses are informed by what they have learned and have become used to as a routinely applied mode of managing stress or pressure, such as when exposed to risk and uncertainty (Fig. 3.1).

The *non-rational* modes are well-known coping strategies, which can have positive effects, for example, in improving healing (Ehrenreich, 2009), while they are often considered negatively as well. They would support passivity or express a lack of motivation. The assumption is that when people pray or hope that things are getting better, they do not actively engage to improve a situation (Renn, 2008). While this might be true, when, for example, people feel that they have no means to influence the future, these *non-rational* modes are also crucial resources for maintaining agency in the face of high risk and uncertainty. This is the case for hoping more broadly as well as for religion (including magical practices), as well as ideology. As we will argue at the end of the section, independent of the degree of institutionalization or cultural embeddedness, empirically unproven imaginaries of the future are in as much a resource to cope with a daunting presence as they are a resource to motivate people to engage in efforts to achieve what might be considered out of reach or "castles in the sky." Many innovations, whether social, technical, or entrepreneurial, require imaginaries of whatever kind to give people's efforts a direction and to mobilize resources for innovation and change. In this way, what we call *non-rational modes,* or *counter-modernity* bearing Max Weber's understanding of the modernization process in mind, might not follow the modern orthodoxy of rationality. However, these are similarly crucial for humans engaging with a world considered open to interests and desires, yet at the same time contingent and uncertain (Koselleck, 1985).

## 3.1 Hope

The importance and positive character of hope for people's life and the management of risk and uncertainty has been proven in many research domains such as in *health sociology* (Alaszewski & Wilkinson, 2014; Brown et al., 2014; de Graaf, 2016; Peretti-Watel et al., 2019; Petersen, 2015), in *gambling studies* (Allen, 2006; Beckert & Lutter, 2012; Lutter, 2010), and *youth studies* (Bishop & Willis, 2014; Bryant & Ellard, 2015; Cook, 2016; Ojala, 2012; Peou & Zinn, 2015) just to name a few.

Whenever the concept of hope is used, work has shown that it is essential to distinguish between two forms of hope with different characteristics (see: de Graaf, 2016; Petersen, 2015). *Passive hope*, with its clear negative connotation,[1] can replace activity. This is evident when, instead of actively engaging in and changing a situation, one only engages cognitively and hopes that things will change themselves. This contrasts

[1] This negative connotation usually reflects the author's modern mindset generally prioritizing action (positive) over inaction (negative).

with the positive notion of hope, which stimulates activity. For example, the philosopher Ernst Bloch argued in *The Principle of Hope* (initially published in German in 1959 and subsequently published in English in 1986) that hope comes with a positive attitude towards the future since it is linked to desired scenarios. He emphasized that this is particularly important when heading towards a not yet known better future. Positive imaginaries, or what we call the "imaginative extension of one's horizon" (Schulz & Zinn, 2023, p. 226), could have a significant mobilizing impact on people's actions, up to and including revolutionary activity.

The dichotomy of passive and active hope becomes more difficult to sustain when an individual lacks resources to change an undesired situation (Zigon, 2009). Research on chronic and terminal illness shows how hope is mobilized to cope with a daunting future and when desperately seeking options to handle a situation (Brown et al., 2015; Mattingly, 2006). Therefore, "passive" hope might not stem from a lack of engagement, but from a lack of means. In this way, hope is also a last resort that helps people tolerate ongoing suffering when they have little or no agency for change, hoping that the situation will change due to external forces. Thus, hope is a vital resource that enables individuals to persevere, keep the possibility of improvement alive, and maintain relatively positive feelings despite struggling with desperation.

For example, Cheryl Mattingly (2006), in her longitudinal ethnographic study of African-American families who have children with severe and chronic illnesses or disabilities, shows how narratives of hope are created, maintained, and revised. She identified a *will to hope,* which was a crucial element when facing suffering as part of their daily life. Because of the moral obligation they felt towards their children not to "give up," parents needed strength to maintain hope. Hoping was therefore not a routinely activated mode of reasoning but an actively and reflexively chosen path. This was anything but an easy and light way of managing the most likely future. Instead, she described the tensions and oscillations between hope and desperation in the face of suffering. This is an important insight. Modes of reasoning, such as hope, might not always be easily or routinely taken. Lacking alternatives and desperation in the face of unpreventable trajectories unfolding, leaves people with only one resource left. Where rationally no positive future is in sight, hope remains as the last resource for expanding the horizon of what is expectable. This tension between a daunting future and the desire to keep a future alive, such as in the case of terminal cancer patients, has been suggested by Patrick Brown (2022) to be critical for the kind of knowledge underpinning non-rational modes of reasoning.

Another example illustrates how young people in Cambodia, who lack knowledge and resources, mobilize hope in managing their transition into the labor market. Chivon Peou (Peou & Zinn, 2015, p. 732), in his study on youth transitions in Cambodia, constructed various action modes to ideal-typically describe their way of engaging with an uncertain future. Many adolescents who attended the university developed clear ideas and plans for their careers through higher education into the labor market. Even when they did not have particularly well-developed plans, they still had an idea and support networks at hand that would foster their transition. However, another group of adolescents, who lacked such resources, experienced their future quite differently. They often took on casual work to meet their needs, without expressing systematic career plans. With the future being highly uncertain and contingent, they were unable to develop concrete plans, but still shared the positive outlook with other youth. However, instead of planning, they were hoping that "something" would happen to change their life for the better.

A different domain where hope is regularly mobilized is gambling. We could even say that hoping is institutionalized in gambling. Authors have suggested that, for example, the lottery represents a commodification of dreams and can thereby brighten one's future. At the same time, gambling also shapes everyday life in the present, such as when people participate in the lottery together (Beckert & Lutter, 2012; Lutter, 2010). Institutionalized hope in gambling might have a crucial function for disadvantaged social groups as well as in societies with large inequalities. Mark Lutter has argued in his study on Germans playing the lottery that it is less about people's belief that they will win the lottery. This would, for example, mean that they stop playing after having won, which is rarely the case. Instead, he argues that the lottery is an example of the *commercialization of dreams*. What motivates people is the real possibility, even if it's only marginally small, that they could win the lottery and their life would change forever. Engaging in activities like playing the lottery and other forms of gambling offers a thrill that is not easily attainable in other areas, such as work, which often involves routine tasks with minimal rewards. Therefore, the process of playing the lottery with others might also have a positive social aspect in the present, as it allows for shared experiences and dreams. This kind of commodification of hope is widespread. Not only poor people, who still have enough money to play the lottery, but also others seeking the thrill of gambling.

There are many examples, which show that hope, like other modes of reasoning, is often mobilized together when engaging with risk and uncertainty. As studies on (illegal) boat migration have shown (Hernández-Carretero & Carling, 2012), hope is rather one among other resources people mobilize when engaging in high-risk activities. Positive *imaginaries* (Castoriadis, 1987) of a rosy future might be one driving force as much as shame for the inability to reach a socially acknowledged status and desperation. The reality of everyday suffering might be the strongest driver for engaging in such dangerous journeys and even accepting or disregarding the severe risks, such as injury and death, associated with boat migration (Hayenhjelm, 2006). In the study by María Hernández-Carretero and Jørgen Carling (2012), young male migrants employed a range of strategies, including actively ignoring information and mobilizing resources such as a talisman for luck and boarding a boat with an experienced Fisherman at the rudder, to survive a high-risk journey. Even when they understood boat migration was a high-risk and possibly deadly journey, they still engaged in it because they saw it as the only option for a change from an unbearable present, sometimes expressing a fatalist outlook.

Considering the often-positive function of hope for people with little other means available to them to improve their social and/or material situation, the negative framing of hope might be due to exaggerated modern norms of calculability and predictability, which we consider later as an *enchantment* of *rationalization* (compare Sect. 8.1). Such norms are powerful in countries where middle-class and neoliberal values dominate. Strong norms of autonomous decision-making accompany these, but neglect the lived reality in lower strata, where people work hard and struggle but still have difficulties making ends meet.

In summary, research suggests that hope has a complex nature. It can inhibit activity, as seen in passive hope, but it can also serve as a reasonable and positive resource. Maintaining hope can be a constant challenge when a threatening future seems unavoidable, with people swaying between despair and hope. The dynamics and tensions involved in hoping are not fully captured by the simple distinction between passive and active hope, which reflects a modern dichotomy favoring active engagement with the world. In this way, active hope is often viewed as a positive attitude towards an uncertain future that one wishes to change. As the next section demonstrates, *magic* functions similarly to *hope* by increasing the perceived likelihood of achieving a desired future.

## 3.2 Magic

Magic plays a similar role as hope, but it refers to objects or rituals that support positive (or negative) expectations about the future. Jarvis suggested that "Superstition [or better magic] is an attitude, or attitudes, individually held by people which relate their existence to the general order of the cosmos, but which are not based upon empirical evidence nor incorporated within the institutionalized belief systems of a society as defined by leading representatives of these systems at any given time" (Jarvis, 1980, p. 291).

In the following, we avoid the expressions "superstition" and "superstitious," which carry an ethnocentric perspective that devalues non-Western, pre-modern, or marginalized groups as irrational and primitive in contrast to Western rational science. As Edward Said (1978) and Talal Asad (1993, 2003) have shown, this rhetoric helped justify imperial domination by classifying colonized people's cultures and religions as irrational. Such a perspective contradicts our approach, which advocates epistemological pluralism and seeks to be sensitive to the role of magic in modern rationality and the reasonableness of magic for engaging with risk and uncertainty (compare also Brown, 2020, 2022).

There is no doubt that throughout history, people have engaged in magical thoughts and practices (Alaszewski, 2015). As the famous Polish-British anthropologist and ethnologist Bronisław Malinowski (1925) observed, lacking control over high risks supports the engagement with religious and/or magical ritual and practices. Referring to his study on Trobriand islanders, he identified different fishing practices in lagoon fishing and open sea fishing (Malinowski, 1925, p. 31). In lagoon fishing, Trobriand islanders can, in a relatively safe environment, rely on their knowledge and skills. For the more dangerous open sea fishing, they are mobilizing extensive magical rituals to secure safety and a good catch. There are also plenty of anecdotes that people today still refer to magical practices: "Throughout his entire career, for example, basketball player Michael Jordan wore his old blue University of North Carolina shorts underneath his National Basketball Association uniform, for good luck. Similarly, tennis player Serena Williams once admitted wearing the same pair of socks throughout a tournament, and golf pro Tiger Woods wears a red shirt on tournament Sundays, which is usually the last (and critical) day of a tournament" (Damisch et al., 2010, p. 1014).

There is enough evidence that shows that "*Magic seems inevitably to be associated with anxiety-causing events, whether its function is to allay the anxiety, as Malinowski suggests, or to generate anxiety where it does not exist and for society reasons should, as Radcliffe-Brown suggests (Homans, 1941)*" (Albas & Albas, 1989, p. 603). Magical practices have been observed among college students and at the university (Albas & Albas, 1989; Rudski & Edwards, 2007), in competitive sport (Buhrmann & Zaugg, 1981; Burger & Lynn, 2005), during military missions (Stouffer et al., 1949), among miners (Wilson, 1942) and gamblers (Henslin, 1967). Therefore, it seems justified to consider them to be still pervasive within modern societies (for reviews, see Jahoda, 1969; Vyse, 1997, 2020).

The reason for turning to such modes might be their efficiency in managing anxieties and focusing on a task, resulting in better performances, as psychological research argues. Lysann Damisch and colleagues suggested, based on an empirical study, that "*the activation of a good-luck-associated superstition [magic] prior to a specific performance task leads to heightened feelings of self-efficacy toward this task, which in turn leads to better performance*" (Damisch et al., 2010). This mechanism can indeed only work when events are not purely chance dependent, as in the case of roulette, but influenced by one's performance (Goffman, 1969). In such cases, even when there is no logical connection between the exercise of magical behavior and the processes in the world, it can still be reasonable to use such practices to improve performance in the face of a difficult task or situation.

This is also true for broader belief systems. For example, it has been reported that many Chinese people believe in lucky numbers. Because this belief can enhance well-being, it might be rational to pay higher premiums for houses with such house numbers (He et al., 2019; Shum et al., 2014), following the well-known dictum of the Thomas theorem, "if men define situations as real, they are in their consequences" (Thomas & Thomas, 1970 [1928], p. 553).

An interesting argument was developed by Colin Campbell (1996), who tried to understand why large proportions of people in modern societies, such as the UK, still engage in magical practices even when they claim not to believe in them.[2] His framework suggests that

> the central importance of the value of instrumental activism in contemporary society and the tension that this necessarily creates in individuals where the 'rational' response is inactivity and resignedness. Engaging in acts which mimic instrumentality under those circumstances, whilst at the same time 'dis-believing' that their actions can, in reality, affect the outcome, is thus identified as essentially a ritual response, one which serves to re-affirm the individual's basic commitment to agency and an optimistic, activist intervention in the world (Campbell 1996, 151)

When people consistently use these practices to deal with stress, even without believing in them and merely following an "instrumental activism" (Campbell, 1996), these practices may still increase the likelihood of success by helping to focus and mobilize positive feelings through the ritual.

In this way, it becomes clear that hope as well as magical practices have been typically interpreted by scholars against the backdrop of modern orthodoxy. There might be some truth in Campbell's model that a normative pattern is ritually reproduced even when people are doubtful

[2] However, one might wonder whether the informants might have responded to the social rationality expectation and might not have admitted an at least marginal belief in the practice.

that it works. Nevertheless, the continuing pervasiveness of magical practices hints at their usefulness. When believed, they remain efficient means for improving outcomes in performance-based activities. There might also be a social component to increase positive feelings in the face of risk and uncertainty when engaging in rituals with others, as we will argue in the case of institutionalized faith and ideology (compare Sects. 3.3 and 3.4).

## 3.3 Faith

Faith is a mode of managing risk and uncertainty that works in many ways similar to hope and magic. It is embedded in broader institutionalized sense-making frameworks, which structure meaning and behavior, and also come with routines and rituals that help to give confidence in the religious understanding of the world. Faith, hope, and magical practices are connected in their provision of a positive attitude towards the future. Strong faith in a religion can mobilize resources in many ways, such as by boosting confidence in one's abilities to manage the future.

Faith, like hope, has been considered in risk studies as a typical attitude that would prevent people from taking necessary action in the face of risk or to explore the causes of a disaster (Renn, 2008). In so doing, this interpretation implicitly follows the modern division between rational and non-rational modes, missing out on the positive aspects of faith, which can, similar to hope, also activate and enable people to act in the face of an uncertain future.

Erich Fromm (1968) approaches the idea of hope by distinguishing between "irrational faith" and "rational faith," linking it directly to the aspect of agency. He explains that irrational faith involves accepting the given situation and circumstances of life. Faith could refer to an idol, a leader, or an ideology that is accepted as correct or true instead of being questioned. In contrast, rational faith results from one's internal activity in thought or feeling and can challenge situations, conditions, or expectations (Fromm, 1968, p. 26).

Interestingly, both faith and hope are understood in terms of modern norms of active engagement versus passive acceptance of the future, or even rational and irrational, as in the case of Fromm, who is more explicit about a modern valuation. In practice, when considering the conditions under which one must engage with risk and uncertainty, these clear boundaries become blurry. As we have seen through several examples (e.g., work migrants, boat people, terminal illness), hope can, even when it is "passive," involve active reflection to harness its positive power. Similarly, as shown, faith may blend with activity in complex ways, encouraging high-risk actions such as work migration. Loïs Bastide (2015), in his study on Indonesian labor migrants, provides an excellent account of how faith can foster engagement with risky futures within a religious framework, which neither involves passivity nor naive exposure to unreasonable risk. As Bastide outlined: "*The practices and conceptualizations … must be understood as the only available means for many migrants to restore a sense of agency in facing serious threats to their health and well-being. In a context where current economic conditions and emerging moral economies render migration increasingly necessary, facing risk is less of a choice than a necessity. And this creative use of cultural resources allows making this relation between threat and necessity morally bearable when there is little choice but to engage in migration routes, regardless of the risk*" (Bastide, 2015, p. 241). In this way, Bastide emphasizes the moral pressures that develop and that must be addressed. Therefore, people deal not only with financial considerations but also with a moral economy.

These migrants developed strategies to manage material and physical risks through social capital and informal insurance practices, such as exchanging information with and assisting other migrants. Simultaneously, their faith helped them overcome fears related to well-known risks of labor migration, including abuse, violence, or even death, in addition to financial exploitation. Viewing the future as determined by destiny, which ultimately is in God's hands, influenced their understanding of risks and misfortune. Sincerely surrendering to Allah became their way of demonstrating faith, while incidents were seen as divine trials testing one's faith in God. In this way, Bastide effectively illustrates how "mixed rationalities" (2015, pp. 241–242) operate in practice to manage various aspects of high-risk activities. These are often overlooked in narrow economic models of decision-making that assume individuals calculate and weigh potential threats against benefits (Williams & Baláž, 2012, cit. in Bastide, 2015, p. 227).

Faith is often linked to magical practices that support and defend the broader religious framework of faith (Douglas, 2003 [1970]). The belief that one's fate is already set helps people deal with high-risk activities by considering external forces that determine the outcome. Several studies have found this view in very different settings, such as in war (Stouffer et al., 1949), aid work (Roth, 2015b), or labor migration (Bastide, 2015). However, these studies also show that most informants still use various rationales to prevent harm and cope with the risk of adverse outcomes.

## 3.4 Ideology

When we discuss "ideology" here, we refer to the original concept as a set of ideas that form a broader belief system (Destutt de Tracy, 1801). These ideas do not provide scientific truth but serve as normative frameworks to interpret the world. Like Karl Mannheim (2015 [1929]), we favor this broader understanding of ideology because it does not carry the negative connotations that are more common today. Our reasoning refers to the human need to make sense of the world, which can sometimes be difficult to justify empirically. Karl Mannheim distinguished between various forms of utopian consciousness that historically developed into liberal-humanist, conservative, and socialist-communist ideas, all providing conclusive frameworks for understanding the same socio-historical reality. However, it is always debatable to what extent ideologies in the broader sense have an empirical foundation.

In the modern understanding of the negative concept of ideology, supporting empirical evidence is usually limited, emphasizing the lack of justification for a worldview (Mannheim, 2015 [1929]). Similar to religion, (political) ideologies give meaning to the world by providing what we call an *imaginative extension of one's horizon* (Schulz & Zinn, 2023, p. 226), which includes various non-rational modes of reasoning. They are reflexive frameworks of varying complexity that interpret the past, present, and future and can offer powerful imaginaries, such as Adam Smith's *invisible hand* of the market. Consequently, they can help justify and shape political goals. For example, the "axis of evil" and the "war against terror" were used by U.S. President George W. Bush in a State of the Union address on January 29, 2002, serving as powerful frameworks to legitimize military and other actions. They provided a way to frame the events of 9/11 and helped prepare and justify the military invasion of Iraq in 2003. Such imaginaries are influential and form part of broader understandings of the world. They are performative, creating a reality that guides both institutional and individual actions. They tend to obscure more complex, ambivalent, or contradictory situations and tend to highlight some gains while neglecting the risks. This is, for example, observable when larger economic projects for improving social resilience are framed in terms of technological and social advancement under postcolonial conditions (See et al., 2025).

Ideologies give meaning to risk and uncertainty in a way that a situation is experienced as bearable or unbearable, and risk-taking, as well as specific responses, are justified to overcome a threat or undesired situation. Such ideologies can be inspired by framing a future differently from the past, or more positively, as the present. They can also, from a Marxist perspective, deliberately frame the world in a specific way, which legitimizes unequal and exploitative social realities, thereby supporting a "false consciousness." Indeed, such a narrative can justify revolutionary activities of high risk and uncertain outcomes.

In this way, the concept of ideology is ambivalent. It not only provokes conflict and asks for change. It can also serve to stabilize societies, such as through religion, by invisibilizing injustice and thereby preventing or channeling social conflict. In such a setting, risks are usually normalized or justified, such as the heightened exposure to risk in specific occupations where lower-class strata of society tend to be overrepresented (BoLS, 2017) or risks of unemployment are justified in a neoliberal framework, individualizing risk, such as in the master narrative of the *American dream*.

Ideologies to different degrees rely on scientific knowledge and expertise, even when only symbolically. The abstract and generalized character of ideologies requires a translation into concrete everyday life practices. When providing orientation for the future, they always come with uncertainties and risks that they are channeling or promise to overcome.

Some political ideologies promise to overcome an undesired present and thereby transform the future into a desirable place (such as Marxism's idea of revolution and the reign of the proletariat).

To the extent that ideologies are supported by science, they serve as frameworks for understanding empirical social reality. However, they can also be regarded as "reality" or a valid way to interpret our lives, even when they lack empirical support, as seen with conspiracy theories. As long as they are deemed valid, they become powerful realities that influence people's behavior. Therefore, ideologies possess transformative power, which can justify taking significant risks both socially and individually, and like religion, they can also help people cope with risk and uncertainty.

As we will argue later, science also requires some (ideological) imaginary, such as the Mertonian norms of the ethos of modern science: communism, universalism, disinterestedness, and organized skepticism (Merton, 1973 [1942]). But science, as we know from research, can fail from time to time, causing unexpected harm. Even then, failure can give way to new insights and knowledge, which might improve future practices and well-being following the logic of trial-and-error learning (Wildavsky, 1988, 1989). Such an understanding of technological advancement can be considered an ideology as well, through which risk is framed positively, and specific action strategies are supported.

## 3.5 Concluding Comments

*Non-rational* modes such as hope, magic, or faith are often referred to for covering the remaining uncertainty every decision has to deal with, since the future always comes with some degree of uncertainty, regardless of the efforts made to reduce and eliminate it. Thus, *non-rational* modes are powerful concepts for coping with and managing situations of desperation when no other means or institutionalized sources are available. Hope seems to be a more fundamental concept among the *non-rational* modes, which is often connected to broader belief systems such as religion and ideology, which may encourage and mobilize hope. Such more complex systems of sense-making, however, differ from hope and follow an independent rationale, typically deeply rooted in the socio-cultural constitution of the social world. Institutions such as the Church and political parties not only provide resources for hope but also serve different social purposes and ways of thinking. They integrate people through social rituals and practices, which structure people's everyday lives more broadly and provide meaning and certainty on a broader social scale. They thereby protect the boundaries of social groups such as believers or party members (Douglas, 1985). Broader belief systems encourage hope, are interwoven with practices of hoping, or are a resource for hoping. Still, hope is the more fundamental concept among the *non-rational* modes, which does not require broader cosmological or ideological frameworks to be mobilized. Since hope can be applied ad hoc and routinely relatively independent of broader belief systems, it can be considered a more secularized form of imagining a positive future in contrast to other forms such as religion and ideology.

As we will argue later, if we want to understand why and how people engage in specific forms of reasoning, it is crucial not to focus solely on, for example, religious and ideological constructs, but on how emotional and embodied practices in everyday life enact these. This is similar to the argument Konrad Talmont-Kaminski outlined in his book on Religion as Magical Ideology (2013), who suggested that social practices and rituals protect the social relevance of religious frameworks.

In general, non-rational frameworks of sense-making broadly provide meaning, which allows individuals to organize the world somewhat independently of empirical evidence. Such an empirical basis might not exist in the case of religion and magical practices or might be limited in the case of ideologies. However, even scientific knowledge relies on theories. These are also constructs or idealized models of the world, not the world itself, and thus involve degrees of interpretation and explanations that are not empirically proven.

Here, Max Weber's key insight is that the calculability of the world is not just an empirical fact but a "belief" or an imaginary that supports and justifies how the world must be understood—as a rationally manageable world in principle (Weber, 1948). The idea that these assumptions are at least partly questionable has been outlined in Chapter 2, showing that they are just one way to frame the processes of secularization and enchantment. Therefore, there is some support for the idea that *rational* and *non-rational* modes we've discussed so far complement or depend on each other, which might already be implied in Weber's skepticism regarding the historical secularization process and the possibility of comprehensive rationalization of the social world.

A similar point has been made by Foucault on a more epistemological level, when describing the co-evolution of reason and insanity (Foucault, 1965). Both Weber and Foucault reject the idea of an ever-expanding, self-contained rationality that eliminates the irrational. Instead, both argue that rationality depends on its counterpart—whether framed as non-rational value commitments (Weber) or as the constitutive exclusion of unreason (Foucault). In this sense, Weber's skepticism about comprehensive socio-historical rationalization parallels Foucault's insight into the co-constitution of reason and insanity.

By now, we have followed a binary of *rational* and *non-rational* modes of reasoning, following broadly a modern distinction of *rational* modes and *other-than-rational* modes. However, the *non-rational* modes such as hope, magic, faith, and ideology do not cover all the modes which are considered irrational from the perspective of the modern orthodoxy. There are several modes that Zinn (2008, 2016) considered to be *in-between* or beyond this dichotomy, which will be discussed in the following chapter.

# 4

# In-Between Modes of Engaging with Risk and Uncertainty

There are several modes that Zinn (2008, 2016) considered to be *in-between* or beyond the dichotomy of rationality and non-rationality. People in daily life often turn to these modes in-between modes such as trust, intuition, and emotions.

One reason people often rely on these modes in everyday life is that they lack the time and resources to examine risk issues in detail, or they lack the knowledge needed to make such decisions. Instead, for example, we consult people (such as friends, experts, or celebrities) or trusted institutions (like NGOs, government agencies, or the media) to find the information we need or to follow their advice. These sources provide clues to help us decide when to become concerned and engage more deeply with one of the risk issues we encounter in everyday life and hear about through the media. Additionally, decision-making research shows strong evidence that people heavily rely on their intuition when making choices. This helps avoid the burdens of searching for relevant information, evaluating options, and weighing different possibilities.

Also, emotions are a vital resource in decision-making. It turned out that every decision has an emotional or affective component that underpins both rational and non-rational modes (Damasio, 1996). However,


J. O. Zinn and M. Schulz, *A New Phenomenology of Risk and Uncertainty*, Critical Studies in Risk and Uncertainty, https://doi.org/10.1007/978-981-95-7405-6_4

emotions can also play a significant role in decision-making as part of an intuitive feeling, which can process more information or do so more quickly than a rational approach that considers and balances many options (Finucane et al., 2000a).

When experts disagree, highlight different aspects of an issue, or when reliable knowledge is unavailable, *in-between* modes are the only resource people can turn to if they do not want to rely solely on hoping for a desired future. In everyday life, it is not clear when routines and practices should be reconsidered or when a decision-making situation is imminent. When people do pause their everyday activities (including information scanning) and turn to reflexive modes, they depend on these *in-between* modes of everyday life reasoning. As we will argue later, these *in-between* modes have a specific (embodied) quality, which is typical for everyday life decision-making in contrast to more abstract forms of reasoning. This is why we will turn to New Phenomenology to systematize the different modes according to their epistemological status (compare Chapters 5 and 6).

In the following, these in-between modes are introduced and discussed in more detail, connecting them to broader research before illustrating how they are combined (Fig. 4.1).

## 4.1 Trust

Within risk studies, trust has proven to be one of the key elements of successful risk management, which includes the critical issue of how experts let the public know about pressing risk issues and the best strategies to respond to them. The modern orthodoxy assumes that only when the public trusts experts risk communication can be effective (Fischhoff, 1995). Brian Wynne has shown over decades that how experts communicate with the public can cause deep distrust and resistance with long-term effects, as seen in his study of sheep farmers in the Lake District affected by the cover-up of the Sellafield disaster in 1957 (Windscale fire) and misinformation after the Chernobyl disaster in 1986 (Wynne, 1982b, 1996).

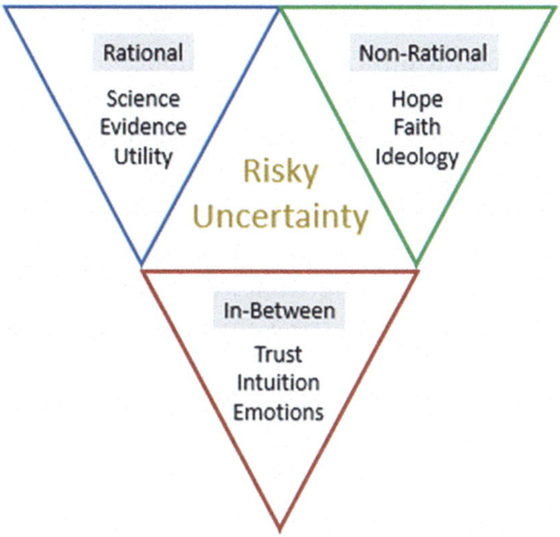


**Fig. 4.1** Modes of managing risky uncertainty

In an earlier study, he had already examined the devaluation of farmers' expertise in disputes about the dangers of Agent-Orange-based pesticides (Wynne, 1989). The devaluation of farmers' local knowledge may also have contributed to the development of deep distrust in science and jurisprudence. Farmers' local knowledge about pesticide application practices was, for a long time, not taken seriously and considered "anecdotal," thereby preventing the ban on the dangerous group of pesticides that continued to cause harm to workers (Wynne, 1989).

Even though some scholars suggest that the public has become more critical of experts and expert institutions (Giddens, 1994b; Strydom, 2002), there is still strong evidence that during times of crisis, large segments of the public turn to experts and their institutions for advice (Hegewald & Schraff, 2022). However, when fundamental social institutions or expert systems are already weakened or challenged by politicians—such as US President Donald Trump (2017–21) or Brazil's President Jair Bolsonaro (2019–22) during the COVID-19 pandemic in 2020—public vulnerability to disinformation and conspiracy theories increases. This is because, in such situations, various institutions, experts, and elected officials—more or less trustworthy—enter into conflicts or debates, offering competing and sometimes contradictory claims about an issue, which makes it difficult for the public to make well-informed decisions and find clear guidance. Nonetheless, there are instances where experts maintain their influence even when politicians challenge expert institutions. For example, during the COVID-19 pandemic, Brazilian governors opposed Bolsonaro's downplaying of the pandemic and instead followed expert advice to prevent the worst outcomes (Sandy & Milhorance, 2020). Similarly, in Hong Kong, the public challenged the slow response of Chief Executive Carrie Lam to the pandemic by adopting mask-wearing and social distancing before regional authorities recommended these measures (Chan, 2021). Trustworthiness follows complex patterns and varies between and within countries. In Hong Kong, the Chief Executive, who prioritized China‘s interests and was responsible for the city's de-democratization, was largely viewed as untrustworthy by many residents. Conversely, during the pandemic, political debates and actions showed that in Brazil, the politicization of COVID-19 led some political figures to trust the WHO's scientific advice more than Bolsonaro's leadership.

However, in many countries, large portions of the population still supported populist views. For example, in the US, many people followed Donald Trump, who successfully shifted pandemic management from an evidence-based approach to an ideological debate. In the early days (January–February 2020), he downplayed the severity of COVID-19 and compared it to the flu, while US experts stressed the seriousness of the virus. In March and April, he promoted hydroxychloroquine, even as the Food and Drug Administration (FDA) and the World Health Organization (WHO) warned, it might be ineffective and potentially harmful. He also contradicted the U.S. Centers for Disease Control and Prevention (CDC) guidance and discouraged mask use. Trump more broadly challenged and sometimes contradicted Anthony Fauci, the Director of the National Institute of Allergy and Infectious Diseases, and Deborah Birx of the White House Coronavirus Task Force, accusing them of being overly cautious, and questioned the FDA's slow vaccine approval, suggesting political motives. At times, Trump sought to support his claims by citing fringe doctors, researchers, or commentators whose positions conflicted with those of the CDC, the WHO, and most peer-reviewed evidence.

Having said this, in crises it is crucial how experts, societal decision-makers (e.g., politicians), and the public communicate about risks. Do decision-makers consider concerns and listen to the public (e.g., Dobson, 2014), which is increasingly diverse and includes different social groups both in the center and the margins? Or do they engage in top-down authoritarian governance with little or no consultation from the public and experts? Therefore, fostering trust in experts and their knowledge, as well as in politicians who make decisions based on available information, is essential for public adherence to laws and expert advice. For example, New Zealand's government was notably successful in communicating COVID-19 risks and explaining epidemiological knowledge and political decisions to the public. This included that the media were giving more space in news coverage to indigenous voices, which contributed to relatively high trust and vaccination rates in the often neglected and higher-risk Māori communities (Morgan et al., 2024). Furthermore, the responsible epidemiologist, Michael Baker (Zega, 2021), and the Prime Minister at the time, Jacinda Ardern (2017–23), were highly liked and trusted during the peak of the pandemic, when strong measures like lockdowns and social distancing were enforced. We will later argue that politicians' and experts' engagement style through social media allowed them to connect personally with people, fostering trustworthiness.

### 4.1.1 Trust in Society

For a good understanding of how trust is involved in people's engagement with risk and uncertainty, it is crucial to see it in its more general role as a kind of glue that holds society (and other social entities) together. Or as Georg Simmel once stated: "*Without the general trust that people have in each other, society itself would disintegrate, for very few relationships are based entirely upon what is known with certainty about another person, and very few relationships would endure if trust were not as strong as, or stronger than, rational proof or personal observation*" (Simmel, 1978, pp. 178–179). If Simmel is correct, the success of managing risk depends on the already established degree of trust within a society when facing and managing a crisis. At the same time, poor management and ineffective risk communication are not only a concern for the outcomes of a crisis but also for social cohesion more generally. These can have destructive effects for societies when people turn away from social institutions, experts, and decision-makers.

Therefore, it is of great interest how social changes influence trust and vice versa, and what character the observable changes in trusting have for individuals and society altogether. There is some agreement among sociologists that individual decision-making has become both increasingly important and more problematic because of the rising complexity and volatility of decision-making situations in late modern society (Beck & Beck-Gernsheim, 2002; Lash, 2002). Individuals have to make fateful decisions in an almost reflex-like manner, without enough time or knowledge available. Therefore, trusting experts and expert systems providing knowledge and skills has become crucial (Mishra, 1996; Seligman, 2000). However, even these have come under pressure, as such institutions struggle to provide certain knowledge and neglect to communicate uncertainty. Not communicating uncertainty in knowledge might be tempting because it can improve trust in the short term. However, when decisions fail, the loss of trustworthiness is larger compared to when uncertainty has been made explicit in the first place (Kreps & Kriner, 2020).

With competing expertise spreading, unconditionally trusting traditional institutions becomes risky. As some scholars argue, the generally observable decrease in trust in many institutions might be an expression of a shift in the way people trust. Rather than unconditionally follow institutions, people would scrutinize the trustworthiness of different institutions (e.g., Walls et al., 2004). This shift has been considered by Anthony Giddens (1994a, p. 14; 1994b) as a shift to *active trust* or by Wolfgang Bonß and Jens Zinn as a shift to *reflexive trust* (2005, p. 196).

Following this assessment, it appears that when trust is most crucial, establishing it becomes more challenging and relies on active negotiation between the trustee and trustor to succeed. Active trust might be even more fragile and repeatedly scrutinized and re-evaluated than the unconditional trust of earlier times. Thus, risk communication scholars have acknowledged that their success increasingly depends on carefully developing a trustworthy relationship with stakeholders and the public (Fischhoff, 1995; Löfstedt, 2005; Renn, 2008; Reynolds & Seeger, 2005).

### 4.1.2 Conceptual Controversy

Debates about trust remain controversial. For a long time, risk studies focused on trust in organizations, institutions, systems, and in people or experts (Renn, 2008). Many studies use surveys that identify different dimensions of trust, with two main factors standing out, perceived expertise and perceived values (Siegrist, 2021). These relate to cognitive and affective elements developed in social relationships, such as emotional bonds, empathy, and identification with others (Calnan & Rowe, 2006; Lewis & Weigert, 1985). Trust has also been a long-standing focus in sociology, seen as the glue that holds social groups and societies together, making it a key factor for social cohesion (Putnam, 2000, p. 137).

However, the concept of trust remains difficult. Some authors suggest that only people can be trusted, whereas with "things" or "systems," we should talk about confidence (Frederiksen, 2016). For some, trusting the money we are using or expecting the car to work the next day when planning to visit a friend seems to make little sense. Therefore, these scholars have proposed reserving trust for relationships between people (Barbalet, 2009) and confidence for "things" (Frederiksen, 2016). Others follow Niklas Luhmann's argument that trust is decision-based while confidence is not (Bonß & Zinn, 2005). The distinction might help to differentiate routines, which are not reflected upon, from reflexive engagement with others, when trustworthiness is assessed. The latter aligns more with intentional or even rational choice approaches within sociology or economics.

However, Michael Siegrist (2021) raised concerns about the conceptual and methodological weaknesses in quantitative trust research, which show difficulties in clearly distinguishing between trust and confidence and related concepts. What is measured when referring to trust or confidence, and whether it is the same construct, remains unclear. One of the reasons might be that some consider trust resulting from conscious decision-making, while others see trust already weakened or challenged when people reflect on the trustworthiness of others or social institutions (Frederiksen, 2016; Lagerspetz, 1998). A state of trusting is, in this perspective, the state of non-reflexive practices, while the evaluation of trustworthiness is a situation of challenge and doubt. Even when trust is a process of evaluating and confidently relying on another person, institution, or thing, it is somehow linked to a subsequent state of confidence and vice versa.

One of the issues in the debate may result from not adequately considering the time dimension. Viewing trust as a static state or condition ignores the complex process of trusting, which involves engaging with one's biographical experiences and reflecting on trustworthiness at specific moments to distinguish it from broader social conditions. Repeatedly experiencing the same events over time, or some form of stability, fosters confidence that things will continue as they are, or we could say, leads to a "normalization" of expectations (Frederiksen, 2016).

Many scholars believe this stability is decreasing in Western societies, which previously experienced a period of relatively high stability and predictability after World War II. Evaluating people's (or institutional) behavior in response to innovative situations is more challenging. Assumptions about a person's character are necessary to imagine how they might respond to future decisions. Here, social factors come into play. This is true for individuals as well as organizations or social institutions (Renn, 2008). However, typical aspects such as affective bonds—including empathy and identification with others—might not be consciously reflected upon but felt more intuitively.

The authoritative analysis of trust literature by Guido Möllering has addressed many of these issues. In *Trust: Reason, Routine, Reflexivity* (2006, p. 111), he defined trust as "*the suspension of uncertainty and vulnerability by interpreting and integrating good reasons, routine practices, and reflexive processes into a leap of faith*". However, we have some reservations about viewing trust mainly as a concept characterized by a lack of knowledge and control that is overcome by a "leap of faith" or "suspension" (Möllering, 2006, pp. 109–110). Many different modes, such as generalized belief systems, hope, or evidence-based reasoning, also involve accepting a lack of knowledge and control. Möllering's review of concepts like *as-if* reasoning, *bracketing*, and the *will to belief* as ways of suspension follows a common deficit perspective in trust literature. However, both Simmel and Möllering recognize different dimensions of trust, such as its connection to reason, routine, and reflexivity. Instead of defining trust by *suspension*, we propose focusing on the epistemic nature of trust and the specific kinds of knowledge that inform trusting (see Sect. 8.3).

In our view, trust is a concept based on experience, even when not grounded in scientifically proven knowledge, and involves embodied emotional elements connected to other social factors. Instead of seeing trust as merely suspension, we suggest recognizing the specific, independent quality of the knowledge on which trust depends. This may align more with Knud Løgstrup's (1997) suggestion to see trusting as a situational phenomenon. However, we believe that the time dimension and social learning are crucial for both institutional and personal trust. Biographical experiences, whether reflexively or bodily perceptible, are key aspects that are activated in particular situations (see Chapter 6). Nonetheless, the question of trust is not simply about doubt, but about understanding that when something is at stake, trustworthiness demands consideration. Otherwise, in everyday interactions and decision-making, we tend not to invest in extensive evaluation of the situation because the risk is minimal. Instead, generalized confidence reduces the need to constantly assess trustworthiness.

Interesting conceptual work on the character of trust has also been provided by Martin Endreß, who combines the phenomenology of Alfred Schütz and Edmund Husserl with Niklas Luhmann's systems theory (Endreß, 2014, p. 56). Drawing on Luhmann's three dimensions of meaning—social, factual, and temporal—Endreß defines trust functionally as establishing a stable framework for social action, reducing complexity, and dealing with issues of social continuity and predictability (Endreß, 2009, p. 26). Since he understands trust as a pre-reflexive mode, there is an affinity to the idea that trust rests on tacit knowledge: it bridges informational gaps and settles temporal problems of continuity and limitation (Endreß, 2014, p. 61). While Endreß emphasizes primarily the cognitive–epistemic role of trust, his phenomenological grounding suggests that it is also pre-reflexive and embodied. Trust, in this sense, is more existential than cognitive, involving tacit, habitual, and affective orientations rooted in the everyday "natural attitude," which is not only thinking but also bodily and emotional being-in-the-world (Endreß, 2012, pp. 494–495). Although Endreß does not develop a systematic phenomenology of emotions as Helmuth Plessner or Hermann Schmitz (with their accounts of *Gefühlsräume* or atmospheres) do, he nonetheless hints at affective dimensions insofar as trust is invested in social relations and sustained by expectations of goodwill, reliability, and familiarity (Endreß, 2012, p. 497).

Returning to our model, we suggest that at least some problems with trust stem from a lack of rigorous epistemological considerations. As we will argue later, after having introduced the framework of New Phenomenology, trusting might combine reflexive cognitive elements with embodied emotional experiences. People can approach trust reflexively, but it remains unclear to what degree they distance themselves from non-reflexive experience, and when doing so, to what extent they connect it to scientific evidence or extended imaginaries of a desired future (compare Sect. 8.3).

Trust partly overlaps with two other modes, *intuition*, and *emotions*, which we also consider as potentially reasonable approaches *in-between* to engage with risk and uncertainty, since they rely on both subjective experiences and broader experience-based assumptions about the world.

## 4.2 Intuition

In everyday life, we often rely on intuition or guesswork rather than detailed rational analysis when making decisions. Research has shown that our intuitive choices are not necessarily driven by wishful thinking or illusions but are based on different factors. They can still be reasonably reliable in situations where rational, reflexive approaches to decision-making are ineffective or fail. The reason for their success, as we can argue with Arthur Reber (1995), is that intuition relates to tacit knowledge and non-reflexive experience of the world.

For example, Stephen Lyng (1990, 2005b, 2008) has argued in his edgework approach to voluntary risk-taking that people who expose themselves to high risks or who are "working on the edge," such as BASE jumpers, skydivers, firefighters, and fighter pilots, all seem to have an ability to understand and respond to dangerous situations quite effectively, even when they have almost no time to consider alternatives. They appear to draw from a pre-rational or even pre-social source to cope with risk and uncertainty. This can be described by the experience of people who, in a reflex-like response to challenges—such as slipping while climbing—find a hold again. In this way, it is the subjective experience of becoming one with the physical environment.

Intuition is a concept that has triggered intense research in the last decades, as professional experts sometimes seem to possess a body of knowledge or senses that others do not have access to. Such knowledge allows them to act more quickly and reliably in preventing harm from happening, even when sometimes erring (Kahneman & Klein, 2009; Klein, 1998). Gary Klein argued that intuition is experience-based and is essentially a part of professional judgment. Through continual practice, professionals would develop an ability to respond rapidly and effectively to complex situations without reflexive deliberation. They acquire an intuitive grasp of situations and the necessary responses. One of Klein's examples is about nurses of a neonatal intensive care unit of a large hospital (1998, pp. 39–40). These nurses developed experience-based, intuitive skills, caring for newly born infants who were premature or otherwise at risk. One of the difficult decisions these nurses had to make was to judge when a baby was developing a septic condition, which becomes almost immediately life-threatening. These nurses could look at a neonate and tell the physician when it was time to start the antibiotics (Crandall & Getchell-Reiter, 1993). Nonetheless, the nurses found it difficult to identify the signs and symptoms that enabled them to identify the early onset of sepsis. Still, in most cases, their initial judgment was subsequently confirmed by tests.

Another example presented by Klein (1998, p. 32) reports from a firefighting crew in the US. In his example, a firefighting crew arrived at a house in a residential neighborhood. When entering the house, the initial situation seemed obvious. The fire was at the back of the house, in the kitchen area. The lieutenant led the hose crew to spray water on the fire. However, rather than controlling it, the fire roared back at them. They tried again, but there was little change. In this situation, the lieutenant began to sense that something was wrong and ordered his crew to leave the building. As soon as they left the floor started to collapse. It turned out that, despite no visible differences from other standard houses, this one had a basement, and the fire's source was located there. Crucial to this example is the lack of reflexive understanding of the situation, which caused the lieutenant to act. He didn't understand what was happening, but he sensed that something was different. Before assessing and discovering what that was, he acted.

Although the examples of nurses and a fire crew lieutenant differ significantly, they appear to involve a similar type of knowledge that relies on a sense of typical situations, enabling efficient action. This development of intuitive knowledge to manage one's everyday life challenges seems to be a common process that provides an additional resource one can rely on. But as with experts, such intuition can also fail and be misleading (Kahneman & Klein, 2009).

On a more general level, all these examples of intuitive activities refer to a sphere of non-reflexive consciousness that seems fundamental to our lives. Without intuitive actions, we would hardly be able to cope with everyday life, whether it is about driving a car, riding a bike, or using a knife and fork. The moment we bodily perform habitualized actions, we do not reflexively follow a script that we work through step by step, but act quickly and routinely, and usually very efficiently, to the smallest as well as larger unpredictabilities without reflexive thinking (compare also Chapter 6).

Decision-making researchers like psychologist Gerd Gigerenzer proposed a different neuroscientific explanation. Instead of focusing on people's experiences, he argued that human brains evolved to use fast and frugal heuristics (Gigerenzer & Todd, 2001) to make quick and efficient decisions in situations with limited knowledge or too much information. Unlike the traditional view of rational decision-making, Gigerenzer and his team at the Max-Planck-Institute for Human Development created many examples that show how, in specific conditions, fast and frugal heuristics can be more effective or serve as an adaptive response to decision-making challenges.

In one study, Gigerenzer demonstrated that stock market experts, when forecasting share prices, can become overwhelmed by the vast amount of information available to them. He proposed that in such situations, using the so-called *recognition heuristic* might yield better results than relying solely on cognitive rationality. He interviewed a group of laypeople on the street about shares from the stock index and created a portfolio based on the companies recognized by the interviewees. His research team then entered and won a competition organized by a well-known financial magazine by assembling the most efficient portfolio. He argued that experts might be hindered by the overload of information about different companies, while laypeople relied only on their limited knowledge of companies they recognized. They therefore selected companies that are more frequently featured in the media (Borges et al., 2001, Gigerenzer, 2007, pp. 27–30). This result might also suggest that the stock market could be better predicted using heuristics rather than rational considerations.

This research provided the insight that the normative rational choice model of decision-making might lack ecological validity (Andrade, 2018). While it is possible to design laboratory experiments where heuristics do not perform well, in real-world situations, they are often superior.

The path-breaking research of Tversky and Kahneman has shown that not only do heuristics shape our judgment, but also how a risk problem is formulated. This so-called *framing effect* should not be observable when people make decisions rationally (Tversky & Kahneman, 1987). Instead, people are influenced by other factors. When provided with the statement that 200 of 600 people have to die, participants of their study tended to take more risks (loss frame). When they were exposed to the message that 400 of 600 people can be saved, they showed risk aversion (gain frame). What is mainly considered an irrational curiosity of the human brain can be interpreted differently from a social perspective. Risk communication not only provides facts but also the communicator's perspective, which may remain implicit and be perceived at an affective level. But it is crucial for understanding a message, including the view of the communicator. Since risk messages are neither neutral, people identify the desired behavior implicit in the message. This means that our intuitive behavior not only considers risks as such but also assesses qualitative elements. This means that the framing effect may capture the social relevance of a risk, whether it is so horrible that it is worth taking an additional risk or not to take any risk to prevent further losses. We sense the more profound social meaning of the statement when listening to a gain frame and a loss frame. This again highlights that because risk is about a valued object at stake, it is a deeply normative concept (Renn, 2008, p. 2), which cannot be separated from its subjective and social meaning.

As a result, psychological research, even when focusing on the neuroscientific mechanisms of the brain, also indicates possible social relevance, since our experiences and valuations are not only a function of our brain but the (social) environment we live in. Drawing on a holistic understanding of consciousness, especially Thomas Fuchs' research (Fuchs, 2011, 2017), emphasizes this point. This perspective is challenging for neuroscientific approaches with their focus on individual brains. In accordance with our model, and with a disciplinary background of philosophy, developmental psychology, and neurosciences, Fuchs highlights:

> The structures of lived experience are inherently mental, i.e., they include spatial, temporal, logical, symbolical, and other patterns which in the course of organism-environment interactions are extracted and ingrained in microstructures of the brain. This results in the formation of neural networks that serve as dispositions for meaningful reactions to similar situations in the future. Thus, in fact, the brain is formed by mental life; from early childhood on, mental structures come to be imprinted in the brain's structure, and the individual increasingly shapes his own brain through his actions and interactions. […] From this point of view, the brain is not a creator, but a relational organ: it is embedded in the meaningful interactions of a living being with its environment. It mediates and enables these interactive processes, but it is in turn also continuously formed and restructured by them. (Fuchs, 2011, pp. 197 f.)

Therefore, biographical experiences and milieu-specific patterns of behavior shape how intuition works out in the practice of people's lives. A central mechanism that structures our risk experiences might be emotions, which shape not only our activities but also how we learn and remember.

## 4.3 Emotion

Until today, the modern orthodoxy with its emphasis on rationality and calculability is skeptical regarding the value of emotions for reasonable decision-making. As Niklas Luhmann suggested in the context of risk, emotions are too personal and too unstable to form the basis for stable social institutions (Luhmann, 1989). Emotions have traditionally been seen as inferior to rationality, for example, when fear of a possible catastrophe leads to risk avoidance (Rohrmann & Renn, 2000). Gerd Gigerenzer (2006) provided an excellent example of how fear can result in secondary disasters. He studied the behavioral shift of people after the 9/11 terror attack on the World Trade Center. Intense media coverage of the event over the year might have influenced people's responses to the terror attack, avoiding traveling by plane and traveling large distances by car instead. Thus, in the year after the terror attack, significantly more people died on the street because of this shift in travel behavior.

However, there is also a different side to emotions, which has become increasingly recognized since neuroscientists demonstrated that emotions are involved in all decision-making. Antonio Damasio (1996) once argued, based on his research on brain-injured people, that their inability to make decisions when a valuation of alternative options was necessary can be explained by the disjunction between parts of their brain that process emotion and cognition.

Consequently, research in psychology, sociology, and risk studies has demonstrated that emotions play a crucial role in how people perceive and engage with risk and uncertainty. Psychological research by Loewenstein and colleagues (2001) suggests that, in decision-making, emotions at a relatively moderate level can serve as a kind of advisor. In psychological studies on risk, the "affect heuristic" has also been extensively examined (Finucane et al., 2000a; Slovic, 1999; Slovic et al., 2002).

Similarly, the significance of emotions in risky decision-making has been demonstrated in qualitative sociological studies (Parker & Stanworth, 2005; Zinn, 2004). For example, some individuals highlighted that they decide when "it feels right to me" (Parker & Stanworth, 2005, p. 321). This emotion-driven approach to decision-making has also been applied to biographical choices (Zinn, 2004) and observed among financial managers (Pixley, 2004). Considering the variety of studies, it is reasonable to conclude that emotions are indeed a common factor in risky decisions across different situations, whether in high-responsibility roles or daily life.

In sociology, emotions have traditionally been understood in relation to social context. Unstable institutional environments (Gehlen, 1988) and the decline of unquestioned background knowledge of the life-world (Schütz, 1972) would lead to anxieties, fear, and distrust (Douglas & Wildavsky, 1982; Gehlen, 1980, 1988; Giddens, 1990, pp. 98, 102, 133), and may even threaten identities. Conversely, stable institutional conditions, including predictable rules and routines, tend to support stable identities and positive emotions.

As Lupton correctly pointed out, psychological approaches overlook the social dynamics of emotions, or what she calls the risk-emotions assemblage (Lupton, 2013, p. 634). In her view, "*both emotions and risk judgments and understandings, rather than being located within the individual, are fluid, shared, and collective.*" She introduced the concept of the "emotion–risk assemblage" to describe a "*heterogeneous configuration of ideational and material, human and non-human elements that is constantly in flux.*" Lupton's sociological critique of psychological explanations helps counter reductionist views of social emotions. However, these assemblages are often much more stable than fluid, shaped by social environments, institutional contexts, manifest social inequalities, and cumulative biographical experiences over a person's life. Still, emotions are negotiated within social settings. Hochschild's (1983) foundational work on emotion management was just the beginning to show how institutions not only influence but also demand certain emotions and ways of expressing and managing them. Nevertheless, a limited number of cultural frameworks are available for people to interpret and handle their emotions in response to risk.

As Zinn has demonstrated in a study with British former soldiers, at least two methods—a dichotomous and an integrative approach—to managing emotions in the face of risk can be distinguished (Zinn, 2012). The following two examples both embed their narratives about emotions within a biographical story to explain how their emotional practices evolved over time. They also reference the institutional expectations and experiences they adapted to. The first example illustrates a discourse of *emotional control* based on a dichotomous separation between reason and emotion. Jo (pseudonym for informant) reflected on his experience of learning to kill. He described how soldiers had to learn ...

> ... to control adrenaline, to control emotions. When you shoot or you take a shot, take three breaths, first, second, third. The third, you squeeze back on the trigger, eye, rear sight, foresight, target, yeah? And by the time the round has hit the target, then you can breathe your third breath out, and that's it. It doesn't matter how excited I can get about something. I'll still have a 48 to a 43 [pulse] depending on what I'm doing. We switch off our emotions. Our target isn't a human being anymore; it's just a target. All it is is a piece of paper with a photograph on it. That photograph might be walking across, yeah, and that photograph's gone, end of story. (Zinn, 2012, p. 4)

However, he placed this narrative within a broader story of experiencing violence at home and growing up with an uncle who lived and worked near a slaughterhouse. He described himself as a "cold-hearted bastard" (Zinn, 2012, p. 5), indicating that this was what he was called when digging out murdered civilians from mass graves in Srebrenica. There was clearly some pride in the story over other soldiers throwing up in the face of the human remains, but it was also a straightforward comment on the personal hardships he had to endure.

Interestingly, there were fewer heroic stories among the informants who controlled their emotions than expected, based on common norms of masculinity and masculine self-identity. Many soldiers shared stories of emotional separation and control, and their struggle to manage emotions with alcohol over a long period.

Other soldiers did not follow this modern pattern. One informant with the pseudonym Albert had a different approach, which was more integrative. For Albert, emotions must be integrated and used. They are an integral part of going into a battle. Controlling emotions for Albert meant using emotions to his advantage. He exemplified his approach by the example of a Corporal who advised him regarding his anxieties before a fight in competitive boxing at the barracks.

> I can remember my corporal saying to me this… I boxed when I was in the Marines. I did 37 fights, and I won the Inter-Championship in the Marines… and I was never defeated, so I was pretty good at this. But I always shook every time. I could never stop my knees and my legs from shaking, …. I was shit scared and my Corporal just kept saying to me this is the same with any man. If they hide it, they hide it better. Pick your first three blows, it doesn't matter if they don't work, by the time you're hit you'll be angry enough to fight back, and he was so right. And I used that in battle with all my men. There's nothing wrong with shaking, it will give you clarity. (Zinn, 2012, p. 4)

While he frames this as a story from the military, he also embedded it into a broader biographical narrative, that he always "*trusted his emotions*":

> If something made me angry, it made me angry, it was wrong and it needed to be fought against, and that's what I did. (Zinn, 2012, p. 4)

He said he learned this from his single mother and always fought when he felt injustice, whether at school or when he saw people misbehaving, like at a bus stop.

> Somebody would shout or pick on a girl at a bus stop, and I would step in and stop them. Somebody would be doing something wrong, and I would speak up against it..hh To take a risk for your future is the natural thing. Why wouldn't you take the risk? (Zinn, 2011, p. 261).

In summary, both managed to control their emotions in the face of risk. While for Jo emotions were something to be controlled to function efficiently, for doing his job, for Albert, emotions were not only an unfortunate issue to be dealt with but also a resource to do his job efficiently. Zinn's study demonstrates that when people deal with institutional expectations and conduct emotional labor (Hochschild, 1983) they find solutions that are biographically mediated (Zinn, 2012a) and are embedded in new social practices and therefore comparatively stable.

Another strong emotion is love,[1] which is a powerful driver of risk-taking, but there are also strategies to prevent the negative side effects of loving. Love is a deep, embodied reality and a form of reasoning that shapes our willingness to take and manage risks. People take risks because of love for others, but they also avoid risks because they feel responsible for those they love. For example, fathers often take fewer risks in leisure sports when they have young children. There are also tragic examples, such as the Hamas hijacking of Israel in 2023, when parents tried to protect their children with their bodies from murderous terrorists entering their homes. Additionally, understanding love influences social relationships and associated risk-taking. Research on safe sex practices shows that when people's feelings for their romantic partners are strong, they tend to be less concerned about AIDS and safe sex (Pilkington et al., 1994). At the same time, insisting on safe sex in a romantic relationship can seriously challenge or even threaten the relationship itself, since it implies that partners could be unfaithful, making protection necessary (Rosenthal et al., 1998). Therefore, love is clearly intertwined with risk practices in daily life. However, love can also be seen as unreliable and a potential source of risk, which calls for precautions. From this perspective, love is combined with rationality, as discussed below. Specifically, the rational management of the financial aspects of a love relationship can provide a foundation for allowing less controllable love to grow (Lewis & Sarre, 2006).

In summary, emotions play a complex role in risk studies of various disciplines. Emotions under some conditions might be misleading, but are central to most decision-making on risk, whether they serve as an advisor, have to be overcome, are instrumentalized (e.g., anxiety), or are a strong motivator for taking risks (e.g., love, shame). Emotions are considered both needing control as well as protection to allow them to unfold.

---

[1] I am grateful to Matthew Burch who asked at a workshop of the Risk Study group meeting of the British Sociological Association in London for the role of love as an in-between strategy.

Emotions are particularly relevant since they are involved with trust and intuition, but may become a motive in their own right, as in love or anxiety.

This leaves us with an important question. How do these different *rational*, *non-rational*, and *in-between* modes with their variants relate to or permeate each other in everyday life?

## 4.4 How Rational, Non-Rational, and In-Between Modes Combine

The growing body of research on *rational*, *non-rational*, and *in-between* modes has shown that a single mode hardly occurs in isolation (e.g., Brown, 2022; Zinn, 2016). Most commonly, people, when exposed to high risk and uncertainty, combine all available resources. They use their skills and knowledge and turn to their intuition or consult experts. They may finally hope and pray that everything works out well. When the stakes are high, people tend to mobilize any resource that might keep them safe. There is, however, some variation in how modes are combined. With degreasing agency, people still try to mobilize sources which involve human agency, such as trusting experts (e.g., doctors), rather than relying on accidental forces and merely hoping for good outcomes. Indeed, ways of handling risk and uncertainty are learned or taken on as part of socialization processes. Furthermore, people are not necessarily passive when hoping or when turning to their faith. They also use such modes actively to shape the future in their favor and combine such modes with others. Even thrill-seekers, who are taking risks as an end in itself, are quite rational in preventing harm from happening to them. Moreover, people often face and manage risks in institutional contexts, which expose them to formal regulations and expectations that must be translated before being put into practice. This is not a smooth process. As research shows, people not only interpret rules and regulations but also reject or bend them according to their views and judgments, as well as the circumstances of a concrete situation, which requires a response. Institutional forces and external pressures can also lead to delusional approaches to risk, resulting in disaster. In the following, we will revisit all these different points by example, which are indeed rather exemplary than exhaustive. They exemplify empirical research found in the literature, illustrating several typical ways in which modes combine. It would be the task for further research to systematize empirical patterns into a comprehensive map. However, we still expect that the presented framework is helpful to examine, characterize, and make sense of further case studies.

Typically, when people engage in high-risk activities, they mobilize all resources available to them and thereby also refer to different modes of reasoning. For example, a study on boat migration from Senegal to the Canary Islands showed that migrants are aware that they are taking high risks when entering a boat, but have decided that they have no other option to change their unbearable situation than to undertake the journey. These mainly young males mobilize all kinds of cognitive, emotional, and practical resources to cope with the risks and uncertainties (Hernandez-Carretero & Carling, 2012). This includes faith in God and acceptance of predetermined fate, a talisman to protect against evil spirits and demons, and trust in an experienced fisherman to prepare the journey with enough drinking water, food, and fuel. Similarly, a study of aid workers has shown that these have to deal with the knowledge of increasing risks of aid work (Roth, 2015a, 2015b). When doing so, they also turn to modes such as intuition and tacit knowledge, and faith or trust. Many are confident that they would be flown out before the situation in a country becomes too dangerous. There is also a small number of aid workers who mobilize the belief in a predetermined fate.

Both examples show that rationality does not always give enough reason or confidence in controlling risks and uncertainties, nor in managing the anxieties that come with them. For instance, when traveling by plane, which is one of the safest ways to cover long distances, many people feel uneasy and must find ways to cope with their anxieties, even when they know the statistics. Therefore, people use additional strategies when choosing to engage in what they perceive as risky activities to achieve their goals. Many examples in the literature show that people often knowingly enter risk situations and use their agency to prevent the worst. This involves relying on various methods, such as making evidence-based decisions and also turning to magical approaches, whether they believe in them or use them as coping mechanisms. When doing this, they also depend on their intuitive judgment about whom to trust, among many other ways of managing risk in everyday life.

Different strategies can be combined in various ways. Rather than giving up, many people try to use and maintain their agency as long as possible, whether factual or illusionary, while the boundaries between the two are blurry. In vulnerable situations, people make attempts to prevent the worst, even when escaping one risk means taking extremely high other risks (Hayenhjelm, 2006), such as engaging with people smugglers to escape poverty, starvation, or political prosecution. Some might even consider selling a kidney to resolve financial disputes. Or women might engage in illegal abortion to escape the socio-legal punishment of the Shari'ah.

When agency decreases, and in extreme cases, such as death, seems no longer preventable when rationally reflected upon, most people tend to cling as long as possible to keeping the possibility of a better future alive before giving in (Glaser & Strauss, 1968). Researchers have shown how, in such cases, trust may combine with other ways of managing risk. For example, Patrick Brown and his colleagues (2015) have argued that terminal cancer patients mobilize trust in doctors or a "will to trust" in professional expertise to cope with the rationally unpreventable. When medical knowledge presents a rather daunting future, trust in a doctor, professional expertise, and medical research help them maintain positive feelings and hope, rather than relying on luck or fate. In such situations, trust in oncologists might intertwine with hope that medical knowledge will develop and new drugs become available. However, patients regularly experience tensions between desperation and hope, as has also been observed by others. The earlier mentioned study by Cheryl Mattingly (2006) on African-American families who have children with severe and chronic illnesses or disabilities show also a reflexive use of hope where the reality of everyday suffering of their children was accompanied by a *will to hope,* which was a crucial element of their daily life, but a struggle accompanied by a feeling of being morally responsible for not giving up on their children.

These examples do not mean that everything is about combining different approaches for better and more efficient outcomes. There are also cases where people oppose a rational perspective, which can lead to death. Ranjana Srivastava (2023) reported on a young patient who had already undergone chemotherapy when her cancer returned. However, she ignored the medical reality and resisted any further treatment. It turned out she believed that her earlier endured harsh treatment would have resulted in "a lifetime cure" to reward her previous suffering. Clinging to this misguided hope ultimately caused her death (Srivastava, 2023). As Srivastava reflected on the challenges in reaching her patient, "the greatest loss was the premature loss of understanding." This raises the vital question of whether there are other ways to combine different modes of reasoning to connect with a person who is shocked and overwhelmed by an unexpected cancer recurrence, rather than sticking solely to a rationalist clinical approach.

Another example of combining different modes of reasoning is thrill-seekers engaging in high-risk leisure sports. They may be viewed as taking unnecessary risks when pushing boundaries and testing their skills through activities like BASE jumping, ice climbing, high-altitude climbing, class five whitewater rafting, mountain rescue work, and other extreme sports. However, as Stephen Lyng (Lyng, 1990, 2005a, 2008) has explained, so-called edgeworkers—those who explore their limits in such activities—are far from careless or negligent about the risks involved. Quite the opposite, they are usually very cautious about their gear, weather conditions, and many other factors. They might seem like "control freaks" because they understand that even the smallest mistake can lead to serious injury or death. Nevertheless, most believe it is within their control and trust their skills to manage the risks and uncertainties successfully. For example, wing-suit divers may not jump if the weather isn't ideal, if they don't feel right, or if they have a sense that it's not their day. In these cases, thrill-seeking, rationality, and intuitive knowledge work together, each depending on the other.

It is interesting to consider the different ways in which rational modes connect with non-rational modes. The example of edgework is characterized by a strong belief in rational control, as well as a sense of an innate ability to manage the risky uncertainties involved. These are effectively transformed into certainty. Our earlier example of emotions presents a different perspective. In a culture of divorce (Hackstaff, 1999), where the instability of intimate relationships is well-known and reflected in comparatively high divorce rates, couples are anxious about the financial implications of moving in with a partner (Lewis & Sarre, 2006). The couples interviewed in the study by Jenny Lewis and Sophie Sarre assume that love is uncontrollable and therefore a backup plan is necessary before they can fully enjoy their love, which they perceive as a risky venture. This contrasts with another study on certainty constructions among middle-aged people in Bavaria, Germany, in which Zinn was involved. One woman he interviewed was in a traditional relationship and fully dependent on her husband. When asked whether she was worried about what might happen to her if she got divorced, she jokingly replied, "I'd be a welfare case" (Zinn, 2004, p. 209). However, she indicated that her loving relationship is beyond doubt and that divorce is not a realistic consideration. She did not seriously entertain the possibility of divorce, adhering to the ideology of marriage as a lifelong bond and relying on her feelings of safety in her relationship with a partner she has known since childhood. Thus, the examples of edgework and intimate relationships illustrate two different ways of managing risk and uncertainty: cognitively transforming it into certainty versus accepting the uncertainty in one domain (physical environment, emotions) while controlling potential negative outcomes in another (finances, sport gear).

Another, though unexpected, example is that of highly professional fighter pilots, some of whom combine a professional attitude and confidence with a belief in luck, fate, and magic (Bonß & Zinn, 2005). They follow the idea that these beliefs help calm people in the face of uncontrollable futures. This contrasts with the example of edgeworkers, who, according to Lyng, often believe in their innate ability to control situations that are chance-determined. In contrast, fighter pilots understand that their training alone can't protect them from enemies who pursue them. Therefore, beliefs in magic might help them manage the unmanageable, at least emotionally. A study on WWII US soldiers (Stouffer et al., 1949) dealing with combat experiences also shows that professionals can sometimes cope with the threat of serious injury or death in less rational ways. Interestingly, many young people working in high-risk jobs—such as soldiers, military paramedics, aid workers, or war journalists—sometimes feel that it won't be them who die, but others.[2] However, as they experience the reality of combat, their work, or grow older, they become more aware that it could be them getting seriously injured or dying. This awareness increases their need for resources to manage their fears.

It would be a mistake to adopt a Westernized perspective that prioritizes rationality as the standard and views non-rational modes as responses to a lack of means to do so. There is sufficient evidence showing how faith-based and religious ways of sense-making are effective when engaging with risk and uncertainty, while intuitive knowledge and rational modes are integrated into a broader faith-based framework. As Loïs Bastide (2015) described in his study on work migration from Indonesia to Malaysia and Singapore, which was discussed earlier in the subsection on faith, religion might provide a broader framework for sense-making. However, people still use available knowledge and their personal experience to manage high-risk situations when applying such a framework in practice. They do not need a delusion of being personally in control or relying on other means, such as alcohol, to deal emotionally with the situation (Freud, 1930). Instead, their faith helps them efficiently cope with their anxieties. Faith provides them with the resources to manage risk and uncertainty both practically and emotionally—through rituals like prayer, which help them stay focused and control their emotions—yet they do not necessarily deny the reality of threats and can still develop reasonable strategies to handle them.

This already indicates that risk management is often mediated and shaped by social organizations, such as religious systems or other forms of institutionalized activity. Max Weber, in his research on modernization, emphasized the importance of the development of bureaucracy for the advancing rationalization and intellectualization of the social world. But also, more recent considerations of a shift from a rationalized commitment to truth to formalized regimes of hope face similar

[2] Neurological research is arguing that the lack of risk awareness of young males is due to a developmental deficit (Steinberg, 2004, 2007). In line with this insight might be a surprising narrative Zinn founds in his study on ex-servicemen (Zinn, 2010, para 46). Some of them explained that at one point they realised that people actually die when doing this job. There is also some other anecdotal evidence from autobiographical reports (Groos, 2011).

challenges (Brown, 2005). The formalization of institutional processes within organizations, which include the rules and regulations to manage risk, requires a translation of desires and political decisions into formalized regulations, which must be applied to concrete situations. That means that, ideal-typically, institutions emerge from practical knowledge and desires, becoming formalized and are brought into practice once again. People who work as policemen, social workers, state administrators, investment bankers, hospital nurses, and others translate formal (risk management) rules into practical activities in their everyday work. When so doing, they use their intuition and practical knowledge or may follow broader institutional imaginaries or corporate identities (Kosny & Eaking, 2008; Sanne, 2008). They may apply discretion, or decide to ignore, reject, or overcome regulations based on their personal experience and judgment.

As we have seen in the example of policemen dealing with issues at a large festival, they balance formalized risk regulation and security measures with their practical knowledge, what may happen when enforcing formal regulations (Horlick-Jones, 2005). The community nurse who must decide whether to risk changing the light bulb against regulations or expose the service user to risk has to make personal decisions about when to follow the rules or bend them (Sawyer et al., 2009). There is good evidence that efficient professional practice is based on both using formalized guidelines and, if necessary, overriding them and applying experience-based "better" knowledge even when this practice has to be concealed (Scamell & Stewart, 2014).

The translation of scientific and formalized regulatory knowledge into everyday life practice is central to both professional risk practice and laypeople's evaluation of the personal relevance of risk and its consequences. At the end of the day, when experts and people in everyday life engage in "well-informed guesswork," they bring together formalized knowledge and regulations, experience-based intuition, and non-rational belief systems, thus mobilizing all three modes even when focusing on one mode more than the other.

The need to translate formal rules and organizational values into practice is well-known. It can also become a primary concern for safety experts seeking to enhance safety in organizations, when applying discretion or bending the rules is a sensible decision. For example, as an industrial electrician in Martin Kosla's study explained, all his colleagues who laughed at him when he wore the protective gear at work are now dead, because not wearing the gear meant being exposed regularly to harmful asbestos dust (Kosla, 2015). A Swedish study described how railway maintenance workers bend formalized safety rules when fixing the railway track, suggesting that they are doing a good job when helping the organization to meet norms of punctuality while exposing themselves to unnecessary risk, which sometimes ends in disaster (Sanne, 2008). In a similar perspective, research on man-made disasters has shown that one of the difficulties in establishing safety is that, for a long time, a shift from safe behavior to exposure to risk might take place unobserved (Turner, 1978; Turner & Pidgeon, 1997). A wrong sense of safety and control might develop out of routines of ignoring better knowledge as long as no major accident occurs. Because intuitive knowledge develops over time, it can turn into overconfidence and unsafe procedures. Diane Vaughan (1996), in her study on the Challenger launch decision, showed that formal safety procedures shifted over time, informally establishing a practice of "deviant decision-making" which finally led to the disaster. Becoming accustomed to negligence as a new normality, along with the personal and organizational ways of misjudgment, is not unexpected. They might be motivated by external pressures but rely on common mechanisms of *in-between* and *non-rational* modes that we apply routinely when exposed to risky decision-making situations.

Whether in everyday life or organizational contexts, different modes of thinking do not only operate in a synchronic view of decision-making at a specific moment. Instead, the future, the present, and the past are interconnected and influence each other. In a modern perspective, orthodox rationality comes with the expectation that knowledge and, consequently, control over the future will increase over time (Parsons, 1980). However, the rationality model of social and scientific progress might be challenged by unexpected side effects of successful modernization, such as climate change (Beck, 2009). Scientific predictions and countries' failure to follow experts' recommendations for reducing carbon emissions provide good reasons to believe in dystopian worldviews. As

Julia Cook's (2016, 2017) study of young Australians' engagement with distant futures has shown, some adolescents and young adults do not subscribe to such a negative outlook, nor do they ignore the facts; instead, they cling to the modern myth that humanity will be able to solve climate change in the future. This non-rational hope, as they explain, helps them find meaning in the present and gives them hope to actively work towards a better future.

There are many other examples where the imaginaries of a utopian or dystopian future inform the present. There are suggestions that sometimes asylum seekers might have exaggerated rosy views of the country of the global West they are heading to, being surprised and frustrated about the reality of asylum centers and the lived reality of racial discrimination. Another example could be whistleblowers who are sometimes driven not only by the reality of the present but by worries about the future. Edward Snowden's view of a just world was compromised by the reality of large-scale global surveillance programs of the NSA in 2013. The imaginary of a world in which populations are increasingly controlled by the state and privacy rights compromised motivated Snowden to speak out and leak high security information about the NSA's surveillance programs to the public. A different example is games of luck in their different institutionalized forms, which combine the possibility of a future gain with the excitement of risk-taking in the present. Dreaming about the future can lure gamblers into financial risk-taking. As we will argue in Chapter 8, not only individuals but also institutions are enchanting the future to motivate and legitimize engagement with risk and uncertainy.

Many of the examples above could give the impression that modes are separate entities with distinct boundaries that can be combined in daily practices. In reality, some social practices effectively blend different modes. For example, religious rituals merge the reflective realm of reasoning with in-between practices. Spiritual activities such as prayer, fasting, confession, and singing together serve various roles within social communities, such as maintaining a sense of belonging and order, and transmitting socio-cultural knowledge and skills. Rituals can help to focus, relax, strengthen emotional bonds, and provide other benefits. Praying the rosary, for instance, has been reported by an interviewee in a study on how people construct biographical certainty (Zinn, 2001). It was used as a daily strategy to stay calm and handle everyday challenges, including responding to and making crucial decisions about risks and uncertainties.

All kinds of rituals have become part of our work and daily life for various reasons, but rituals are also important when engaging with risk and uncertainty: focusing before a task, staying calm, and preventing emotional overwhelm. Soldiers, therefore, practice rituals to remain functional in combat situations. Even when waiting for the next mission, one interviewee in a study with British ex-servicemen mentioned his rituals during the wait for the next callout. In the barracks, he checks all his gear and weapons to ensure everything is in order and finally cleans his boots. If the boots are already clean, he makes them dirty again so that he can clean them again (Zinn, 2010).

Rituals are so widespread in modern societies and organizational risk practices that we often don't notice them, such as being told about safety procedures on a plane in an emergency. Informing people about important events, including escape routes in case of fire, has become a routine activity at many universities in Europe and beyond. Rituals are essential in organizational risk management. However, as we will discuss later, these rituals can sometimes become flawed, as in the case of the Challenger Launch Decision in 1986, which led to a disaster (Vaughan, 1996).[3]

Thus, rituals are both socially established practices and individually performed routines that serve various social functions while also being essential for managing risk and uncertainty. They sometimes play a role in transmitting knowledge from generation to generation, a function traceable back to Homo neanderthalensis as an important way of passing down technological skills and knowledge over time (Nielsen, Langley, Shipton, & Kapitány, 2020).[4]

We tend to see rituals as crucial for responding to risk and uncertainty because of their social role and their effectiveness as a subjective way to

---

[3] Compare as an example: https://www.riskcoalition.org.uk/blog-posts/bringing-risk-into-the-heart-of-the-organisation-using-rituals.

[4] I am grateful to Professor Francesca Fulminante who pointed out to me this historically very early function of rituals during my time at the Hanse Wissenschaftskolleg in Delmenhorst, Germany, in 2023.

handle risk and uncertainty. In our model, they might result from reflexively evaluating a situation, but when turning into a routine or ritual, may increasingly become part of our stock of possible responses to a situation. Consequently, rituals are embedded not only in formal procedures but also in subjective, embodied experiences.

## 4.5 Concluding Comments

Chapters 2, 3, and 4 have provided examples and research from different disciplines that showed how *rational*, *non-rational*, and *in-between* modes have all their typical forms of reasoning, which come with advantages and disadvantages. They are not only specifically powerful when facing situations of risk and uncertainty. They seem to complement and combine when dealing with different challenges systematically. They may help stay focused, manage or use emotions, trust expertise, stay motivated when the stakes are low, and much more to support and direct one's activities.

Insights from disciplines such as psychological research on decision-making suggest that some mechanisms are better understood in terms of their social function and relevance. For example, the *framing effect* (Tversky & Kahneman, 1987) indicated the high sensitivity of humans to social aspects of language. They did not respond merely to mathematical likelihood, but to the implicit hint embedded in the language about the expected response. Rather than being irrational when responding differently to a task presented in a gain frame or a loss frame, people are susceptible to the linguistically implied preference for risk aversion or risk-taking. This comes as no surprise since humans construct their world collectively by language through which they negotiate "truth-claims" about the world (Berger & Luckmann, 1967; Habermas, 1984). In this way, the experiments of Tversky and Kahneman can also be seen as a confirmation that people's responses to risk require some sensitivity for both the "soft" social processes as well as the "hard" rationality of numbers, which are difficult to separate.

The former chapters have shown that the different modes or rationales of engaging with risk and uncertainty are connected. There is good evidence that the modes mutually complement, and there is also a clear indication that they all have their own epistemological status. The *in-between* modes are less a mix of *rational* and *non-rational* modes but an independent quality of reasoning. In-between modes, in our view, refer to a specific kind of knowledge that distinguishes the *in-between* from the *rational* and the *non-rational* modes of reasoning to be outlined in the following chapter. There is evidence that a good balance between the different modes is necessary for reasonable decision-making, and each mode appears to have a specific function within the broader decision-making process. People exploit these modes of reasoning to realize their aims.

What is missing in the conceptual outlines reviewed so far is a clearer conceptual grounding of the different modes, one that considers the epistemological differences of each group to allow for a more concrete systematization of how they relate to one another. For this purpose, we introduce New Phenomenology in the following chapters, which will be used to clarify the epistemological qualities of the knowledge underlying the different modes of reasoning and will help understand how they connect. The phenomenological perspective emphasizes subjective experiences and being situatively embedded when engaging with risk and uncertainty, taking as a starting point the embodied, pre-reflexive dimensions of sense-making, priming, and shaping the reflexive.

In the final chapter, we will expand the perspective to the institutional and organizational level to examine how institutions might exploit or encourage specific mechanisms. We will also see how forms of reflexive knowledge produced in different social institutions require a connection to people's embodied experiences in their life-worlds to become meaningful for them (compare Chapter 8).

# 5
# Neo-Phenomenological Foundations

As we have argued in the earlier chapters, it is empirically inadequate to disregard the *non-rational* and *in-between* modes of dealing with risk and uncertainty. In contrast, each of the three modes (*rational*, *non-rational*, and *in-between*) is reasonable under certain circumstances, which requires a more differentiated approach. For this purpose, the following sections turn to New Phenomenology with its original epistemology to develop an empirically grounded understanding of subjective acting under risk and uncertainty that allows us to consider the reflexive and the tacit forms of knowledge, as the latter play a crucial role in such situations. We begin by introducing some key aspects of New Phenomenology, which was founded by the German philosopher Hermann Schmitz (1928–2021), and then apply it to the forms of knowledge underpinning the modes of reasoning discussed in the former chapters.

New Phenomenology, in general, refers to the tradition of the philosophy of bodiliness or corporeality (in German "Leiblichkeit"). By refining the research of Edmund Husserl (2012), Maurice Merleau-Ponty (2002 [1945]), and especially Martin Heidegger (1967 [1927]), Schmitz



J. O. Zinn and M. Schulz, *A New Phenomenology of Risk and Uncertainty*, Critical Studies in Risk and Uncertainty, https://doi.org/10.1007/978-981-95-7405-6_5

profoundly investigated the dimension of involuntary subjective experiences. Essentially, this approach offers an analytical perspective that allows us to consider methodologically all the forms of noticeable certitudes, for example, hunger, fear, joy, pain, shame, intuition, trust, and so on, as they play a crucial role in our daily life. While trust is essential for decision-making and the management and communication of risk, other forms of embodied knowledge are less positively framed in this field of research, such as different kinds of emotions when ruling out "superior" rationality. In contrast, New Phenomenology allows us to take these empirically relevant aspects of decision-making seriously. Indeed, they are subjective, but at the same time, they are as certain to the experiencing person as they could be and are highly relevant for decision-making under risk and uncertainty.

As mentioned in the introduction to this book, New Phenomenology allows us to gain insight into the deep structure of sense-making as it proceeds throughout daily life. This process can be distinguished along the two main poles of *reflexive* and *non-reflexive* forms of knowledge. While reflexive knowledge, understood as the result of symbol-mediated thinking (especially language and numbers), is the result of social institutionalization, the non-reflexive forms of knowledge derive from involuntary bodily perceptions and are partially shaped by personal biography. This non-reflexive knowledge might be "merely" subjective, but it is as certain as it could be to the person who is affected. This perspective reveals a phenomenological gap between the sphere of subjective and involuntary[1] experience on the one hand, and their symbol-mediated interpretation by abstract and objectifying thinking on the other. Following this, the sociologically relevant categories of an individual and an institutional level arise along the differentiation of non-reflexive (individual) and reflexive (institutional) certitudes. By objectifying reflexively all that occurs to us in the sphere of bodiliness, we (re-) initiate the process of socio-cultural institutionalization of the individual, subjective experience, and thereby also gain intersubjectivity.

[1] We refer to all embodied experiences as involuntary in so far these are happening to us and are not voluntarily induced.

This process of symbol-mediated objectivation provides the basis for all forms of abstract and increasingly more technically advanced knowledge production that has resulted in highly functionally differentiated modern societies. As subjects living in a modern world, we are confronted with different forms of highly objectified knowledge. Each form of reflexive knowledge is a distinct way of making sense of a given situation. Thus, the modern self is challenged by a vast variety of possible orientations for its action. This will lead us, beyond other aspects, to the question of relevance that a concrete person ascribes to various forms of objectified knowledge. Taking the sphere of subjectivity in this sense empirically and epistemologically seriously, it becomes possible to analyze afresh the inner relation between the three observable modes of dealing with risk and uncertainty. Finally, and as a consequence, we will argue that this perspective allows us to fathom the tension between *reason* and *rationality*, which also seems important in the context of the modes of engaging with risk and uncertainty. Dealing reasonably with such situations, as we will argue, depends on considering the involuntary perceptible as a relevant sphere rather than merely trying to dominate or overcome it rationally. In that sense, our approach aims to address constructively the crisis of Western thinking as it has been diagnosed by the late Husserl (1970), a crisis that consists in an increasing decoupling of the subjectively experienced life-world on the one hand, and the results of scientific "progress" on the other. Even if involuntary perceptible experiences remain highly subjective, as in cases of *intuition* or *trust*, they could enforce one's ability to engage with risk and uncertainty, which might, as is the case with hope and firm belief, sometimes even improve outcomes as we have argued earlier (Chapter 3), for example, in the case of better health outcomes, when performing under pressure and to engage in challenging tasks, such as high-risk migration. For the moment, and to introduce New Phenomenology with its rather unusual epistemology, we will firstly provide an insight into the relations of this approach to some selected writings of Alfred Schütz, who can be seen as the founder of phenomenological sociology. To this purpose, the following two subsections turn to his early writings on the one hand, and to his model of analyzing the problem of relevance on the other, taken from one of his latest books. Thereafter, we present the neo-phenomenological model of self-givenness, subjective factuality, and situational embeddedness.

## 5.1 The Sphere of Non-Reflexive Knowledge in the Early Writings of Alfred Schütz

As mentioned initially in this chapter, it is worth distinguishing two basic classes of knowledge, the reflexive and the non-reflexive (compare Fig. 5.1). This is, of course, a preliminary and rather rough differentiation. In the following subsections, this distinction will be expanded into a three-dimensional model. We later differentiate *objectified knowledge*, resulting from reflexive thinking, into *rational* and *non-rational* forms by using the categories of being anchored in the subjective life-world and the level of empirical foundation.

However, by remaining firstly at the rough differentiation, the reflexive knowledge denotes all forms of creating objectivations by symbol-mediated thinking, whereas the category of non-reflexive represents what undoubtedly occurs to the subject on the level of involuntary sensations. Though New Phenomenology hardly refers to phenomenological sociology, it nevertheless seems to be helpful to briefly turn towards the early writings of Alfred Schütz to clarify the proposed distinction.

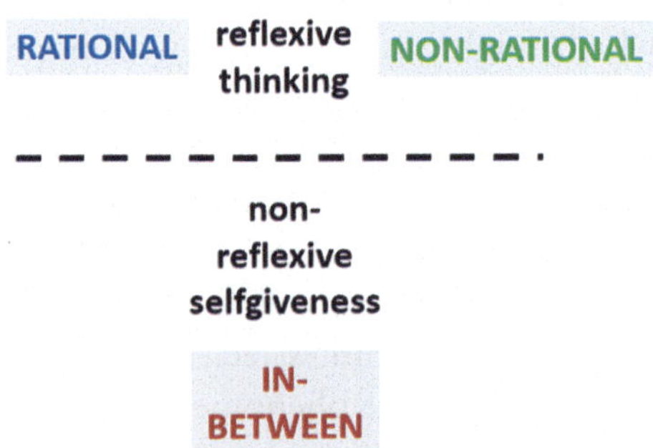


**Fig. 5.1** Reflexive thinking versus non-reflexive self-givenness

Before finally turning to the (classical) phenomenology of Edmund Husserl, Schütz (2013) started an attempt to work out his ideas in the early 1920s under the influence of the time-theoretical investigations of Henri Bergson. The key issue for Schütz at the time was the analytical problem that, to generate meaning structure by symbolic thinking, there logically needs to be a prior level of subjective experience. Otherwise, the process of unfolding meaning structure through symbolic representations would lack any content to reflect on. Schütz (2013, p. 31) hence speaks of the "basic difference between experiences as such and the reflection about experiences—a difference important for many reasons," which, following Schütz, was firstly acknowledged by Henri Bergson. However, as Schütz, in accordance with Bergson, highlights, the non-reflexive sphere of experience, understood as the pure duration of the I, can hardly be grasped by symbolic representations. Schütz stresses:

> Our experiencing is almost ever coupled with reflection about the experience. We control ourselves by our thinking; often we are unable to see the image on account of the concepts. Our consciousness of the stream of duration holds on only timidly to the unambiguous 'now' and 'thus', using them as rigid boundaries between which we squeeze our experiences-turned-into-concepts. (Schütz, 2013, p. 31)

Although this is obviously a conceptually problematic notion for classical epistemology, Schütz, inspired by Bergson and following logical considerations, distinguishes two ultimately incommensurable spheres of experience. On the one hand, we have the "continuum of changing experiences of quality" which never stops and, hence, pertains to the "realm of duration" (Schütz, 2013, p. 35). On the other hand, due to our capability of reflexive thinking, we classify these constantly flowing experiences by using symbolic abstractions, and, in this way, create a "delimited realm of concepts" (Schütz, 2013, p. 35).

By exploring the tension between the symbol and the symbolized, he develops a model that posits an identity of these two dimensions at the next lower level of the so-called life forms. Finally, the most irreducible sphere of this chain of reference is, inspired by Bergson, the pure duration of the I (Schütz, 2013, p. 57). Accordingly, Schütz, in his early writings, posits a basic tension between two distinct levels of experience: the involuntary occurring on the one hand (non-reflexive sphere), and the symbolically itemized on the other (reflexive sphere). This becomes clear in particular in the following passage, which is crucial for the context of this book and the elaboration of our model. Regarding the relation between the highly subjective, non-reflexive experience of quality differences on the one hand and its symbolic-mediated abstraction by reflexive thinking on the other, Schütz ascertained:

> With every positing of a symbol, the I steps more [and more][2] out of pure duration and into an objective world. To symbolize an experience means to rob it of its [character as a highly personal experience and its] belonging to a specific Now and Thus and, instead, to endow it with general validity. (Schütz, 2013, p. 70)

To summarize these early findings of Schütz, objectifying an experience by reflexive thinking is about robbing its subjective dimension step by step. Symbolic-mediated objectivity refers inevitably to non-reflexive experiences, which are always highly subjective. Though the non-reflexive knowledge hence constitutes the base of any objectivation, this whole sphere for Schütz, as a Neo-Kantian thinker, necessarily remained epistemologically problematic. To solve it, in the late 1920s, he started to turn towards the classical phenomenology of Edmund Husserl. Although he dropped his strong Bergsonian perspective in this sense, the early influence remained remarkable throughout his whole work. As we will show later in our argumentation, the described contradiction between the symbol and the symbolized plays a crucial role in explaining why people in situations of risk sometimes do not simply turn to the socially offered, rational knowledge about the respective risk. To anticipate the argument for a moment, abstract forms of knowledge are not founded in the respective life-world of the affected person, or, in other words, it achieves not overcome the internal contradiction of the

[2] Unfortunately, the English translation of this passage is incomplete. We added the missing parts in square brackets because they are crucial for our argument. For comparing the original source compare Schütz (1981, p. 140).

sphere of subjective experience on the one hand and its symbol-mediated objectivation on the other.

## 5.2 Schütz's Study on the Problem of Relevance

In the context of dealing with risk and uncertainty, it is worth referring to another of Schütz's publications, namely the late and unfinished "Reflections on the Problem of Relevance" (Schütz, 1970). This is of great interest for our argument due to at least two reasons: Firstly, it combines the Bergsonian approach mentioned above with the findings of bodiliness that meanwhile had been published by Maurice Merleau-Ponty (Merleau-Ponty, 2002 [1945]). Any process of sense-making, as Schütz (1970, pp. 171ff.) highlights in accordance with Merleau-Ponty, refers to the basic spatial location of our implicit embodied knowledge of self-being. Hence, Schütz complements the pure duration of the I, understood as the ontological ground for all the qualitative experiences, by a spatial dimension that is given through our bodily sensations. Both dimensions together form what he then terms the sphere of "existential knowledge" (Schütz, 1970, p. 144). It is a part of all the stock of knowledge at hand that accompanies any situation of subjective action.

The second, and for our investigation even more worthy contribution of Schütz's late book is the analytical differentiation regarding the phenomenon of relevance. As shown, in his early writing, he primarily focused on the epistemological question of the identity of the symbol and the symbolized, whereas the itemization itself remained a relatively open process. At this early point of his work, he describes this process of sense-making by using the metaphor of a prism, which refracts the beam of white light into its spectral colors. The original experience (beam of white light), subjective to the highest degree, is dismantled into its components by our capability of reflexive, and symbol-mediated thinking (Schütz, 2013, p. 56). However, in his late study, which deals with the problem of relevance, he steps deeper into this interpretative process of symbolically refracting experiences. He emphasizes the questions of what we consciously focus on, by what kind of concepts, and based on what purpose?

To answer these questions, Schütz (1970, pp. 26ff.) distinguishes three forms of relevance: (1) topical relevance, (2) interpretative relevance, and (3) motivational relevance. We will shortly present these three forms to use them later for our argument:

Topical Relevance: Schütz's analysis starts from the "field of consciousness" (Schütz, 1970, pp. 3ff.) that is characterized by a thematic core and a horizon, embedding the topic that is brought to the center of awareness. The field of consciousness, as Schütz (1970, pp. 21ff.) stresses in concordance with Husserl, is structured by familiar and hence unproblematic phenomena, and others which come with a field of problematic possibilities. In the latter case, we do not know precisely what the respective phenomenon is and hence turn our awareness to it—we give it topical relevance. However, Schütz, to avoid a misunderstanding of Husserl, stresses that these "*activities themselves have their history: they are the sedimentation of previously experienced events and are thus themselves constituted and interconnected into an experiential framework of context*" (Schütz, 1970, p. 5).

Interpretative Relevance: Following this insight that our conscious experience is structured by familiarity and strangeness, it is clear that we proceed involuntarily, what Husserl terms "passive synthesis of recognition" by applying our knowledge about typical or non-typical qualities. Thus, as Schütz highlights, we recognize its unfamiliarity, which is always a contextual experience, and begin to interpret it. However, not all the vast amount of knowledge at hand is relevant for this process. There are only "a few coherent types of previous experiences with which the present object might be compared—that is, interrelated by sameness, likeness, similarity, and so on" (Schütz, 1970, p. 36). These aspects, which help grasp the sense of the by then unfamiliar phenomenon, in Schütz's terms, gain interpretative relevance. The categories by which this process is realized are the question of typical or non-typical features of a phenomenon, a categorization that strongly depends on the given context of appearance.

Motivational Relevance: This interpretation of the phenomenon can be pursued to an exhausting level of empirical saturation or can stop at a relatively superficial level, depending on its situational importance to the affected person. Sometimes it might be enough to know that an object in the corner of a room that I am entering (an example that Schütz uses) is not dangerous. I might only want to know whether I need to act immediately (e.g., in case of a threatening animal) or if I can ignore it. In the latter case, I will stop the process of interpretation and release the phenomenon from the thematic center of my attention. Due to its low degree of importance, it sinks back into the horizon of the field of consciousness. We can decide to leave the phenomenon in a stage of either-or, a stage in which the level of interpretation "might be considered as having quite satisfactory plausibility" and "our curiosity or 'interest' in this problem and its interpretation might simply be exhausted" (Schütz, 1970, pp. 46 f.). The question to which degree we proceed with this process of becoming familiar depends mainly on our motivation. This sphere of motivational relevance, Schütz (1970, pp. 48ff.) differentiates into an "in-order-to-motivation" and a "because-motivation." The first one is mainly related to the future. By projecting our actions, we strive to achieve a state of affairs that appears necessary or desirable. The "because-motivation" is more closely related to the past, specifically the biographically shaped reasons behind the questions, which we then project as "in-order-to-motivations."

This relatively brief summarization of Schütz's study of the problem of relevance should merely give a first impression of the three dimensions of relevance as we will use them to analyze the subjective acting under risk and uncertainty. Regarding to Schütz's model, three general additional aspects are worth mentioning:

Firstly, he differentiates all three forms of relevance along the distinction of intrinsic and imposed relevance. A topical relevance, e.g., can be either voluntarily picked out of the horizon (intrinsic), or it can thematically come to the fore involuntarily, as is the case with sudden occurrences (imposed). Interpretative relevance, moreover, can be chosen intrinsically by selecting specific features that seem helpful in navigating the process of comparison, particularly in distinguishing between typical and non-typical instances. However, the phenomenon itself imposes a variety of characteristics that are relevant for its interpretation, e.g., in cases of physical objects, weight, color or spatial extension. Additionally, even a specific way of interpreting a given situation can turn into an imposing structure of sense-making as well. The whole process of modern rationalization, with its depreciation of any other form of understanding the world, for example, can be seen as a tendentially imposing form of interpretative relevance (compare Chapter 2). Finally, as mentioned above, motivational relevance is closely tied to the significance of a phenomenon. This importance may come from my intrinsic attitude, e.g., being fearful or bold, or it may arise due to the character of an event that provokes immediate, subjective action. Interestingly, in the context of our study, in this latter case, Schütz exemplifies his model by a potentially life-threatening phenomenon, which comes along with "vital importance for planning the man's future behavior" (Schütz, 1970, p. 46). We will come back to this aspect later.

Schütz, secondly, stresses with all clarity that these three dimensions of relevance are inevitably interconnected with each other. Though they could be ideal-typically investigated in the order presented, they phenomenologically never arise separately. Motivational relevance can influence the thematization of an aspect, and the interpretative relevance can shape the motivational alignment of a given situation. Hence, we are constantly immersed in a system of intrinsic and imposing circumstances of *topical*, *interpretative*, and *motivational relevancies*.

Thirdly, it is evident that this whole system of relevance is strongly connected to the process of habitualization (Schütz, 1970, pp. 167ff.). The situational given stock of knowledge at hand depends on the cultural circumstances on the one hand, and on the individual experiences made in these circumstances on the other. Thus, the biographical history of a concrete person shapes not merely motivational, but also interpretative, and due to this, the topical relevance as well. The theme a person focuses their awareness on, and the categories of being—whether typical or non-typical—and the motivation behind it, are highly complex issues. We will use this frame later to describe how decisions under risk and uncertainty can be analyzed.

To summarize these selected aspects of Schütz's thoughts, acting in general is something that connects the sphere of the involuntarily occurring (non-reflexive knowledge) and its itemization (reflexive knowledge). To get deeper into the non-reflexive ground of subjective experience, we will now turn to New Phenomenology, which offers a profound understanding of this.

## 5.3 The New Phenomenology and Its Understanding of Subjective Self-Givenness

Hermann Schmitz, the founder of New Phenomenology, revived the field of phenomenological studies, especially those of bodiliness ("Leiblichkeit" in German) and worked out a highly elaborated epistemology. In general, and as is typical for phenomenological research, the resulting approach aims to take a critical attitude in relation to concepts of natural science and traditional thinking habits. Besides various philosophical traditions, Schmitz elaborates this criticism also in regard to the classical authors of phenomenology, namely Husserl and Heidegger (Schmitz, 1996). Given the fact that the New Phenomenology of Schmitz and especially his critique of the tension between objectified and involuntary perceptible embodied factuality derives from his studies of self-consciousness, we will make a short excursion into this field.

One of the key issues of New Phenomenology, as mentioned, is to elaborate an empirically founded understanding of our lived experience that is not, or at least as minimally as possible, shaped by classical and scientific thinking habits. To do so, Hermann Schmitz develops an innovative understanding of subjectivity. The key argument is that there are empirically two forms of self-consciousness, or in other words, "*two sources of my access to acquaintance with myself*"[3] (Schmitz, 2018a, p. 72). Thus, he aims to overcome an old paradox of self-consciousness that has been famously formulated by Immanuel Kant, the somewhat

[3] All quotations in this book, which are taken from sources in German language, are translated by the authors.

problematic idea that self-consciousness is an experience in which one is simultaneously subject and object of his or her own contemplation (Schmitz, 2010a, p. 25). This notion of self-consciousness emerged from the tremendous influence that René Descartes had (and still has) on Western thinking. The subjective self, following Descartes, is primarily defined as a thinking entity: "*I think, therefore I am.*" What Schmitz stresses, however, is the question of who is the first "I" in this sentence?

Traditionally, this question was aimed to be solved by a never-ending spiral of characterizations, famously presented by Johann Gottlieb Fichte (2000) at the turn of the nineteenth century (compare as well Schmitz, 1992). In criticizing this, Schmitz shows that it is not possible to confirm the concrete subjective self-being by accumulating a range of objectifying attributions. While the definite description of other phenomena, as Schmitz (2011, p. 248) argues, does indeed work by means of ascription, this does not work related to self-consciousness. What is to be identified in the latter case must already be known to avoid an infinite regress. Schmitz highlights:

> Only in the case of self-ascription must the reference of the identification (what something is identified with) already be known prior to the identification. Otherwise, e.g., in my case, the result would be a progression to ever new characterizations, e.g., from a man born in Leipzig in 1928 to a professor emeritus of philosophy, in each case with the addition of information sufficient for definite description. In no case would it turn out that it is precisely I who is this individual; for all appropriate specifications of, on the one hand, Hermann Schmitz and, on the other, Alexander the Great contain nothing that would indicate that I am, e.g., Hermann Schmitz and not Alexander. (Schmitz, 2011, p. 248)

The neo-phenomenological studies of Schmitz show that the classical understanding of self-consciousness sets in too late, assuming that there is already somebody knowing of his or her own being. By means of objectifying attributions, may they be as differentiated as possible, we will never be able to define that concrete subjective self that each of us inevitably is. Logically, there must be a form of self-givenness that precedes all the self-ascriptions as they are typically stressed in the philosophy of consciousness. Schmitz formulates the key argument as follows:

> Why should I be just Hermann Schmitz and not, for example, Alexander the Great? All objective facts, which one can state about Hermann Schmitz, carry no trace of the information that this man of all men is what I am. I know it only through my affective involvement, in that something comes close to me, which I can pursue with prudence, with the result that I find a range of circumstances in which I am entangled or, as Heidegger would say, in which I am thrown. This applies to every conscious entity, even to the one who, like an animal[4] or an infant, cannot even say 'I' or even speak. (Schmitz, 2010a, p. 22)

The own existence, Schmitz argues, is not a positive fact, but on the contrary a highly subjective occurrence that happens to us by being bodily perceptibly affected. This embodied self-being is what Schmitz describes in the former quotation. It is something that occurs to the self on the non-reflexive level of bodily sensations. Schmitz (Schmitz, 2010a, p. 14) calls this "being conscious of oneself" (in German "Sichbewussthaben"). Only based on this, is there anyone at all who can ascribe objectifying attributions to him or herself, like name, age, profession, gender, and so on. This second level Schmitz terms as "to be conscious of oneself as something" (in German "von sich als ein Etwas Bewusstgehabtwerden"). This second sphere of objectifications is of course result of social interactions. Understanding oneself as something, e.g., a male, a sociologist or a person born in Germany is not imaginable without the process of socialization as it has been investigated by George Herbert Mead (1934). The very important aspect in the context of our book is that the level of pathic self-givenness is, in an involuntary way, subjectively evident. In case of doubt, embodied certitudes are experienced stronger than any objectified knowledge. Schmitz stresses in this context:

> So self-ascription is only possible if it is based on self-consciousness without identification. And such self-consciousness genuinely exists in the form of affective involvement. If I am, e.g., in pain, I immediately know it without having to find a sufferer to whom I ascribe identity with myself. Furthermore, there are states of upheaval or shock with increased

---

[4] Being bodily affected in that sense is the most basic form of subjective self-being that, as Schmitz often highlights, also applies to at least any mammal. Being bodily, he shortly defines, means being able to startle (Schmitz, 1996, p. 34).

> or, on the contrary, reduced motion in which the conscious subject has no access to themself as the referent of an identification but nonetheless distinctly feels themself in the intensity of excitement or derangement e.g. raging anger, panicked fear, mass ecstasy, devoted struggle in the heat of the moment, being sunk in melancholy. (Schmitz, 2011, p. 248)

To summarize this argument, self-consciousness without self-ascription occurs to us by bodily sensations like pain, fear, hunger, tiredness, shame, or by being seized by feelings (Schmitz, 1996, pp. 23). Nevertheless, this dimension of embodied self-consciousness should not be misunderstood as something that lies beyond the sphere of social interaction. In contrast, neo-phenomenologically, we find ourselves always already immersed in processes of embodied communication, a form of pathic relatedness to the (social) world (Fuchs, 2000; Schmitz, 2018b). With regard to the former subsections, these neo-phenomenological results are consistent with the category of "existential knowledge," as Schütz (1970, p. 144) terms it. The fact that this non-ascriptive self-consciousness has been neglected so long in philosophy and in other disciplines is certainly connected with its epistemologically problematic status. So bodily sensations are in the moment of affectedness as evident as possible. On the other hand, it is at the same time as subjective as something could be, which makes it epistemologically suspicious. However, the whole sphere of pathic self-givenness is, neo-phenomenologically considered, the most evident and ultimately the most relevant level of our lived experience. As we will show in the following subsections concerning situations that seem to be existentially threatening, this applies in the context of risk and uncertainty as well. For the moment, however, it is of great importance to mention that the neo-phenomenological concept of non-reflexive self-givenness by bodily sensations is not merely a logical deduction by a philosopher sitting in his armchair, doing philosophy of consciousness. On the contrary, the insights of Schmitz have already been fruitfully applied in various fields of research, e.g., in medicine (Burger, 2008; Danzer, 1993; Langewitz, 2008), in clinical psychology (Moldzio, 2006; Wendt, 2015) or developmental psychology (Fuchs, 2000, 2008).

Finally, the first fruitful contribution of New Phenomenology to the topic of this book is the empirically grounded systematization of non-reflexive knowledge, which plays a vital role, especially in the in-between modes of engaging with risk and uncertainty. While this sphere of subjective experience, as we have mentioned earlier, in Schütz's early writings, remained a logically necessary but epistemologically somewhat problematic dimension, with New Phenomenology, it becomes conceptually systematizable and empirically verifiable. In this context, the presented model of a two-dimensional subjectivity offers an empirically grounded understanding of subjective experience that can help to conceptualize non-reflexive yet clearly perceptible forms of certitudes like emotions, intuition, or trust. Up to this point, we have taken the first step towards an analytical model to examine the relevant levels of knowledge as they are crucial in the decision-making process under risk and uncertainty. Aside from different forms of objectified knowledge (which we will address later), there are embodied certitudes that involuntarily arise to the individual through bodily sensations. Since such perceptible certainties are as evident as they are subjective, Schmitz refers to this as a dimension of "subjective facts."

## 5.4 The Neo-Phenomenological Distinction of Subjective and Objective Facts

Contrary to the classical notion of the human self, New Phenomenology turns Cartesian Dualism around: I am (bodily perceptible myself), therefore, I think. As phenomenological and psychological research (e.g., Fuchs, 2000, pp. 19 f.) evidently shows, we are primarily pathic entities which, only based on embodied and non-ascriptive self-consciousness, are able to unfold the sphere of reflexive thinking. The latter one constitutes the means of objectivation which can be either experience-based and empirically founded (rationality) or is rather metaphysical in the sense of an *imaginative extension of one's horizon* (hope, faith, and ideology) (compare Fig. 5.2). Both levels of knowledge, *reflexive* (rationality, hope, and faith) and *non-reflexive* (intuition, trust, and emotions) forms of certitudes (see Fig. 5.1), as the risk-sociological research shows, are highly relevant for decision-making. Given that non-reflexive certitudes, as is the case in any form of subjective affectedness, are merely bodily sensible by the affected person itself, Schmitz calls them "subjective facts." On the other hand, the reflexively generated and intersubjectively accessible knowledge, independent from its character of *rational* or *non-rational*, neo-phenomenologically, is part of the whole dimension of "objectified facts." Actually, the underlying epistemological tension was already brought to debate in Husserl's latest work (Husserl, 1970, p. 132) where he stated "that there are two sorts of truth: on the one side, everyday practical situational truths [...]; on the other side there are scientific truths, and their grounding leads back precisely to the situational truths, but in such a way that scientific method does not suffer thereby in respect to its own meaning, since it wants to use and must use precisely these truths."

Returning to the elaboration of our model, we speak of intuition, trust, and emotions as forms of being bodily affected, which means that they arise as subjective facts in the sense of Hermann Schmitz. However, this differs from the common understanding of the affective as a form of largely erratic behavior. Instead, such experiences result from one's subjective biography. Their affective character consists of an embodied involvement that occurs involuntarily and seemingly spontaneously. This sphere of subjective factuality, however, contrasts with the symbolically mediated and objectified knowledge, even though the latter is reliant

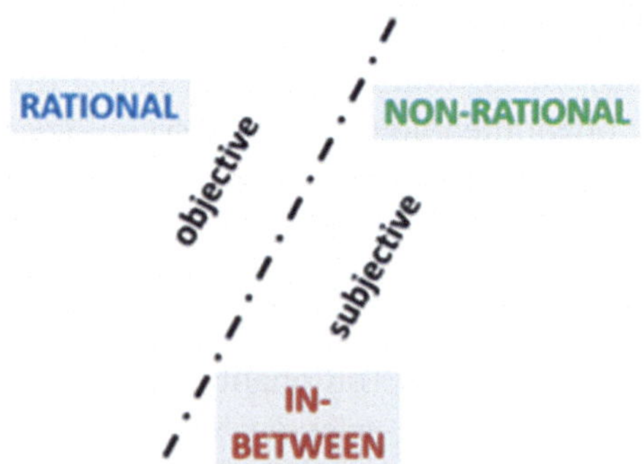


Fig. 5.2 Subjective versus objective facts

precisely on the former. Consequently, these two levels of certainties are neo-phenomenologically considered as subjective and objective, or more specifically, objectified facts.[5] The seemingly contradictory term "subjective facts" is closely linked to the theory of self-consciousness presented above and is defined by Schmitz as follows:

> Such self-consciousness without self-ascription is made possible by the subjective facts peculiar to affective involvement. In their plain factuality, they already contain reference to oneself, respectively to the experiencer. As a result, they can be predicated by, at most, one person under their own name. This stands in contrast to objective or neutral facts, which can be predicated by anyone, granted they know enough and are sufficiently articulate. The facts that are subjective for someone are richer in containing this subjectivity than the pale and neutral ones that result from the former by grinding down subjectivity. (Schmitz, 2011, pp. 248 f.)

Schmitz uses the scientifically provocative term of "subjective facts" to emphasize, contrary to positivist transfigurations, that a fact, epistemologically, is always a fact for someone. This is strongly reminiscent of the former distinction described in Schütz's early writings between the "continuum of changing experiences of quality," on the one hand, and the symbol-mediated "delimited realm of concepts" on the other (Schütz, 2013, pp. 35ff.). Nevertheless, especially with regard to Hermann Schmitz's approach, it is crucial to understand that the aim of his distinction of subjective and objective facts is not to neglect the importance of gaining intersubjective verifiability by objectifying the embodied experiences. However, considering that the ideal of objectified knowledge aims to ensure that no personal bias contaminates the outcome of scientific investigations (Porter, 1995, p. 74), Schmitz emphasizes the sphere that is intentionally neglected in positivism. By doing so, he intends to avoid a simple belief in the dream of pure objectivity. In this sense, he develops the term "subjective facts" to categorially clarify the relation between the sphere of subjectivity and objectivity along empirical observations

[5] In the coming section, we will sharpen the distinction between the two forms of objectivations generated by reflection, namely rational ones on the one hand, and non-rational ones (hope and faith) on the other. The two crucial differences are the degree of empirical foundation and the level of being anchored in the subjective life-world.

and epistemological coherence. Hence, this approach shows that our lived experience, in accordance with Alfred Schütz, is characterized by a kind of ontological gap between subjective and objectified facts which can only be suspended, if at all, by direct embodied experience (Schütz, 1970, pp. 37ff.). As we will show in the coming sections, this tension of subjective and objectified facts becomes even more problematic in cases of risk and uncertainty in which the object to be familiar with does not yet exist.

Although positivist science pretends to neglect the sphere of subjectivity, it remains the epistemological ground even for science, as, e.g., Bruno Latour illustratively reconstructed along empirical observations (Latour, 1993). To get to the level of objectifications, one could say that the initially subjective facts must be deprived of their subjectivity by means of symbolic representation; they have to reduce as much as possible the inherent subjective bias of any empirical facticity (Porter, 1995, pp. 11ff.). However, this practice of objectification is an ambivalent capability of human subjects. As the philosopher and psychiatrist Thomas Fuchs argues in this context, depreciating or even completely ignoring the non-reflexive but bodily perceptible sphere of subjective certitudes provokes a highly problematic and potentially pathological self-and world-relation. Fuchs highlights:

> Without affective contact the world gets 'on the other side' and freezes in empty existence, in dead facticity. This emptying falls back on the subject and contradicts Descartes' cogito: A human being who only thinks, who is not bodily-feelingly connected with the world, no longer 'lives', namely in the sense of the living existence that underlies all cognitions. The complete subject-object-separation, the stripping of all own from the alien, would therefore not produce the certainty of pure selfhood, but a nightmare of alienation. (Fuchs, 2008, p. 272)

To generalize this, our ability to objectify embodied facts through symbolic representations, from the perspective of a concrete person, can lead to a subjectively meaningless factuality. The production of objectified knowledge, as Theodore Porter (Porter, 1995, p. 85) formulates, requires a kind of outsider position: "*Unless you become like outsiders, you shall never enter the domain of quantitative science. The ultimate outsider is the machine, and it is rapidly becoming the greatest in the kingdom of quantification. [...] Inevitably, meanings are lost.*"

While this process of objectification is of great social importance, not merely for natural sciences, but also, e.g., for the moral legitimation of modern political decision-making (Porter, 1995, pp. 74ff.), it inherently exhibits the potency of turning into a completely abstract frame of data that does not contain a relation to anybody in concrete, and therefore, subjectively arises as meaningless. The more successful *subjective facts* are neutralized, the more they lose their connection to the person who is affected by the processed problem. In other words, that which is on the one hand the impressive achievement of, e.g., statistical techniques, widens on the other hand the ontological gap between subjective and objective facts, and hence, between the concrete self and an accumulation of more and more objective, but increasingly meaningless data.

A short example can illustrate this gap: In situations of life-threatening circumstances, the objective fact that, e.g., 95 percent of the population survives a medical treatment, contains no definite information about my future survival. Of course, these data show that, for example, if I had cancer 100 times and received the appropriate treatment just as often, then I would survive, let us say, 95 times. But this is a pure probabilistic and highly abstract knowledge, whereas my survival is a unique and concrete case. Such knowledge is obviously of substantial importance from a macro-perspective, but phenomenologically, it arises detached from the existential threat as it is experienced. Hence, even the most sophisticated statistic does not response to the ultimately relevant question "what does this say about my very concrete case?" Such situations of a subjective catastrophe can provoke complete risk aversion (Luhmann, 1993, pp. 2, 150 f.). The affected person then does not accept any probability, and to regain the capability to act, he or she turns to hope and faith or to modes of in-between.

This example demonstrates an aspect that is of great relevance for a neo-phenomenological perspective to engagement with risk: The gap between subjective and objectified facts, which is always problematic, becomes even more complicated when the respective case consists of a future-related issue. No scientific approach, no matter how elaborate, can answer the question of what the future will bring in my particular case. The observation of Theodore Porter (1995) that the social handling of numbers is deeply connected with the question of trust in such cases becomes decisive. Depending on their individual biography, people can trust the respective statistical insights, try to intuitively evaluate them, or reject them (in some or all situations) altogether, and instead turn to faith, hope, or ideology. Moreover, as we will argue later in this book, for risk information, it is highly relevant to reflect this epistemological lack of information about a concrete case. In other words, the concept of risk and its elaborate scientific processing itself produces proper uncertainties, which have to be taken seriously. Otherwise, the collective efforts and achievements of dealing with risk may turn into irrationality by overplaying its internal epistemological limitations.

Finally, in situations of risk and uncertainty, the eventful openness of the situation positions us in a dialogue between the embodied and the objectified forms of certitudes, between reflexive and non-reflexive forms of knowledge. Both of these types of certainties, as we will show in Chapter 6, form the situational frame of a concrete decision under risk and uncertainty. Before this, however, we will apply the presented understanding of the two relevant categories of knowledge, reflexive and non-reflexive ones, to the ideal-typical, three-dimensional model of *non-rational*, *in-between*, and *rational* modes of engaging with risk and uncertainty.

## 5.5 Characterizing Different Risk Rationales by Three Forms of Certainty

Following the insights of New Phenomenology, beyond the factuality of being affected as a concrete person (subjective facts), human beings are confronted with the collectively shared sphere of objectified knowledge. If I, for example, feel severe pain (subjective fact), in the case of an adult person, this experience is accompanied by the whole dimension of socially mediated expert knowledge of modern medicine (objectified knowledge). Using my medical knowledge, I can decide whether I need to go to a hospital or not. If I am not sure how to deal with it, I can hope that this pain will turn out to be harmless. This hopeful imagination, neo-phenomenologically, is a form of objectified knowledge as well, whereas it is, of course, founded differently. Hence, in situations of risk and uncertainty, such objectified knowledge can be further distinguished along the most relevant categories, namely *rational* and *non-rational*. We also refer to the latter as "objectified knowledge" because it is a result of the human capability of reflexive thinking. Due to this categorial overlap, we now propose a scheme for categorially distinguishing these three forms of knowledge (embodied, rational, and non-rational) and subsequently applying it to empirical examples. The two crucial dimensions for our distinction are the level of being anchored in the subjective life-world and the degree of empirical foundation of the respective knowledge.

We begin with the aspect of being rooted in the subjective life-world. An entirely rationalized fact, such as, for example, the survival probability of a medical treatment, initially appears to the self as somewhat abstract from a phenomenological perspective. Although it is the product of scientific research and can be considered helpful to the affected person in a theoretical sense, this form of knowledge mainly feels alien and disconnected from the subjective life-world (see the previous subsection). As Porter (1995, p. 4) states, such facts are "reasonably disinterested" of the person and their specific problem. For instance, when a person faces a situation of risk with statistical evidence, they initially encounter a cold factuality that must be integrated into their sphere of meaning. Using the terms of late Alfred Schütz, scientific data should be viewed as a specific part of the stock of knowledge available. However, how much this knowledge gains interpretative relevance depends on aspects like the individual's pre-existing biographical assumptions, or the manner in which such knowledge is communicated and explained.

In contrast, the other forms of objectified knowledge, namely the metaphysical ones, such as hope and faith, arise from the subjective life-world or are more flexible in adapting to it than their rational counterparts. Though they are objectivations as well, generated by reflexive thinking, they have a different relation to the life-world. *Hope*, for example, can be seen as an imaginative extension of one's horizon towards a desired future and thus offers a perspective that might be important for the motivation to succeed in daily life. Hope, faith, and ideology help the self to cope with a subjectively experienced situation of risk and uncertainty. From the perspective of modern rationalization, these gain relevance especially in situations where the self is confronted with a lack of agency. However, as we have argued with Bastide (2015), these modes are in general powerful resources to engage with a notoriously uncertain future as well as to cope with undesired and harmful outcomes.

For instance, the hope that everything will work out somehow and that I will survive a serious illness, is an empowering extension of my horizon towards the desired future. This means that hope, in contrast to rational objectifications like statistical data, does not have to acquire interpretative relevance first. Considering that such knowledge emerges from the subjective life-world itself, it becomes clear that the interpretative relevance from its origin accompanies it.

Moreover, there are institutionalized forms of non-rational knowledge as well, such as faith or ideology. Though they epistemologically go back to reflexive thinking, like hope as well, from the perspective of the affected person in situations of risk and uncertainty, they arise as part of the socially offered stock of knowledge at hand and thereby provide a broader framework of sense-making and meaning that helps to cope with a situation but includes the capacity to act. They can be seen as an extension of one's horizon, which—differently to hope—unfolds a collectively shared sense. Religion might be one of the most obvious examples of this; the denial of climate change might be another. In such cases, a specific way of interpreting the world becomes part of the stock of knowledge at hand that offers possible orientation to the affected subject. Insofar as they achieve a power of conviction, jumping from one subjective life-world to another, they proliferate their capability of collective sense-making—or in Schütz's words, they acquire interpretative relevance. This is the case with religious ideas, ideologies, or conspiracy theories.

To distinguish the two forms of objectified knowledge (rational and non-rational), as mentioned, there is a second aspect that is analytically helpful. Rational facts on the one hand and non-rational ones, such as hope and faith, on the other are characterized by a different degree of empirical foundation (compare Fig. 5.3). To clarify this point, one could once again refer to the example of medical treatment and the probability of subjective survival: While the statistical knowledge about the effectiveness of a treatment is based on empirical data from the past, the hope that I, as a concrete and affected person, will survive is strongly related to the future. Thus, both forms, rational and non-rational knowledge, are indeed a result of the human capability of reflexive thinking. Still, they can be distinguished according to their level of experience saturation. Considering that, e.g., rational facts are strictly bound to former observations, they have to follow specific rules of generalization. This is because they aim to displace the "subjective contamination" epistemologically. As Porter explains, "*rules are a check on subjectivity: they should make it impossible for personal biases or preferences to affect the outcome of an investigation*" (Porter, 1995, p. 4).

In contrast to this, non-rational results of reflexive thinking are connected to empiricism in a quite different way. Hope, on the one hand, is focused on a desired and imagined future, and hence, is rather future-related. It refers to the empirical presence merely insofar as it takes it as a starting point for the respective imagination. Faith or ideology, in contrast, are often connected with empirical observations and concrete practices as well, but they do not follow the mentioned rules of displacing the subjective bias as in case of rational knowledge. Faith, for example, is sometimes even strongly motivated by experiences which are highly subjective and build the ground for the interpretative relevance of a

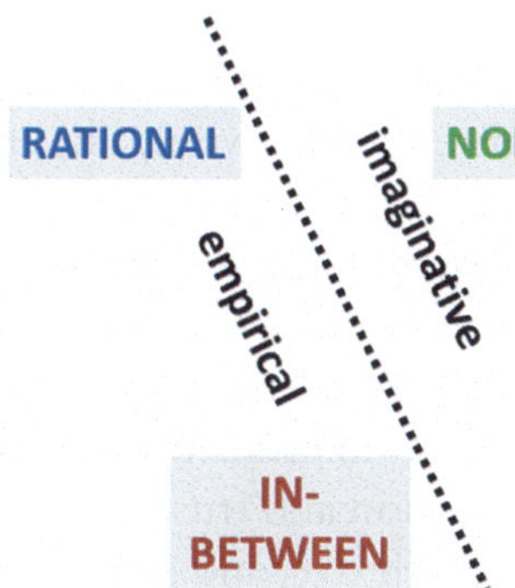


**Fig. 5.3** Empirical versus imaginative foundation of knowledge

specific religious worldview. Collective prayer, religious rituals, and other forms of spiritual collaboration might be empirically based on experiences that play a significant role here. Ideology, by contrast, is very selective in dealing with empiricism. It selects only those aspects that fit its own interpretation of reality, leaving others aside. Thus, ideology relieves people of rather unpleasant aspects of the empirical world and opens a more subjectively appropriate perspective. Nevertheless, even ideology might provide grounds for commonly shared practices, whether discursively realized (e.g., specific uses of terms) or in the form of political gatherings.

In summary, there are two categories by which the objectified forms of knowledge can be distinguished. Firstly, due to its level of abstraction, rational knowledge is often experienced as something that is detached from the subjective life-world. Such knowledge arises for the subject firstly as a potentially meaningless factuality that must be re-entangled with the subjective living conditions of a concrete person. The other forms of abstract thinking, namely hope, faith, and ideology, in contrast, seem closely linked to subjectivity. While hope arises from the life-world of the affected person, institutionalized forms of non-rational knowledge, like faith and ideology, are selectively connected to it. The second aspect of distinction is the degree of empirical saturatedness. While rational knowledge is mostly related to former observations and follows strict rules of generalizations, the non-rational knowledge is much more flexible in addressing and including empiricism into the generated meaning.

Turning now to the third form of certainties relevant for managing risk situations, namely the modes of in-between, like trust or intuition. As they depend on bodily perceptibility, to a large degree, they could be seen as non-reflexive forms of orientation. We call them *subjective facts* because they are experienced involuntarily at the level of embodied sensations and can hardly be objectified. However, they share some categorial similarities with both of the former-mentioned categories of objectified knowledge: On the one hand, intuition and trust arise to the self as something bodily perceptible and non-reflexive, and consequently, is of course strongly connected to the subjective life-world as faith and hope are. On the other hand, intuition and trust are founded in former experience and

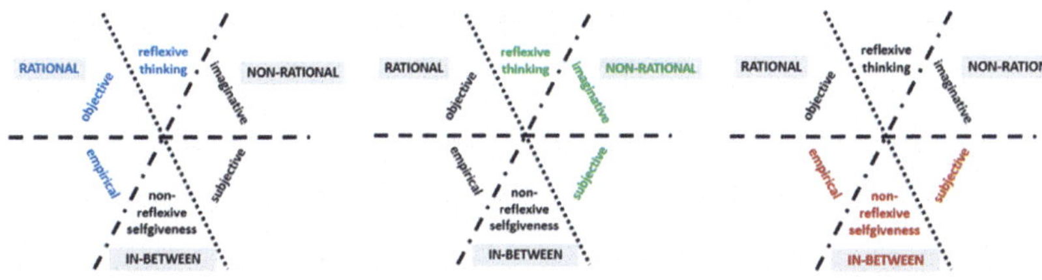


**Fig. 5.4** Dimensions of rational, non-rational and in-between forms of knowledge

thus are empirically grounded as rational knowledge, whereas they do not follow the rules of generalization. To summarize this, one could say that rational and in-between modes of managing risk are firmly grounded in empiricism in the sense of being empirically evident. The difference of such forms of acting is merely whether the relevant knowledge appears to the self on the level of reflection (rational) or on the level of bodily sensations (in-between). Compare Fig. 5.4 for an overview that summarizes the key characteristics of each of the forms of knowledge related to *rational*, *non-rational*, and *in-between* modes of reasoning.

## 5.6 Concluding Comments

After having specified the three modes of dealing with risk and uncertainty along the epistemological categories of *reflexive* and *non-reflexive* knowledge, the following subsection will dynamize the model, which has been introduced as a rather ideal-typical categorical system. For this purpose, we will turn to the empirical circumstances of decision-making as experienced by concrete, socially and biographically embedded persons. To do so, we present the neo-phenomenological understanding of situations, which allows us to clarify how the three modes of dealing with risk and uncertainty interact, depending on the respective person and the circumstances that enable and determine their action.

# 6

# Embedding Decision-Making Under Risk Into Its Situational Frame

For systematizing subjective action in a concrete situation of risk and uncertainty, we dynamize the former reconstructed model with its three dimensions of knowledge. From a sociologically informed viewpoint, any action is rooted in a socio-cultural context. This context includes not only institutionalized knowledge, such as social norms, but also individual biographical experiences. To consider these different decision-making aspects, we begin this chapter with a discussion of the neo-phenomenological understanding of situations. It provides an analytical view where decision-making appears as a dynamic interaction between individual and institutional elements of sense-making. Using this perspective, it becomes possible to analyze the entire process as it unfolds in daily life (and is shaped by biographical factors) with empirical adequacy.

As discussed in Chapter 5, the three modes of managing risk and uncertainty (or forms of reasoning) can be divided into non-reflexive forms of knowledge, which refer to *in-between* modes, and reflexive forms, which relate to *rational* and *non-rational* reasoning. From this perspective, the individual aspect of decision-making is choosing to rely



J. O. Zinn and M. Schulz, *A New Phenomenology of Risk and Uncertainty*, Critical Studies in Risk and Uncertainty, https://doi.org/10.1007/978-981-95-7405-6_6

on one of these three relevant modes—a decision that comes from practically weighing reflexive and embodied knowledge. However, the chapter will show whether a person turns to *rational* or *non-rational* modes or trusts their gut feeling (*in-between* modes), is often not a result of reflexive decision-making. On the contrary, the process of practically weighing different modes is mostly involuntary and closely related to biographical circumstances.

Considering this, the entire dimension of the non-reflexive, previously regarded as one of three equally important reasoning spheres, becomes crucial for understanding decision-making under risk and uncertainty. As demonstrated earlier, *in-between* modes are just as empirically grounded as rational knowledge. The main difference is that *in-between* modes originate from subjective experience, while rational modes draw from a collective and objectified body of knowledge. This insight may be crucial for effectively managing and communicating risk.

## 6.1 The Transformation of Situations Into Constellations by Language-Based Representation

It is common in social science that any subjective action is inevitably embedded in a situational context. Theoretical approaches to this issue can broadly be categorized into two traditions. On the one hand, there are positivist approaches that see situations as a collection of facts that a more or less rational actor recognizes. These facts are considered genuinely objective, meaning they are viewed as unaffected by subjective perception. On the other hand, social constructivist approaches emphasize that the very situational frame of action is largely shaped by subjective activity. Particularly feminist (Haraway, 1988) and postcolonial (Mignolo, 2009) epistemologies stress that what we perceive in a given situation is not an objective fact, but rather a product of socially and historically mediated categories of perception. These categories, due to cultural imprinting, have sedimented in our way of perception and shape what we acknowledge or do not acknowledge as "given" (Schütz &

Luckmann, 1973, 1989; Berger & Luckmann, 1967).[1] The sociological elaboration of the concept of life-world, among other aspects, denotes this sphere through which the results of perception arises subjectively self-evident.

Instead of turning towards one or the other side of this debate, the understanding of situations, developed by New Phenomenology, is a third way of conceptualizing the frame of human action. It follows the general aim of phenomenology in that sense that it intends to develop "*a science of the universal how of the pregivenness of the world, i.e., of what makes it a universal ground for any sort of objectivity*" (Husserl, 1970, p. 146). Of course, it is not possible to reconstruct the whole neo-phenomenological model and its epistemological foundation. In a nutshell, human action is considered a transformation of *situations* into *constellations*. This means that we are always and inescapably immersed in situations (sphere of embodied subjective facts), which can be considered in the first place as a chaotic and manifold mixture of significance. Schmitz speaks of a "*diffuse but holistic meaningfulness*" (2005, p. 9), which occurs to us on the level of bodily sensations. Moreover, due to language-based explication, as humans we are able to "*lift out of the wholeness single aspects, which can be associated by intelligent cross-linking to constellations in order to reconstruct the inexhaustible situation approximately and to get a grip on the essential features*" (ibid.).

Situations, as this quotation shows, are neo-phenomenologically defined as a holistic frame in which we are bodily perceptible immersed in any moment of our conscious life. In this context, Michael Großheim (2002, p. 280) speaks of "situations being charged with primary, i.e., *non-projected meaningfulness.*" Only based on such involuntary experiences of quality, as the early Alfred Schütz would term it, we are capable of developing a representation of reality by symbol-mediated thinking. The process of transforming quality into the "*delimited realm of concepts*"

[1] In recent years, this important critique of feminist epistemology has been combined with classical phenomenology; an interdisciplinary process from which emerged the currently growing field of "critical phenomenology" (e.g., Guenther, 2021; Magri & McQueen, 2023; Salamon, 2018). Though it would be a really interesting project to combine the approach of critical phenomenology with the neo-phenomenological instruments, this lies beyond the scope of our book.

(Schütz, 2013, p. 35) is what Schmitz in the former quotation calls to "*lift out of the wholeness single factors.*" The hence reflexively isolated aspects of the involuntary experienced can then be related among others by "intelligent cross-linking" to gain a categorially differentiated, but abstract image of the situational given. The representation, gained in this way, Schmitz calls *constellations* because it consists of singularized items, picked up from the holistic meaningfulness of a fluid and chaotic situation. Consequently, one should speak of "deriving sense" rather than "making sense" on the base of the situational given.

This approach, which Schmitz (1994, pp. 215ff.) terms, in a broader sense, an "epistemological explicationism," is of great importance if one seeks to fathom the tension between non-reflexive and reflexive knowledge, as it plays a key role in acting under risk. Like the early writings of Alfred Schütz, New Phenomenology also stresses the transformative aspect of reflexive thinking by highlighting the ontological gap between *subjective* and *objectified facts* (compare Sect. 5.4). However, due to its foundation in the philosophy of bodiliness, Schmitz's approach offers a more differentiated model. Both authors, Schütz and Schmitz, highlight that even if we transform the situation into a constellation by developing a symbol-mediated representation, we remain inescapably entangled with the surrounding aspects. From this perspective, sense-making in general denotes the process of itemizing the embedding circumstances through language-based thinking, or in other words, by transforming non-reflexive into reflexive knowledge along socio-culturally offered forms of doing so. In this way, we extrapolate single aspects from the manifold meaningfulness of a given situation and relate them to each other. The result of this is a *constellation*, or better said, various *constellations* that help us translate the firstly chaotic experience of any fluid situation into a symbolic-mediated universe of meaning (Schmitz, 2010b, pp. 44 f.). *Constellations*, hence, are the basic formation for the whole process of sense-making[2] and offer a scheme of possible orientation for any human action.

---

[2] In rejection of radical manifestations of social constructivism, New Phenomenology stresses that "sense-making" is always the result of the situational given (subjective facts) on the one hand and its culturally shaping (and shaped) itemization (objectified facts) on the other.

With regard to the previously mentioned primary and non-projected meaningfulness, situations essentially contain facts, problems, and programs for solving them (Schmitz, 1994, pp. 56 ff.). This means that any situation confronts us, in the first place, with subjectively embodied facts in a fundamental sense (to exist, to be here and now, etc.). In a similar vein, Schütz (1970, p. 144) speaks of a bodily perceptible "existential knowledge" that forms a crucial part of the stock of knowledge at hand. A *program*, moreover, is a routine handling, which phenomenologically is as well part of the given situation, as is the *problem* to solve, based on its subjective factuality. Such programs, accompanying the concrete situation, are often realized involuntarily. This means that we follow them without considering other forms to deal with what is given in the concrete moment. This is regularly observable in routine practices or in threatening situations, which we have learned to handle. If we face, for example, a rapidly approaching object or a rapidly rising tide (problem), we involuntarily dodge it or flee to a safe place (program). Given this example, such programs are often realized without taking the detour via reflexive thinking. Schmitz (2010a, p. 87) in such cases speaks of non-reflexive programs of "bodily intelligence."

Sociologically, with regard to these programs, we would speak of social norms. As they originally go back to the capability of reflexive thinking, they are based on constellations—constellations, which have become institutionalized. Successively, many of these institutionalizations get habitualized and enable us to realize a program without thinking about it. One could say that a subjectively incorporated norm is a constellation which has been reintegrated into the personal situation (compare Sect. 6.2) and furthermore arises as an aspect of the involuntarily given. If one aims to clarify why people in situations of risk and uncertainty turn to rational or non-rational modes—or, in the presented terminology, transform risky situations into a specific constellation to gain orientation for subjective action, it seems worth combining this model with the late Alfred Schütz. Considering his findings, a situation contains imposing and intrinsic aspects of thematic, interpretative, and motivational relevance. Depending on the respective circumstances, when a specific theme is imposing, the affected person is urged to realize a particular way of interpreting it along motivational aspects. Thus, the process of transforming a situation into a constellation is highly structured by the individual biography, which shapes motivational and interpretative relevance. In accordance with this, Schmitz highlights that the person themselves must be seen as a part of the holistic meaningfulness of the respective situation as well. We come back to this in the following subsection.

Social norms, especially with regard to the question of how to deal with situations of uncertainty, are structuring programs, transforming a situation into a constellation. In Schütz's words, a social norm is a specific way of understanding the given circumstances, a way of sense-making that acquires interpretative relevance. To deal rationally with a situation of risk and uncertainty, for example, is such a culturally shaped and shaping norm that structures subjective acting.[3] Combining the findings of Alfred Schütz and Hermann Schmitz, one could say that a constellation is an objectified knowledge and, given that it acquires interpretative relevance, an objectifying knowledge at the same time. If I understand an event as a risk, for example, that could be handled rationally, then I refer to objectified knowledge, resulting from thousands of former observations, and at the same time, I objectify this very concrete present event as a case of the respective probabilistic population.

The combination of these two approaches allows us to sharpen the analytical view for the upcoming and perpetuating forms of culturally shaped practices of sense-making. During socialization, humans learn to explicate situations in a culturally mediated way and hence perpetuate a specific set of constellations. Socialization in this sense means giving particular forms of itemizing a situation an imposing interpretative relevance. That specific forms of deriving meaning from the occurring are often realized involuntarily and hence are somehow an imposing process of embodied sense-making. This has also been sociologically addressed beyond classical phenomenological sociology, for example, by Pierre Bourdieu. In the context of this book, the point of reference between Bourdieu and Schmitz lies in the phenomenological

---

[3] As mentioned before, Schütz highlights that such forms of interpretative relevance can be either intrinsic or imposing. Following this, the process of rationalization, as it is characteristic for modern society, comes along with an imposing interpretative relevance insofar as it devalues all diverging forms of interpreting a given situation.

background of both authors, emphasizing the sphere of bodiliness, taken originally from Maurice Merleau-Ponty. Similar to Schmitz, the latter was an important phenomenological source for Bourdieu (1986) as well. Merleau-Ponty's work allowed him to reconstruct the sedimentation of interpretative schemes as the development of an incorporated cultural capital, conceptualized in the process of embodied habitualization.[4]

In that sense, the formation of the habitus is an inscription of a socio-economically influenced variety of knowledge on how to transform situations into constellations. This knowledge becomes tacit and remains in the subjective sphere of the involuntary. Once sedimented as forms of bodily intelligence, they become part of the non-reflexive programs that we follow in already known or vaguely familiar situations. And as we will argue later, these inscriptions are important too for the understanding of how people combine *rational*, *non-rational,* or *in-between* modes. Such programs for dealing with a given situation, developed during socialization, gain significant relevance for the respective person. For example, can the same situation of uncertainty appear either as a spiritual test or simply as a pure coincidence. However, for the affected person, it is rather difficult or even impossible to switch between these two ways of understanding the circumstances. Their biography has structured the way of making sense of the occurring events by the inscription of specific interpretative patterns. Finally, during everyday experience, these inscriptions arise to us due to the sphere of emotion, intuition, and trust (including distrust). And lastly, it is also observable that some people habitually reject social norms in general, an aspect that is of great importance, especially for the social engagement with risk and uncertainty.

At this point, it seems useful to briefly expand the discussion of the presented model of situations with the findings of classical phenomenological sociology. As mentioned above, social norms can be considered as programs that, phenomenologically, are part of the meaningfulness of a given situation as a concrete person experiences it. They outline a possible way of dealing with the circumstances, but without entirely

[4] The far-reaching influence of Maurice Merleau-Ponty on Bourdieu's concept of the habitus is often overlooked, but is that important that Loic D. J. Wacquant (1996, p. 41) called Bourdieu a "sociological heir" of Merleau-Ponty.

determining the provoked action. To clarify this sociologically, we turn to the work of Berger and Luckmann (1967). In their phenomenological investigations of the social epigenesis of institutionalized norms, Berger and Luckmann emphasize that any form of non-random action, in its origin, results from face-to-face interactions. Evolving from the subjective practices of learning by trial and error, specific forms of dealing with given situations that turn out to be empirically adequate become a shared routine. From the success of handling a problem, the practices go through a process of institutionalization, enabled by our capability of reflexive and symbol-mediated representation. Such institutionalized forms of knowledge gain relevance across different situations of social order. A social norm in this sense, on the one hand, produces the sphere of social meaning. The latter orders sociality across present, spatially absent, or even completely unknown persons. On the other hand, microtheoretically, it offers a collectively shared structure of knowledge by which one understands how to orient herself/himself in the socially ordered world as it occurs to us situatively throughout daily life.

These insights from Berger and Luckmann can analytically be sharpened with the presented understanding of situations, taken from New Phenomenology. From this perspective, an institutionalized social norm is a specific practice of transforming a situation into a constellation, a form that gains cross-situational effects on social order. It is a constellation that has detached from a specific situation and, hence, can be applied to any similar one. Such institutionalized constellations are evident in our daily lives as various culturally offered forms for making sense of a given situation. And individually, a specific set of institutionalized constellations sediment in the subject itself (habitualizations) and involuntarily structure the decision of acting along *rational*, *non-rational*, or *in-between* modes. Even if the set of constellations at hand does not fit exactly to the respective actual situation, it offers a rough frame of orientation that serves as a counterpart to sensed certainties in the course of the subjective search for an adequate form of acting.

Finally, the upcoming and perpetuating socially formed meaning can be understood as something that is realized (anew) in every moment. The social sense of a situation derives from its reflexive and embodied interpretation of the involuntarily experienced wholeness. That means we have learned to interpret situational contexts in a specific way, which allows us to identify some aspects as relevant and others as not. It is this process by which the socially formed meaning is brought into the respective concrete situation of our daily life. Considering that any situation is always at least a little bit different from all before, and that the process of sense-making depends on the respective person who realizes it and its biographical background, the advantages of a dynamic perspective like that of Schmitz come into play. It helps to avoid what could be termed as a kind of social theoretical robinsonade.[5] This is because any member of society grows up in a context in which the collective store of possible sense-making is already there. From childhood onwards, we are confronted with various constellations, and each of them offers a more or less distinct form of interpreting situations, or in other words, of sense-making. If one seeks to understand the subjective ways of dealing with risk and uncertainty—the focus of this book—we suggest grounding the analyses in the presented phenomenological insights.

To summarize the presented model, by symbol-mediated representation, we can unfold a kind of reflexive user interface that allows us to plan, and hence, to deal with risk in a fundamental sense. Risk itself, as we will argue later, is a result of the described situational itemization. Only by reflexively systematizing a situation and recognizing overarching similarities do we derive causality and hence develop an understanding of what risk itself is.

We have already stressed that we limit ourselves in this book to a summary of some key aspects of the neo-phenomenological understanding of situations. Nevertheless, it is worth highlighting that Schmitz (Schmitz, 1994, pp. 75ff.; 2005, pp. 24ff.) analytically distinguishes different types of situations. Besides the "actual situation" which describes the respective moment of experiencing (similar to the everyday understanding of what a situation is), we find ourselves confronted

[5] The literary term "robinsonade" originally denotes, e.g., novels whose plot is about a lonely person or a quite small community, living in socially isolated circumstances as it was the case with Robinson Crusoe. In social and especially in economic theory the term exists as well to describe models that start with the action of one or the interaction of two individuals and generalize the insights of such fictitious circumstances towards the macro level. Even if Berger and Luckmann reflect it critically, they work with such a foundation of social interaction as well (Berger & Luckmann, 1967, p. 71).

with aspects that proceed throughout various situations. Schmitz terms the latter ones "continuous situations" ("zuständliche Situationen" in German). Such continuous situations are, e.g., the stock of social norms or the collectively used language. Neo-phenomenologically, these phenomena are situations as well because it would be in vain to attempt listing all aspects of the normative frame of a society or all grammatical rules and potential phrases of a language; in other words, it is impossible to exhaustively transform the situation of the normative basis or the language into a fully explicated constellation. Instead, such phenomena must be described as a diffuse but holistic meaningfulness in the neo-phenomenological sense. The same is the case with the personality of a person, an aspect to which we come back in the following subsection.

Moreover, and of importance for the question of dealing with risk and uncertainty, as a special case of continuous situations, there are "shared situations" in the sense that in many circumstances a kind of collectively perceptible atmosphere is overarching people's daily life, and hence, involuntarily influences concrete actions. This concept aligns with the notion of the risk-emotions assemblage proposed by Deborah Lupton (see Sect. 4.3), which also highlights that risk judgments and understandings are not solely individual phenomena. Lupton, however, stresses the fluidity of such emotional and collective circumstances, while the neo-phenomenological understanding of shared situations is open to a bodily felt societal embeddedness that is continuing throughout a more or less long period of time. An example of such shared situations, in the neo-phenomenological sense, is the ambiguous feeling between menace and ignorance that gripped people, especially at the onset of a pandemic, or the observable techno-euphoria stemming from the (rarely reflected) notion of a more or less immediate connection between technology and social progress. Even rationalism itself, understood as a holistic frame for social acting and knowing, could be considered an example of a shared, continuous situation. Such shared continuous situations, hence, can provoke an atmospheric tinge that shapes the actions of the people who find themselves embedded in specific circumstances. Due to this, shared continuous situations are crucial for the question of whether individuals and collectives turn to one way of sense-making or to the other.

That means that, neo-phenomenologically, besides the individual biography, the social norms, and the institutionalized forms of knowledge, the collectively shared and bodily perceptible atmosphere that proceeds throughout an actual situation has a notable influence on which form of knowledge at hand gains interpretative relevance, and which does not. Social change or innovation, from this perspective, is then the result of the mutually dependent dynamic of the situational and atmospheric setting on the one hand, and the culturally offered and concretely realized forms of sense-making on the other.

Generally, all types of situations in the neo-phenomenological sense are characterized by the impossibility of fully systematizing a concrete situation—that is, transforming it completely into an objectified constellation. As Schmitz (Schmitz, 2005, p. 9) emphasizes, epistemologically, there remains a gap of knowability between what we can understand through reflexive abstractions and what happens to us involuntarily concerning the wholeness of a situation. When connecting this model to the topic of risk, it's clear that this gap is not only related to what is currently given but also to the future. In other words, if reflexive thinking—along with its rational or non-rational outcomes of objectified representations—cannot exhaustively account for what is presently available in a situation, it is even less likely to encompass what is not yet present. In this context, one can also refer to Theodore M. Porter's words (1995, p. 74), who states: "Objectivity as impersonality is often conflated with objectivity as truth." Especially when it comes to future-related knowledge, where the actual outcome of a specific case remains definitively unknown, this limitation of objectified and rationalized knowledge becomes critically important. We will revisit this point later when discussing the enchantment of rationality.

Finally, there are at least three crucial analytical advantages for investigating subjective action under risk and uncertainty, as understood in the context of New Phenomenology. Firstly, the presented perspective enables us to comprehend the tension between reflexive and non-reflexive forms of certitudes, which are particularly relevant for decision-making in situations of risk and uncertainty. Secondly, and closely related to this, the neo-phenomenological approach is characterized by sensitivity to the problem that, even if the systematization is as elaborate as it could be, there always remains a residual. The latter derives from the ontological gap between subjective facts and objectified facts, between non-reflexive and reflexive forms of knowledge. And thirdly, this allows us to investigate the limits of rationalization by reflexive thinking critically. During the process of symbol-mediated abstraction, processed through our capability of mental representation, we transform qualitative experiences into objectified images. Phenomenologically, it is this mental jump from experienced qualities to their symbolized forms, from the embodied to the symbolic level, which, even if the subject itself does it, generates a more or less considerable distance. New Phenomenology allows a detailed analysis of this process. Given that everyone throughout the day engages in this act of social sense-making, we devote the following subsection to the individual level, namely, the development of personality emerging from a negotiation between the reflexive and non-reflexive forms of certitude.

## 6.2 Realization of Meaning as an Oscillation Between Subjective and Objectified Facts

As we have shown, social sense-making must be considered as a highly dynamic process, done by a person who finds themselves inevitably immersed in a situational frame. We now introduce the neo-phenomenological model of being a person, before clarifying the whole argumentation in the context of managing risk, using a fictitious example. Regarding the question of being a person, the insights of the former subsections can be brought together. While introducing the neo-phenomenological distinction of subjective and objectified facts, we referred to Schmitz's studies of self-consciousness (compare Sect. 5. 3). In this context, he stressed two levels of being oneself. On the one hand there is the embodied experience of "being conscious of oneself" (subjective, and involuntary perceptible fact). On the other hand, due to our capability of symbol-mediated thinking, human beings are able "to be conscious of oneself as something" (abstract, and objectified facts) (Schmitz, 2010a, p. 14). Finally, considering that we can never become consciously aware of ourselves without being embedded in a situational frame, the understanding of being a person combines these two neo-phenomenological insights. Regarding the question of personality, Schmitz writes:

> A person is a conscious entity with the ability of self-attribution, which consists in understanding itself as a case of several genera, on which it can distribute accents of affiliation and disaffiliation, and which it can connect or separate in various ways. Hence, the person gains a scope for flexible self-determination and for making a statement. (Schmitz, 2017a, p. 114)

This model of being a person stresses that, from birth, we are involuntarily conscious of ourselves due to all forms of bodily affectivity like joy, hunger, fear, tiredness, desire, and so on. Based on this sphere of subjective self-givenness, while growing up, and of course in interaction with others, we learn to objectify all these phenomena of affective experience by language-based forms of reflexive thinking. Hence, we successively gain distance to the sphere of our affectedness and develop a reflexive relation to ourselves—a process that was famously investigated by George Herbert Mead (1934). However, New Phenomenology, with its elaborate understanding of bodily sensations, offers a categorial framework to investigate more adequately this subjectively realized interaction between embodied forms of self-givenness and their culturally shaped formation towards a personal identity.

A key insight of New Phenomenology is that the daily experience of an adult person constantly oscillates between the sphere of bodily affectedness and its reflexive interpretation due to language-based (or even numerical) abstractions. For this dynamic process of being a person, Schmitz (2017b, p. 114) introduced the terms "personal emancipation" (reflexive abstraction) and "personal regression" (return to bodily affectedness). We will go into this model in more detail in a moment, but it must be emphasized that the terms "emancipation" and "regression" in no way should be understood as normative ones. In contrast, Schmitz (2007, p. 263) developed this dynamic model to overcome the highly reductionistic modern notion that human subjects were merely rational and sovereign entities (reflexive thinking = desirable versus subjective sensations = problematic). In rejection of the underlying human hubris, Schmitz consequently stresses the fact of being reliant on the sphere of embodied self-givenness. His philosophy, in general, is motivated by an epistemological rehabilitation of involuntary sensations to overcome a reductionist conception of the human being.[6]

Coming back to the model: As mentioned above, we experience ourselves as an undoubtedly existing entity due to all kinds of bodily sensations. Personal emancipation, in this context, means to gain distance from what happens to us involuntarily by means of language-based thinking (Schmitz, 2007, p. 277). This process of emancipating from being trapped in situational circumstances, however, is something that could only be done partially. Though we are able to reflexively systematize what happens to us, in other words, to transform the situation into a constellation, we remain inevitably immersed in the situation itself. What changes is our capability to deal with it in a reasonable and foresightful way (Schmitz, 2011, p. 77). Reflexive thinking, from this perspective, is about the ability of (re-) constructing the "meaning" of a given situation and, hence, acting adequately and reasonably.[7]

However, this personal distancing by reflexive abstraction is only half of the truth of human experience. In situations of subjective affectedness, for example, in situations of sudden shock, of overwhelming emotions, while heavily laughing or crying, we return successively to the sphere of involuntary perceptible self-givenness. Such experiences are, of course, extreme cases in which the bodily sensations come to the fore. In everyday life, they continuously accompany our perception and act without being so dominant, or even without being realized by the affected person at all. However, Schmitz uses the extreme situations in which a person loses his or her composure to clarify the basic

---

[6] This reductionism has been problematized, for example, in the context of the pandemic and with regards to health economics by Schulz (2020).

[7] "Adequate" and "reasonable" should not be misunderstood as objective categories. Instead, they are characteristics that could only be attributed to a specific action by considering the subjective situation (compare our conclusions in Chapter 9 as well).

dynamic of being a person in the neo-phenomenological sense. Objective facts, in such extreme situations, lose their relevance for orientation while we are confronted with the highly subjective sphere of bodiliness. This return from the abstract level of reflexive orientation towards the sphere of bodily sensations, Hermann Schmitz calls "personal regression" (Schmitz, 2017b, p. 114). Besides such extreme situations, which are of course merely exceptions, our everyday life proceeds more or less in the middle of completely objective or entirely subjective facts. Schmitz speaks of different degrees of emancipation, which change continuously, depending on the respective situational context. Our perception of the world under normal circumstances is not merely a neutral apprehension of one objective (or better, objectified) fact after another, but is always accompanied by an embodied dimension of personal attunement. This can be briefly exemplified: While I am, for example, bad-tempered due to an incredibly stressful working week[8] (bodily perceptible attunement), I am sitting in the office listening to the ringing phone (occurrence of an objectifiable event). Of course, this personal attunement is of significant relevance for the outcome of the respective situation. It mediates how I respond to the world at hand: I might either leave the call unanswered or I might answer it in an unfriendly tone of voice. The latter response, shaped by my embodied attunement, could impair the subsequent social interaction and, in turn, provoke further events—such as my supervisor complaining about my unacceptable behavior. In this way, the bodily felt disposition resonates throughout the situation and contributes to the unfolding of its social consequences.

Finally, being an adult person is the always ongoing process of oscillating between the two spheres of subjective and objectified facts, whereby a detachment of one sphere from the other is impossible—and potentially pathological (Fuchs, 2008, p. 272). The patterns of symbolically mediated thinking and the embodied self-givenness remain in a mutually dependent relationship. This coincides with the results of research regarding decision-making (compare, for example: Damasio,

[8] Strictly speaking, attributing the embodied experience of stress to what happened during the last days is already an interpretative abstraction. This shows how we always oscillate in our self-perception between the sphere of bodiliness and reflexivity.

1996; Kahneman & Klein, 2009; Klein, 1998). Finding a balanced equilibrium between these two spheres of self-being is not something that is done once in the episode of socialization. On the contrary, it is a task that must be mastered continuously throughout one's whole lifetime. Considering that the underlying tension is one of subjectivity (bodily sensations) and objectification (reflexive thinking), it becomes clear that this issue is strongly linked to socially mediated sense-making in general. Practically, subjective experience must be brought into dialogue with objectified forms of intersubjective knowledge. Being a person who lives in society is about solving that tension by using the culturally offered forms of (self-) objectivations. Hence, concerning the reformulation of Berger and Luckmann, one could say that building up a socially mediated identity can be considered as a form of self-institutionalization or self-socialization when over time, individual responses to institutional contexts build up in both a subjective and institutionalized structure of a biography (Heinz, 2000; Hoerning & Alheit, 1995).

As we have argued in the former section, this neo-phenomenological understanding of reflexive and non-reflexive certitudes is of great importance for the field of risk research. For elaborating this argument and to analyze sociologically why concrete persons act in situations of risk in specific ways, this approach seems promising. In this context, another aspect that we have already mentioned briefly is important. Schmitz's approach considers that the subject's own biography, with all its imprinting influences, arises involuntarily. This means that one's own personality is something that can hardly be made exhaustively available by reflexive thinking, as the situation is in general. Due to this observation, Schmitz (2017b) tends to avoid the term "personality" and prefers to speak of a "personal situation" that processes throughout every actual situation that we experience. Our biography fundamentally shapes the way we interpret the given circumstances, and this process of shaping is part of the holistic meaningfulness of any situation as well. At this point, it could merely be mentioned briefly that this perspective is strongly connected to the findings of the late Alfred Schütz, who stressed the biographical influence on the experience of familiarity and strangeness, and to the emergence of topical, interpretative, and motivational relevance (Schütz, 1970, pp. 53ff.).

Regarding Schmitz's model, however, the distinction between bodily sensations and the socio-culturally shaped ways of itemizing a given situation should not be misunderstood. They are neither two completely separate dimensions of subjectively experienced reality nor an indistinguishable mixture. The first option would suggest a problematic essentialization of bodiliness, while the second would lead to a strong form of structuralism that leaves no room for action by the affected person. To avoid this misleading view, the cultural and historical forms of interpreting a situation should be understood as parts of its complex yet chaotic meaningfulness as experienced by a concrete individual. Although any situation, in this sense, contains potential social order and biographical residue, it does not determine which aspects are to be highlighted or how they should be interconnected into a web of meaning (see also Chapters 9.4 and 9.5 in Schulz, 2024). In other words, one cannot choose who I am, but it is at least partly possible to choose what I want to be—or, more generally, it is not possible to choose the situational context with its manifold meanings I find myself in. Still, it is at least partly possible to choose how I want to handle the circumstances I face.

However, it is of course not the case that a person independently and freely decides which of the culturally offered forms to use to unfold a personality. On the contrary, as Bourdieu prominently elaborated, a sociologically highly relevant aspect of subjective sense-making is the whole sphere of the involuntary. As mentioned in the former subsection, during the process of socialization, we learn to act in specific situations in a culturally prefigured way and hence do not think about such forms of adequately handling them (bodily intelligence). Social knowledge sediments in the personal sphere of involuntariness (personal situation) and becomes effective from here. While growing up, we learn to re-enact specific forms of itemizing situations, whether due to reflexive thinking or mimetic reproduction. It is this intersection of embodied certitudes, physical circumstances,[9] and society's store of possible forms

[9] As we have highlighted earlier in this book, New Phenomenology distinguishes analytically the sensed bodiliness from the dimension of physical bodies. While the latter ones are touchable and visible things—for other persons as well as for the respective "owner" of it—the felt bodily sensations can merely be experienced by the affected person itself. Of course, most of these

of sense-making—understood as the more or less problematic clash of individuals and institutions—that ultimately leads to the subjective action as it is empirically observable, and hence, is of utmost importance for managing, communicating and researching risk.

Just as it is true for any everyday situation in general, the presented understanding of reasoning must be considered as the intersection of an individual and an institutional level. The innovative aspect of Schmitz's philosophy is its complex perspective on how the reproduction of institutionalized knowledge is practically achieved through the development of an abstract representation of ourselves and our surroundings (epistemological explicationism). Individual and institutional elements of acting interplay along the difference of embodied and reflexive knowledge, whereas the embodied level could also be at least partially formed by institutionalized programs of structuring meaning (for a detailed sociological view on the subject-theoretical interplay of sensing and thinking, compare Schulz, 2024). Due to these insights, this approach allows us to sharpen the analytical view for the development and perpetuation of culturally shaped practices of sense-making. During socialization, humans learn to explicate situations in a culturally mediated way and hence perpetuate a specific form of interpretation (social norms). From this perspective, such habitualizations are an inscription of constellations into the subjective sphere of the involuntary (Schmitz, 1994, p. 184; 2007, p. 169). Once sedimented there, they become part of the non-reflexive programs that we follow in situations that are either well-known or vaguely familiar. During everyday life, they prominently occur to us due to phenomena like emotions, intuition, or trustworthiness. Interpretative relevance, as Alfred Schütz terms it, can hence be unfolded deliberatively as well as involuntarily. As we will show, this is also highly relevant for the question of whether we turn to *rational* or *non-rational* constellations in situations of risk. In the following section, we will provide a more detailed illustration and exemplification of the argument.

---

sensations are accompanied by measurable somatic reactions of the physical body in the sense of an object. Though, how the intersection of these two spheres of factuality can be thought together is subject of further phenomenological and epistemological debates.

## 6.3 A Neo-Phenomenologically Inspired Example of Handling Risk and Uncertainty

This subsection illustrates how the different conceptual decisions might work out in practice when applied to an empirical example. For this purpose, we introduce a fictitious adolescent person, named Lars, who is making first experience with drugs at a party. The situation in which Lars finds himself contains a hardly countable variety of possible forms of acting (manifold and not exhaustively explicable meaningfulness). Such forms of explicating different aspects of the given circumstances would be, for example, going to the dance floor in the living room, playing a board game in the kitchen, or simply going home because of being tired or bored. One of these possible options as a pastime is the cultural practice of burning tobacco leaves and inhaling the smoke.[10] Though smoking, considered socially, is of course a routine practice, we assume that for Lars at the party, it is the first encounter with this practice.

According to our model (Schulz & Zinn, 2023), ideal-typically, three modes of dealing with such a situation, if considered risky, are relevant, namely *rational* (scientific evidence), *non-rational* (hope and faith), and *in-between* (trust and intuition). As it is the category most closely associated with the subjectivity of the acting person, especially the latter mode is highly connected to biographical formation. If, for example, a good friend of Lars who offers him a cigarette, due to former shared experiences, is in his view of great trustworthiness and tells him that nobody has ever become negatively affected by trying it once, it might be that Lars decides to follow this recommendation.[11] In contrast, if a person in whom he has great confidence for many years has told Lars that smoking

[10] All such forms of pastime are knowledge-based institutionalizations in the sense of Berger and Luckmann (1967) and build, together with an uncountable variety of alternatives, the socially shaped but implicit background of a given situation to which a concrete person finds itself always exposed to.

[11] This example is, of course, a simplification. Lars could indeed differentiate the trustworthiness of his friend, depending on the respective topic or former experiences. If Lars, for example, knows that addicts often downplay the harmful effects of drug consumption, he would be cautious with this very concrete advice, while still trusting his friend in many other situations. Moreover, the inner-group interactions could, of course, influence Lars's decision remarkably,

is dangerous, he supposedly would not try it. Moreover, the same is the case with intuition in the sense of an involuntary attitude to the topic of drug consumption. If, for example, Lars' parents have smoked for as long as he can remember, and until today, nevertheless enjoy the best of health, this can cause an intuitively open-minded attitude to drugs in general. Or finally, if a well-known person in Lars' life has died due to smoking or other forms of drug consumption, he potentially would reject such habits fundamentally.

In all of these ways of acting—albeit in a largely involuntary manner—a specific mode of deciphering the given situation gains interpretative relevance.

What makes a decision under risk so complex is that all three modes of acting are, at least potentially, reciprocally related to one another. Depending on the biography of a concrete person, the motivation of reasoning and acting *rationally*, *non-rationally*, or within *in-between* modes varies. Lars, for example, can orient his actions along the rational mode, namely the scientific insights about the harmful consequences of smoking. However, and this is the reason for the complexity mentioned, there are three different motivations[12] for doing so. He can act along the rational mode (1) because of having critically reviewed the offered knowledge, (2) because of hoping that scientific insights are right, or (3) because he follows involuntary sensations like trust or intuition. The situation itself, as the neo-phenomenological model shows, does not determine a specific way of dealing with it. However, all these programs of potential orientation are already inherent in the situation itself (compare the neo-phenomenological concept of the holistic but diffuse meaningfulness described in Sect. 6.1).

As we will argue later, these three motivations of acting in a specific way are related to the three overall tendencies of *rationalization*, *enchantment,* and *subjectivation* (compare Chapter 8). Regarding our example, the decision that Lars will make is strongly linked to biographical

e.g., under group pressure or if only one of his friends recommends trying smoking, while most of the other people around him hesitate or reject it.

[12] At this point, we limit ourselves to some exemplary *because-motivations* and leave aside the dimension of *in-order-motivations*. (Schütz, 1970, p. 45)

experiences and habitualized tendencies of transforming situations involuntarily into constellations. This means that the question of whether a person turns to rational or non-rational modes—or, in Schütz's words, which itemization acquires interpretative relevance—is often the result of an *in-between* decision, resulting from the personal situation of the respective individual. This refers to the high importance of developing an understanding of the *in-between* modes of reasoning and acting. In the last consequence, even the decision to turn to *rational* or *non-rational* modes, may this be done reflexively or non-reflexively, is shaped by *in-between* modes of reasoning such as emotion, intuition, and/or trust. Another motivation for acting in one way or another, especially with regard to young people, is to impress a member of the respective peer group or simply to try something new. Additionally, atmospheres can play a crucial role in involuntary decision-making, so, e.g., in Lars' example the euphoric mood of a party, or a rather queasy atmosphere in an ambiguous situation, located in a poorly lit and sparsely populated neighborhood.

Regarding the institutional perspective, *rational* or *non-rational* modes of handling risk situations compete for interpretative relevance. Which of them are eventually chosen, as we exemplified with the case of Lars, depends on the subjective experience over time and the concrete situational circumstances. This competition of different forms of interpreting a situation comes with important insights for the management and communication of risk. *Rational* as well as *non-rational* modes, for the affected subject, are abstract ways of managing risk. Institutionally, the respective mode must go through a process of subjectivation to unfold its power of structuring subjective action. This means, for example, that communicating risk effectively involves adapting the way one interprets a situation to the sphere of subjective experience. Only if reflexive risk knowledge gains in this sense interpretative relevance for concretely affected persons, rational or non-rational patterns of orientation turn out to be effective. Suppose Lars, for example, sees the deterrent images on cigarette packets while thinking about trying to smoke for the first time. In that case, the scientific knowledge about the risk of smoking is brought closer to his daily life. Insofar as he decides not to do it based on such a bodily felt impression, the respective knowledge acquires interpretative relevance. Such a successful realization of institutionalized knowledge through subjective action is what we call *subjectivation.*

## 6.4 Concluding Comments

What is finally of great importance for the question of how people act in a given situation is the tension between subjective and involuntary experience on the one hand and the individual relation to the culturally offered forms of objectifying a situation on the other. This, of course, could not be answered definitively for any concrete case, but the presented model helps to take into account the process of decision-making as it is practically conducted alongside the respective personal situation. In reality, the latter includes many more dimensions than we have mentioned in this brief example. For instance, beyond the exemplarily mentioned dimensions, the personal situation of a concretely acting person comprises other sociologically highly relevant aspects, such as class, gender, race, socio-economic status, educational background, and so on. The aim of the example, however, was merely to illustrate the largely theoretical explications of Chapters 5 and 6 and to demonstrate the complex interplay of the three modes of acting under risk. The neo-phenomenological concept of situations and their transformation into constellations, in combination with the understanding of interpretative relevance taken from the late Schütz, allowed us to develop a dynamic model that represents the complexity of acting in general, and of acting under risk and uncertainty in particular.

Independent of this theoretical model, a key problem in the management and communication of risk is that, sometimes (as with climate change), a significant number of people neglect the fact that a risk exists. However, there are specific experiences that make such denials difficult. The more the threatening circumstances get closer to the sphere of bodiliness, as we will argue in the next section, the more difficult it becomes to ignore them, whereas it is of course possible to interpret the respective situation of risk quite differently. For example, it is hardly imaginable to neglect that there is a problem if a forest fire or a flood is getting closer and closer to one's house. Phenomenologically, however, the concrete problem depends on the realized form of making sense of such an experience. Subjectively, it could be the result of climate change, as well as the expression of divine providence or simply a coincidence. This leads us to an important aspect of the concept of risk in general: What we talk about when addressing risk issues can be traced back epistemologically to the sphere of embodied experiences as it is investigated in New Phenomenology.

# 7

# From Embodied Threat to Abstract Risk—The Significance of Subjective Experience

As we have argued, the management and communication of risk is at its core about the entanglement of the offered patterns of sense-making with the subjective life-world. Considering that phenomenologically risk is an abstract representation of a potential (but in case of occurrence very concrete) threat that affects a person subjectively, it becomes clear that this process of subjectivation refers to an idiosyncratic sphere of bodily experience. This field of experiences, that in the terms of the late Alfred Schütz touches the level of our existential knowledge and has a "*vital importance for planning the man's future behavior*" (Schütz, 1970, p. 46), is neo-phenomenologically characterized by the undoubtable and non-reflexive certitude of being personally affected as somebody who is inescapably here and now. Without such embodied experiences that are known to anybody to a more or less intensive degree, risk was a merely abstract representation and remained meaningless. From this perspective, risk analysis, risk management, and risk governance are a culturally shaped interface of managing human life to overcome situations of possible harm or threat.

Following these epistemological insights, unlike an abstract risk, a tangible threat accompanied by bodily sensations is not negligible.



J. O. Zinn and M. Schulz, *A New Phenomenology of Risk and Uncertainty*, Critical Studies in Risk and Uncertainty, https://doi.org/10.1007/978-981-95-7405-6_7

The core issue is how to interpret this subjective experience and how to respond to it. Recognizing this aspect clarifies that managing and communicating risk involves engaging with the highly personal sphere of individual affectedness. However, some people do not change their behavior or protect themselves even when harmed because they do not link the concrete experience to scientific understanding; instead, they follow their similarly learned but non-rational interpretations. For instance, even when people with COVID were in intensive care, not all switched to an expert perspective. Many remained influenced by deep distrust of social institutions and clung to non-rational ideas, such as conspiracy theories. According to our model, it seems unproductive to focus solely on a person's current actions in such cases. Instead, only a historical view of the individual's biography can foster a deeper understanding of why specific ways of interpreting a situation become relevant while others do not.

The process of entangling the *rational* and *non-rational* reflexive knowledge in the sphere of non-reflexive subjectivity has similarities and differences. This is due to the inner epistemological structure of these two basic modes of reasoning (compare Sect. 5.5):

*Rational* reasoning faces the challenge of connecting abstract (scientific) risk knowledge to concrete experiences of harm, or at least promoting trust based on positive experiences with experts. This is because the concept of risk is basically an abstract and reflexively formed matrix of processing what (most) subjects involuntarily experience as a significant threat. Visualizations of harm, concretely experienced by others, such as the visual reporting of overcrowded hospitals during the COVID-19 crisis in Italy through the media, helped to transform an abstract notion of risk into a concrete threat that becomes bodily experiential.

*Non-rational* itemizations, in contrast, do not have to overcome this gap between an abstract risk and the bodily experience. Hope, for example, which we termed an "imaginative extension of one's horizon" (Schulz & Zinn, 2023, p. 226), consists in the optimism that the problem thematized in the risk will not turn into a subjective threat. Following our description, it arises from the personal situation itself and hence is connected to it from the first moment. Faith or ideology, as we argued in Chapter 3, selects aspects from subjective empiricism to develop an image of the world (often with reference to institutionalized forms of sense-making) that fits more flexibly than rational knowledge into the corresponding living circumstances of the respective person. Such ways of dealing with risk are in some situations so successful because they are much more adaptable to the subjective life-world due to neglecting (partially) empirical reality and fitting the subjectively desired. Moreover, hope, faith, and ideology can also be the consequence of a situation that is experienced as desperate and hence comes along with a significant impression of a lack of subjective agency in combination with a bodily felt threat. Considering all this, these non-rational modes of reflecting on the respective circumstances are generally characterized by a closer relatedness to the personal situation which prevents the described gap that is typical for rational knowledge.

With regards to the latter aspect, our neo-phenomenological insights reveal a systematic problem that all management and communication of risk face. It must establish the connection between non-reflexive and reflexive certainties efficiently, which becomes particularly difficult when risks are new and there are not yet concrete realities risk communication can refer to. In such situations, rational knowledge might lack even more plausibility, as it cannot simply refer to former experiences of the (not yet affected) subjects. Epistemologically, this problem relates to what Alfred Schütz (1970, pp. 78ff.) in the tradition of Husserl's phenomenology calls the difference of polythetic and monothetic knowledge. To the affected self, the experience of a threatening situation arises monothetically, which means it is not built up over time. It is not the result of a long-term reflection but is imposed at once. The existential knowledge of subjectively being here and now and being bodily affected by an event is such a monothetic certainty. Abstract risk knowledge, in contrast, is developed through a large chain of empirical observations and conclusions, conducted by a myriad of different persons whom I may not even know. It is polythetic, which means that it involves numerous steps of analysis. Therefore, phenomenologically, monothetic knowledge is characterized by a higher degree of plausibility than polythetic knowledge. In cases of unfamiliar risks, this widens the described gap between abstract knowledge on the one hand, and the personal situation on the other.

Of course, theoretically, it is possible that the not yet affected person retraces the single steps of analysis that constitute scientific findings, but this is not merely a question of time, but especially of technical and methodological expertise. This problem of translating aspects of the vast collective stock of knowledge at hand into subjective empirical observations is exacerbated in modern societies with their high level of functionally differentiated rationalization (Luhmann, 1995).

Research shows that the concrete and monothetic experience of embodied threat convinces many people that the risks are real, and therefore, they prepare for the future. The increasing frequency of extreme weather events, e.g., has also raised awareness of the problem of climate change in Western countries. The abstract knowledge of climate research becomes bodily perceptible knowledge when forests die due to drought or rivers burst their banks with growing frequency and increasingly devastating consequences. The former abstract polythetic understanding of climate change turns into a monothetic and highly subjectively evident certainty.

Since scientifically generated certainties that underpin abstract risk knowledge are often not directly experienced but indirectly approached through trusted experts, it is comparatively easy to fall for authoritative representatives or charismatic leaders of *non-rational* knowledge systems, such as religion or ideology. When people, through lifelong socialization processes, become accustomed to relying on forms of reasoning that fail to connect embodied, concrete experiences to critical empirical rationality, they can become vulnerable to charismatic leaders or conspiracy theories.

That the use of symbols of trustworthiness other than scientific ones can be effective, when connected to embodied experiences of one's life-world, might also be relevant for Iain Wilkinson's (2005, p. 57) argument, when conceptualizing the experience of suffering. He pointed out that charismatic leadership might be alluring because it offers meaning to otherwise meaningless suffering.

Indeed, trusting scientific expertise or charismatic scientists can pose a similar risk. Unconditionally following such a trusted individual makes us susceptible to being enchanted by scientific authority, especially when these experts no longer rely on evidence. They may instead become captivated by their own expertise, driven, for example, by overconfidence.

It makes the situation of managing and communicating risk rather complex, as institutions as well as individuals use and try to shift between different ideal types of *rational*, *non-rational*, and *in-between* modes of reasoning. Positioned within the broader framework of historical social change, the controversial debates and institutionalized forms of *rationalization* and *(dis)enchantment* can be connected to phenomenological observations when complemented by the aforementioned importance of *subjectivation* and reflexive forms of knowledge. It can then be demonstrated that modes of *enchantment*, *rationalization*, and *subjectivation* continue to play a significant role in how people and institutions navigate the risks and uncertainties of the future. As we will argue and illustrate by examples in the following section, these processes complement and are dependent on each other.

# 8

# Shifting Modes: Rationalization, Enchantment, and Subjectivation

We began our book by linking risk studies to modern rationalization, suggesting that managing and communicating risk should be viewed as socially and historically embedded processes. One could say that risk studies are a child of the ongoing rationalization of modern societies. They are part and parcel of an effort to manage an open and therefore uncertain and potentially risky future (Koselleck, 1988) in a reasonable way using systematic, evidence-and purpose-based strategies (Fischhoff & Kadvany, 2011). Indeed, systematic strategies to manage risk and uncertainty existed already in ancient times, such as in the Roman World (Toner, 2024), but were more based on experience than theoretical knowledge, while large parts of the world were still considered to be shaped by Gods and transcendental forces. With advancements in various social domains, the modern imaginary (or modern orthodoxy) of a world being determined by humans through all-encompassing rationalization has become increasingly influential, even though this dream has never been fully realized (Latour, 1993). Max Weber and many of his contemporaries, as well as his successors, were concerned about how far this process could advance and whether the rationalization of the world would lead to humanity becoming detached from its nature, and



J. O. Zinn and M. Schulz, *A New Phenomenology of Risk and Uncertainty*, Critical Studies in Risk and Uncertainty, https://doi.org/10.1007/978-981-95-7405-6_8

under certain conditions, might even turn into irrationality. However, we are nowadays in good company when identifying clear limits for rationalization on the macro-, meso-, and micro-level. For example, there is evidence that religion and magical practices have not disappeared and remain much more pervasive than modernists such as Karl Marx, Emile Durkheim, and Sigmund Freud might have expected. Therefore, many scholars have suggested that the societal disenchantment hypothesis of modernizing societies goes too far (for example, Bennett, 2001; Berger, 1967; Ritzer, 2005), and a more differentiated perspective is needed (for example, Wohlrab-Sahr & Burchardt, 2012). When shifting perspective, it becomes clear that flaws are also observable on the micro-level of the realm of rationality. In the heartland of rationality, such as economics, decision-making research has highlighted systematic limits to the paradigm of rationality. Cognitive psychologists have demonstrated that the normative model does not align well with the descriptive model of decision-making (Tversky & Kahneman, 1974, 1987), which has led to the development of modifications such as *bounded rationality* (March, 1988; Simon, 1982) and *behavioral economics* (Thaler, 2016). When digging deeper into history, it became clear that there had already been scholars who doubted and challenged the dominant paradigm of rationality, such as Vilfredo Pareto, an economist who later moved into sociology (Pareto, 1916, 1963).

When we systematized the growing body of qualitative studies, which examined how in everyday life people manage risk and uncertainty, we followed Zinn's (2008, 2016) suggestion to distinguish modes, which ideal-typically follow the *rational* orthodoxy and separate them from *non-rational* modes, which rest on other factors not related to the causes of an outcome but wishful thinking or an extension of desires into the future. But these *non-rational* modes were not the only ones that may be considered "irrational" from the perspective of *modern orthodoxy*. What could be understood as being *in-between* the *rational* and the *non-rational* is also suspected to have a rationality deficit, such as *emotions*, *intuition*, or *trust*. Indeed, we were rather critical of such a dichotomous view and considered all modes of reasoning to be reasonable under specific conditions, which include formalized rationality as well as faith, hope, trust, intuition, rituals, and many more. However, rather than giving up on the modern distinction between *evidence-based reasoning* and *wishful thinking*, which seems so dominant not only for modernizing societies (Krohn & Krücken, 1993), we emphasized the importance of *in-between* modes. These follow their independent logic of experience-based reasoning, which seems central to people's engagement with risk and uncertainty.

The triangle of *rational*, *non-rational*, and *in-between* modes of reasoning in the face of risk finds support in a growing body of research that makes sense of people's responses to risk and uncertainty (for example, with a focus on more recent publications, Albers, 2023; Ardissone, 2024; Berning & Hardon, 2016; Bikker et al., 2019; Bredewold & van der Weele, 2025; Brown, 2016, 2022; Calestani et al., 2024; Chiu & Yu, 2019; Clancy et al., 2022; Clark et al., 2025; Dixon, 2023; Jackson et al., 2025; Joelsson, 2019; Kiriscioglu & Ustubici, 2025; Kiriscioglu & Van Heelsum, 2024; Larsen et al., 2023; Manca, 2018; Mellini & Mileti, 2022; Porsanger & Magnussen, 2021; Qui, 2024; Reuter, 2018; van der Molen & Brown, 2021). The central insight of these studies is the importance of different modes, each of which plays a distinct role when people engage with risk and uncertainty. Most of the time, these modes mutually complement each other in complex ways and must be considered to understand how people manage the risks and uncertainties they face. Reflexive reasoning characterizes differentiated social domains such as science, economics, religion, and law, which rely on abstract forms of knowledge and are relatively detached from the embodied, subjective experience of everyday life. However, we suggested in Chapter 7 that to become socially meaningful, these reflexive and comparatively abstract forms of knowledge must be reconnected to the more immediate experience of people's life-world (Schulz & Zinn, 2023).

Most important for understanding the different modes, as each is ideal-typically an independent form of reasoning, is their knowledge base. *Rational* reasoning refers to proven or provable evidence, and *non-rational* modes are empirically relatively independent claims. In contrast, *in-between* modes rely on tacit, embodied knowledge, connected to everyday practices in a socio-material world.[1] Using New Phenomenology, we outlined the epistemological basis of these ideal type modes of reasoning and developed a framework to systematize the relationships between them (compare Chapters 5 and 6). In so doing, what was initially implicit has become more emphasized. That is the rooting of the *in-between* modes in the embodied experience of the world of everyday life. This contrasts with the reflexive forms of knowledge, such as science or religion, which both require a connection to people's embodied reasoning to be convincing, a connection that we term *subjectivation.* We assume that the embodied knowledge of the life-world is experienced more directly, providing a strong sense of validity.[2] Even science only convinces when this connection is established, for example, by trusting the experts or "the numbers" (Porter, 1995), and the same is the case with religion. One could say, for example, the embodied experience of faith is a key element for "true faith" or faith becoming rooted in one's subjective experiences (for example, by everyday religious rituals). Our argument finds support in the work of Philip Mellor and Chris Schilling (2010, p. 31), who have argued that "the cognitive, theological and normative dimensions of religion cannot gain social and cultural significance independently of bodily practices." In their later work, they have also highlighted, similarly to us, the challenges of establishing and maintaining this connection between the reflexive and embodied sphere (Mellor & Schilling, 2014).

Reflexive knowledge might not rely on evidence, as in the case of the *non-rational* modes, or it might sometimes be too abstract or too specialized, as in the case of *rational* modes. In both cases, it would only be possible to follow an argument metaphorically. Truths are then felt rather than reasoned and are rooted in tacit knowledge rather than deliberative decision. For example, most people do not understand the abstract

[1] This includes the embodied sensing of the digital world as in the atmospheric experience of video games (Andiloro, 2023).

[2] This does not exclude the possibility that an academic loves abstract models and has a similar feeling as a result of this practice. It is also possible that the reflexive insights contradict the feelings one has, which can lead to cognitive dissonance (Festinger, 1962). A good example is an interview with an ex-serviceman of the British Forces who stressed the emotional dishonesty of the military or the incongruity between official narratives and emotional reality of combat (Zinn, 2012).

mathematical climate change models, but they do understand what it means to experience more and increasingly severe floods, droughts, and other extreme weather events, or that we experience warmer winters and hotter summers, and can connect these embodied experiences to experts' communication of scientific research. In the case of a faith community, the sense of truth is less dependent on empirical evidence than shared practices and support, as well as authoritative figures such as the Imam, Priest, or Rabbi, who support specific interpretations of the world.[3] For example, during the COVID-19 crisis, some religious leaders tried to convince their followers that, contrary to established religious doctrine, vaccination was a more sensible approach to tackling the pandemic than prayer. Daniel Estrin (2021), for instance, reports on rabbis in Israel who sought to persuade orthodox Jews to get vaccinated.

As we argue in this chapter, the earlier considerations presented in the book have important ramifications for understanding societal modernization, as well as the management and communication of risk. With our epistemologically informed model of *rational*, *non-rational*, and *in-between* forms of reasoning and related forms of knowledge, we are now able to draw a more differentiated picture of how modern *rationalization* is complemented or even dependent on (*re-*) *enchantment* processes. In our view, the modernization process itself depends on *enchanting* its rational orthodoxy and also drives the *rationalized enchantment* of the modern world (Ritzer, 2005). Such macro-level enchantments can be fostered by producing a dream world, such as George Ritzer has suggested when researching consumer culture in the *cathedrals of consumption*, and, for example, the Disneyland Park in California (USA) (Ritzer, 2005). Even the ideal-type framing of a scientific culture as outlined by Robert K. Merton, emphasizing claims of truth, objectivity, and independence (Merton, 1938), mainly represents an *enchantment* of the practical reality of research as has been shown in laboratory studies (Latour & Woolgar, 1979). *Institutional enchantment* offers opportunities for micro-level *enchantment* of various kinds, but also alienation when they fail to connect with subjective experiences. For example, the

[3] The difference to science, in which ritualized practices also play a major role in the constitution of truths, lies in the possibility that, at least in theory, the foundations of truth in the scientific system can be, or should be, empirically verifiable by anyone.

visitors of Disneyworld might feel bored rather than enchanted, while researchers might feel frustrated and disillusioned about the power games and political influence in academia (Jauch, 2021).

In the following, we outline and illustrate how our framework enables a better understanding of the ways risk relates to *rationalization* and *enchantment* as multilevel processes, and how, through *subjectivation*, a connection must be made that these dynamics make sense to people in everyday life. The framework differentiates between processes at the level of institutions or social systems, relating to rather abstract and reflexive forms of knowledge on the one hand, and the embodied experiences in people's life-world on the other. This also includes attempts to connect subjective experiences to broader social frameworks to manage emotions and find explanations for the overwhelming stream of everyday life experiences (Freud, 1930). Thereby, the framework provides arguments for the consequences when, as Max Weber was worried about, the *rational* is no longer connected to the life-world's everyday reasoning or when *purpose-based* reasoning becomes detached from social imaginaries and potentially provokes irrational outcomes. It also raises the problems that occur when reflexive knowledge is mainly guided by illusions and desires rather than empirical evidence, as has been and still is witnessed in populist polemics and ideologies.

To prevent any misunderstanding, the suggested modes of reasoning are analytical ideal types. The typology of *rational*, *non-rational*, and *in-between* modes is a tool for describing empirically observable tendencies and dynamics, rather than pure forms. For example, purpose-based rationality is rarely found as pure rationality, which is not even what Max Weber might have imagined. Instead, it requires the other modes as well, but to different degrees. These modes are discursively and practically available ways of reasoning that people, organizations, and social institutions utilize or rely on when shaping the world and may differ depending on the social domain. For example, scientific research is indeed driven by scientific norms, but at the same time by the passion of scholars, competition with others, and an interest in developing something that makes a significant contribution to scholarship. However, economic interests might also play a role when the financial potential of medical innovation is considered in the decision on which line of research to pursue further.

In this way, scientific advancement might even become significantly shaped by economic interests rather than scholarly curiosity (Masters & Nutt, 2017). Institutions also relate to social groups or even specific individuals in different ways, constituting social inequalities, for example, when wealthy people can access some treatment not available to others or when new medicine is mainly tested by underprivileged people who risk their health for getting access to income (Cottingham & Fisher, 2016). These issues are indeed relevant, highlighting that risks are connected to options available only to resourceful individuals. Additionally, modes can be used as a last resort when other modes are inaccessible, such as when resources like money or skills are insufficient (Chapter 3).

The following explores and illustrates the various tendencies of *rationalization*, *enchantment,* and *subjectivation* through empirical examples, before reflecting on the dangers of different forms of reasoning becoming detached from one another.

## 8.1 Subjectivation and Enchantment of Rational Reasoning

This section considers two tendencies in rational modes, such as scientific, evidence-based, and purpose-based reasoning. Firstly, a tendency of (*re-*) *enchantment* that goes beyond Max Weber (and also Charles Taylor, 2007) with a focus on myths, religious rituals, and beliefs in spirits, demons, and divine forces. Instead, we see it as the general attentiveness to *non-rational* belief systems as we identified in the modes of hope, belief, and ideology (compare Fig. 8.1), which refer to the *imaginative extension of one's horizon*. This includes, indeed, the modern exaggeration of rational controllability and knowledge-claims when going beyond what is deliverable in the face of an open future characterized by complexity, uncertainty of knowledge, and ignorance. But it is also the case when idealized imaginaries, social values, and ethical standards shape institutional and individual engagement with risk and uncertainty. This means that the imaginaries of science as a practice, which are mainly driven by the desire to advance knowledge, are not the same as the reality of the scientific system's practices when scholars compete for resources and recognition, prioritizing economically lucrative inventions over others. In this way, the *imaginative extension of the horizon* is not justified by the (empirical) practices but externally, for example, by idealized normative standards of the scientific production of "truth" (Latour & Woolgar, 1979; Merton, 1938).

Secondly, as reflexive modes in general, *rational* modes require connecting to the life-world and embodied forms of reasoning (*subjectivation*). As risk studies have proven over decades, it is not enough to provide a rational explanation for a risk and its management to the public (Fischhoff, 1995; Renn, 2008). It also must "feel right" to people. Therefore, institutional offerings and attempts to connect to the life-world are crucial. But this is difficult to the degree that social domains are detached self-referentially organized systems (Luhmann, 1995) and, as a result, produce systematic tensions between specialized forms of reflexive reasoning and people's lived reality (Habermas, 1984) (compare Fig. 8.1).

There is a wide range of examples of *enchantment* practices within the social sphere. Famous ones are the *enchantment* of scientific progress, the promises of technological innovation, the equality principle in modern societies, and the *achievement principle* underpinning the *American Dream* and other neoliberal models of the world. It is essential to

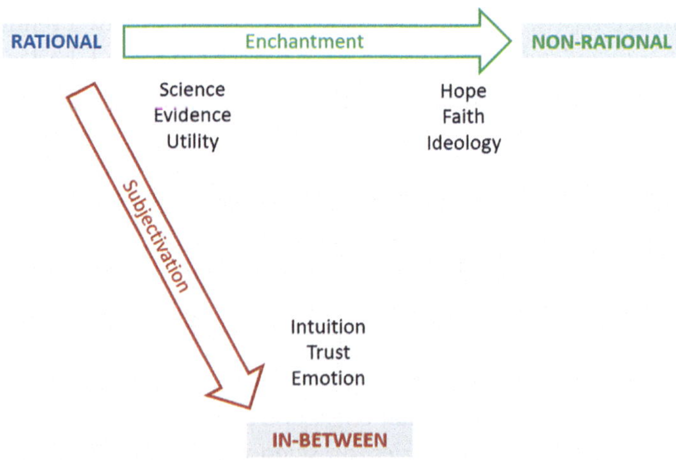


**Fig. 8.1** Enchantment and subjectivation of rational modes

note that *enchantment* is not only a general social condition of the social world but can also be strategically employed in domains such as the economy or politics for specific purposes. In this understanding, institutional enchantment is relatively independent of subjective experiences. This contrasts with approaches that primarily view enchantment as a subjective experience or assume that macro-level enchantment automatically implies micro-level enchantment, while rationalization is directly linked to alienation. Instead, we recognize the possibility that institutional enchantment can relate to both being subjectively enchanted and being subjectively alienated. This approach allows us to examine work on alienation, as described in Marxist scholarship, as well as (re-) enchantment, following Ritzer (2005). Before exploring examples from the economic realm, we demonstrate that science—often regarded as the producer of evidence and reliable knowledge—is also caught up in complex *institutional enchantment* and subjective *disenchantment* practices. A substantial body of research provides examples of the ongoing *enchantment* of scientific knowledge, particularly in the context of technological innovation and disasters. Over decades, Brian Wynne (1989, p. 37) conducted numerous studies on the enchantment of expertise produced in laboratories or derived theoretically, as we will discuss in more detail below. Similarly, Nik Brown in his research on a *Sociology of Expectations* has shown how technoscience operates not just through scientific evidence but *enchantment* of scientific knowledge, referring to affective, mythical, and promissory dimensions of innovative technologies such as transgenics, predictive medicine, reproductive science, and bioinformatics (Brown, 2003; Brown & Rappert, 2000). More broadly, a large part of Science and Technology Studies (STS) is concerned with enchantment tendencies. An example would be laboratory studies such as Sharon Traweek's (1988) classic ethnography of high-energy physicists. In *Beamtimes and Lifetimes,* she describes the mythology and practices of "an extreme culture of objectivity: a culture of no culture, which longs passionately for a world without loose ends, without temperament, gender, nationalism." From a different perspective, but similarly addressing enchantment processes, is the concept of *socio-technical imaginaries* introduced by Sheila Jasanoff. Such imaginaries are "collectively held, institutionally stabilized, and publicly performed visions of desirable futures, animated by shared understandings of forms of social life and social order attainable through, and supportive of, advancing science and technology" (Jasanoff & Kim, 2015, p. 4).

Such ideas of enchantment of science also align with Bruno Latour's historical analysis (Latour, 1993). In *We Have Never Been Modern* (Latour, 1993, pp. 15 and following), he emphasizes that at the start of natural science and laboratory experiments during the seventeenth century, it was not automatically assumed that observed phenomena had effects outside the laboratory setting where they were studied. For example, the early exploration of the vacuum, as Latour argues, relied on the subjective testimony of socially prominent individuals. Gradually, such testimony became less necessary as the technology was exported, and experiments were repeated in different locations. Since these phenomena can now be observed wherever laboratories are reconstructed, scientists today often see the vacuum (or any other laboratory result) as a universal fact that exists independently of social and political contexts. This enchanting assumption, which is a key reason for the high level of abstraction in laboratory knowledge, is questionable—especially in experiments involving humans not merely as witnesses but as active participants in the investigation setting itself (see, for example, the replication crisis in disciplines such as psychology or economics (e.g., Baker, 2016; Schmidt, 2009).

We consider the way laboratory knowledge is intruding into people's everyday lives and shapes the social sphere as *institutional enchantment* to the degree it systematically exaggerates its validity. In a study of Agent-Orange-based pesticides, Wynne demonstrates that the enchantment of scientific expertise can alienate people on a subjective level. In the case of pesticides, the National Union of Agricultural and Allied Workers (NUAAW) lobbied for a ban on Agent-Orange-based pesticides because of their harmful effects on the health of the workers applying them. However, during the 1970s, the official government Pesticides Advisory Committee (PAC) concluded that there was no scientific evidence to support a legal case that these pesticides are harmful. The union workers' concerns would only be based on unscientific anecdotal evidence. At this point, the subjective experience of daily life and scientific knowledge clashed in the sense that they do not connect meaningfully but follow largely disconnected rationales. Relying only on an idealized, enchanted imaginary of scientific truth, the repeated attempts to obtain a ban were juridically rejected in 1979 due to a lack of scientific evidence. The official review stated:

"*The use of brush killers containing pure 2,4,5-T offers no hazard to users, to the general public, to domestic animals, to wildlife or to the environment generally, provided that the product is used as directed ... The use as directed of brush killers ... poses no risk provided that the maximum allowable level of the TCDD contaminant is not exceeded*" (Wynne, 1989, pp. 36–37). Thus, the use of the pesticide would be "*safe so long as it was produced and used under the proper conditions*" (Wynne, 1989, p. 37).

The judgment referred to risk analyses which were underpinned by laboratory knowledge but came with several idealized assumptions, such as:

> Farmers and farm workers were always able and willing to use the chemical according to prescribed conditions of preparation and use: such as full instructions and the time to read and follow them; correct dose; the correct base solvent; full protective equipment; proper pressurized valves and spray nozzles; spraying only in certain climatic conditions. (Wynne, 1989, p. 37)

However, these descriptions did not relate to the experiential knowledge of the farm workers, who considered these assumptions so unrealistic that a Workers' representative stated:

> it was like asking someone to work in a laundry, but to keep out of the steam. (ibid.)

The reiteration of the patronizing distinction between superior scientific rationality and inferior subjective life-world knowledge, or in our words, the disconnection between reflexive rational knowledge and embodied subjective knowledge, resulted in a significant loss of public credibility and supported the development of growing public distrust (1989,

p. 38). This example, in our view, shows two things. Firstly, *institutional enchantment* can occur when legal experts focus solely on the idealized imaginaries of scientific expertise, rather than considering how such knowledge is integrated into people's life-world through its practices. When referring only to the sphere of reflexive scientific knowledge, the court neglected to consider the epistemological limits of this knowledge. In this way, the court followed uncritically the authority of the *modern dream* and failed to see how it *enchanted* scientific practice or became *enchanted* by science. Secondly, the *enchantment* of science during modernization pushed the social world into a trajectory during which the public becomes increasingly *alienated* from the reflexive societal systems. As a result, the subjective *alienation* from science might, in the aftermath, also extend to the legal system when uncritically taken over by enchanted versions of social reality rather than connecting these to people's lived experiences. Historically, we might say that the *enchantment* of science has already contributed to an increasing detachment of science from people's experiences. In this way, the gained authority of science simultaneously contributed to losing touch with the life-world and led to the erosion of scientific authority. Reversing this trend would require a continuous reconnection of abstract to embodied knowledge. This contrasts with calls for the public to put more trust in science but suggests the need for science to engage with the people's life-world to overcome the gap between abstract and embodied knowledge.

Brian Wynne's work (e.g., 1982a, 1982b, 1989, 1992, 1996) was primarily concerned with how local knowledge was disregarded within the hierarchy of scientific knowledge vis-à-vis lay knowledge, rather than socio-structural forces such as gender, class, or race shaping the opportunities for social groups'knowledge to be recognized. The fact that the *enchantment* of abstract forms of objectified knowledge invisibilizes and sidelines other forms of knowledge has been a central topic for a growing body of research. Famously, Donna Haraway and Sandra Harding both propagate the significance of the perspective of marginalized social groups and people, since "*partial perspectives provide more adequate, richer, better accounts of the world*" (Haraway, 1988, p. 590). Therefore, from a gender perspective, "*starting thought from women's lives will generate less partial and distorted accounts not only of women's lives but also of men's lives and of the whole social order*" (Harding, 1991, p. 119). In practice, however, similar to Wynne, in the study of Michelle Murphy (2006) "*women workers' accounts of their illnesses were dismissed as subjective and unreliable, yet their standpoint revealed systemic risks otherwise invisible to management and regulators*" (p. 87). Similar points have been made in postcolonial studies, which challenge Western imaginaries of superiority, enlightenment, and modernization while invisibilizing, devaluing, and marginalizing indigenous knowledge (Anderson, 2002). It is not only credibility but also the availability of interpretative concepts that are skewed or missing as a result of the *enchantment* of objectified scientific knowledge. Thus, the problem is not only one of acknowledging other forms of reflexive knowledge, but the lack of such institutionalized knowledge being available, which people from disadvantaged groups could relate their embodied experiences to. With our distinction between *rational* and *non-rational* forms of reasoning, we can differentiate between specific kinds of empirical knowledge and non-empirical forms of sense-making (e.g., ideology, faith), which can efficiently *enchant* such knowledge and thereby systematically disadvantage other forms.

Another example sheds light on the process of institutional enchantment of science in a more positive light. A growing number of authors are scrutinizing debates about the advancements in gene-technology. Some companies capitalized on the enthusiasm surrounding these rapidly developing technologies by offering to freeze cord blood stem cells, thereby allowing for the potential development of future medicines in case the child develops genetic illnesses later in life (Brown, 2005). In this way, it is an imagined precautionary measure that these companies sell. As some scholars have proposed, given the missing evidence suggesting advancements will be achieved in the near future, their products are based on *hope* rather than *evidence* (Brown et al., 2015; Petersen, 2015). Therefore, in our framework, we consider this as an expression of technological *enchantment*. This might be interpreted from the perspective of the *rational orthodoxy* as a deficit and an undesirable shift away from evidence-based reasoning. Often, the underlying motivation for such enchantment is the aim of acquiring financial resources for the research enterprise. In that sense, the respective institutions shift to marketing strategies, rather than adhering to the framework of scientific sobriety. However, the strategic enchantment of science used by the companies is willingly taken up by people who have the money to spend in support of such an imaginary.

Finally, people can also become enchanted by social institutions, such as science, when attempting to make sense of a daunting future with climate change, as we will discuss in Sect. 8.3. An enchanted future can also help to manage the present, which is crucial in many cases. It is vital when the future is likely to be disastrous, as in the case of climate change. Julia Cook (2016, 2017) provided an example with her study on young Australians' expectations regarding a distant future they will not experience themselves. Even though they are not personally affected, the possibility of dystopian development in the face of climate change requires many young people to cope with the possibility of human extinction. Some used the *enchantment* of technology as a means to consider the present meaningful. For them, it was necessary to believe that technology would be able to finally manage the challenges of climate change, even in the distant future. This allowed them to experience their life as still meaningful and to enjoy and engage in a life they value in the present.

Other examples come from the body of scholarship that builds on George Ritzer's work on the "cathedrals of consumption" (2005), show how attempts to enchant consumers and employees strategically take place in practice. The study of Nada Endrissat and colleagues (2015) argued by the example of a US organic supermarket chain that not only are consumers being enchanted in the *cathedrals of consumption,* but staff can become enchanted as well. This allows at least two interpretations. From the perspective of Marxism, it represents a wrong consciousness when workers are unaware that the exploitative mechanisms are covered up, which must be made visible to allow critique and social change to take place. In contrast, the insights from Endrissat and colleagues' study raise the question of whether employees might prefer feeling good rather than feeling alienated when being exploited by the capitalist economy and thereby embracing the possibility of enchanted work experiences.

Moving to non-profit social service organizations, the complexity and ambivalence of enchantment mechanisms on the organizational level vis-à-vis the subjective level can be demonstrated. In an ethnographic study on three social service organizations for social groups in need (homeless, drug addicts) in Canada, Agnieszka Kosny and Joan Eakin (2008) showed how the enchantment of work manifested in a specific work culture and discourse within the company. This constitutes an ambivalent situation. The work culture contributed to a valued identity among employees, but at the same time, it came with significant health risks from overwork and stress. At the core of the organization's mission was the notion of being prepared to go "the extra mile" (2008, p. 154) and to be available for the people in need even after work hours. Having internalized the mission, many workers willingly and enthusiastically followed patterns of self-exploitation to provide help to marginalized and disadvantaged clients. Thus, institutional enchantment was successful in making sense of one's work in the company (being subjectively enchanted), but the encouraged self-exploitation came with heightened health risks to the employees. This is a good example to show that the enchantment processes are often contradictory and ambivalent. An institution can offer opportunities for subjectively enchanting yet exploitative work practices and thereby increase feelings of self-worth; however, it can simultaneously invisibilize or devalue the risks faced by employees. Thus, enchantment might also come with the risk of losing feelings of self-confidence and self-worth when struggling to meet internalized expectations and experiencing burnout and health issues as a result. In this way, enchantment can even increase and heighten exploitation.

Another case of economic enchantment is gambling (compare Sect. 3. 1). The gambling industry, similar to the argument of the *cathedrals of consumption* as introduced by Ritzer's work, is enchanting its customers by promising the possibility of escaping their daunting lives. The gambling palaces, as well as the different forms of lottery, all in one or the other way enchant the subjectively experienced present and connect it to a wished-for future. There is a systematic connection between forms of gambling and social structure. Games of luck or gambling are a pervasive activity in many countries and are specifically popular in lower social strata (Beckert & Lutter, 2009; Griffiths, 1993; Wardle et al., 2014). It seems to serve a social function and may therefore often be supported by governments, which, through taxes, also generate significant revenue. Despite the "irrationality" of gambling—the costs are much higher than the possible gains gamblers make—a large body of gamblers spend as a group a significant amount of money on gambling. The Lottery can serve as an example, which is well socio-culturally embedded in many countries. For example, the Spanish Christmas lottery, *El Gordo*, is a state institution that is celebrated publicly and regularly mentioned in the news elsewhere in the world. In Germany, the "6 out of 49" with weekly drawings is similarly well established. However, since the public does not calculate mathematically, it is the marginal possibility of winning the Lottery that allows the player to dream of a life changer. In this way, it is indeed the enchantment that is sold through the lottery, or as Mark Lutter suggested, these are "*markets for dreams*" (Lutter, 2010). There are specific social groups, which consider playing the Lottery and dreaming about the future as a meaningful response to a life situation where other options seem not open and a change is welcome and desirable. But rather than the change itself, it is the reality of dreaming that allows them to be *enchanted* in a disadvantaged life or the exploitative reality of a life in a capitalist economy. Thus, the importance of the social function of an *enchanting* future lies not only in the power to allow dreams to turn into reality, which seems otherwise unreachable. More important than opening options for a change in the future is framing the present in a positive light.

Enchanted rationality is not only observable in relation to science and the economy but also in the political sphere. An obvious example is the war propaganda, such as during World War II or the current War of Russia against the Ukraine. But the way social crises are framed more generally, such as during the recent COVID-19 pandemic, illustrates the mobilization of imaginaries for enchanting the world for crisis management. New Zealand's response to the COVID-19 pandemic can serve as an example for strategic political enchantment that worked out well. The primary reason for the successful campaign was, in our view, the systematic connection between strategic enchantment of a scientifically legitimized response and its connection to the subjective level. This resulted in an internationally comparatively high rate of compliance.

New Zealand's response was indeed as evidence-based as possible at a time of relatively high uncertainty, informed by epidemiological knowledge and consultation with countries with comprehensive experience in managing the SARS virus, such as Taiwan (Manch, 2020). However, the approach has been internationally praised mainly for two reasons. Prime Minister Jacinda Ardern was able to develop a convincing narrative of managing the pandemic as a joint enterprise, "*we are all in this together*" (Hirwani, 2022; McGuire et al., 2020). Indeed, this is a rhetorical but critical imaginary that neglects the remaining inequalities in the effects of lockdowns, particularly when large families have a comparatively small living space or when casual workers no longer have an income. Therefore, the imaginary *enchants* the social reality of social differences and inequalities, which had to be addressed separately, such as the involvement of the Māori Community (Muriwai et al., 2024; Royal Commission, 2024; Te Hiringa Mahara, 2023). The government's campaign supported the sense of being in this together. The Prime Minister, along with the main epidemiologists, explained the situation and the basis for the decisions made. They demonstrated three key attitudes: serving the population to the best of their ability, providing accurate information, and explaining the science behind the responses and regulations implemented. This was complemented by the Prime Minister's daily social media presence. Using social media, Ardern spoke with the public in the evening from home, explaining the reasoning behind the decisions and their implications for them. She presented herself as being part of the shared effort, being affected herself, and as an authentically honest person, which altogether fostered the enchantment narrative of "*we are all in this together*" (Hunt, 2021; McGuire et al., 2020). This communicative performance was complemented by a broad media campaign, as well as additional symbolic actions. For example, when the Health Minister, David Clark, ignored lockdown regulations, Ardern rebuked his attitude, and he later had to resign from his duties (Roy, 2020a, 2020b). This response to non-compliance supported the broader narrative and certainly helped motivate people in a society with significant inequalities to come together in response to the COVID-19 pandemic. Thus, institutional enchantment was successfully connected to the micro-level where people personally experienced and suffered under lockdown. It might have given them a sense that their hardships are recognized and acknowledged. In this way, the government presented itself as trustworthy, and the polls showed that during the extreme hardship of lengthy lockdowns, these were broadly accepted, and trust in government increased to the highest levels ever, even in international comparison (McClure, 2021).

The presented examples demonstrate various ways in which strategic and institutional enchantment and subjectivation of rational modes are realized in practice across the scientific, economic, and political domains. The examples referred to different and contradictory dynamics of becoming *enchanted* and being *alienated* at work or in relation to scientific expertise. The political response to the COVID-19 crisis in New Zealand might also have alienated some groups of people who suffered most under the lockdown. The examples also illustrate the significance of the time dimension. For managing significant risks institutionally and subjectively, even when imagined only in a distant future, enchantment seems an essential element to reasonably engage not only with the future but also with the present. However, subjectivation remains crucial for both the rational handling of risk and coping with a daunting future.

Similar to Chapters 3 and 4, the examples demonstrate how analytical categories can help identify and analyze the various ways in which different modes of reasoning combine and inform engagement with risk and uncertainty. For instance, in the case of an acute crisis, such as the COVID-19 pandemic, the presented tendencies of *enchantment* and *subjectivation* overcome the ideal-types' neglect of systematic tendencies and dynamics of reasoning among the modes.

The following section originates from the *non-rational* forms of managing risk and uncertainty to illustrate how tendencies of *rationalization* and *subjectivation* of *non-rational* modes combine in providing support for (reasonably) engaging with risk and uncertainty.

## 8.2 Rationalization and Subjectivation of Non-Rational Reasoning

This section examines how *non-rational* modes of reasoning can reveal tendencies of *rationalization* and *subjectivation*. In this context, we see *rationalization* as the process by which wishes, dreams, and mythologies become more systematized and valuable for managing risk and uncertainty. This rests broadly on Max Weber's conceptualization of the *rationalization* process, which encompasses not only secularization and purpose-based reasoning but also the growing systematization and formalization of belief systems, such as through bureaucratization (Weber, 1930, 1978). Specifically, faith and ideologies provide reflexive bodies of knowledge that help individuals navigate risk and uncertainty, as well as rituals and practices that facilitate everyday life *subjectivation*. These provide confidence and a sense of truth that is relatively independent of empirical evidence. Before discussing institutionalized forms of *non-rational* modes, we turn to *hope* as the more fundamental attitude towards a risky future (Fig. 8.2).

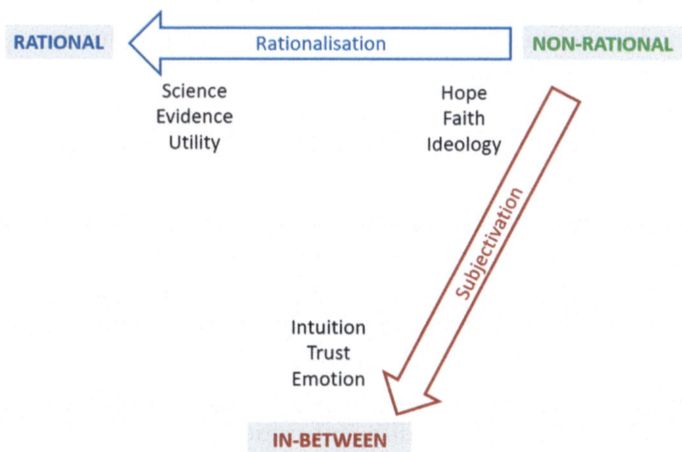


**Fig. 8.2** Rationalization and Subjectivation of Non-Rational Modes

Among the *non-rational* modes, we have characterized *hope* as the most basic form of reasoning about risk and uncertainty. It is considered from the perspective of rationality as *non-rational* or even *irrational*. However, as we have already argued in Chapter 3, there is good evidence that hoping in the face of risk can have positive effects, and therefore hoping is indeed a reasonable way of responding to risk and uncertainty, particularly when little knowledge and resources are available. Even when there is no causal relationship between a particular illness and the hope to overcome it, research has shown that, on average, a positive attitude can improve healing and well-being (Snyder et al., 1991; Yıldırım & Arslan, 2020) and therefore justifies encouraging hope as a rationalizable strategy to improve health outcomes. Indeed, the placebo effect is effective because a positive attitude has positive health effects (Hall, 2022).

It is important, however, to note that there is a difference between hoping in the context of risk as random events or engaging with risk as action (Goffman, 1969). With the latter, results and success depend on one's attitude, motivation, and performance. In contrast, for example, when playing roulette, hope will not influence the outcomes, but rather how we feel about them. But in cases of performance-based risk engagement, modes such as hope, faith, and magic, which foster a positive attitude towards the future, can, on average, improve outcomes. In this way, *non-rational* modes can profit from rationalization when encouraging a positive attitude. For example, the utilization of resilience-based approaches in combat preparation for soldiers follows this approach. The resilience training aims to improve soldiers' resourcefulness in the face of high risk and uncertainty. Strengthening resilience systematizes and rationalizes, among others, *non-rational* modes of engaging with risk and uncertainty. This becomes an increasingly desirable strategy when knowledge about the future is limited, or when the future is to a large degree uncertain, as in the case of soldiering. Pat O'Malley's (2012, pp. 59–60) list of titles for the different sections of an US army resilience training program shows that spirituality and optimism (including hope) are among the key aspects:

> Positive emotions (optimism and humor); Emotional regulation (fear, anger etc.); Cognitive flexibility (positive explanatory style, positive reappraisal and acceptance); Coping style (active approach vs. passive/avoidant); Spirituality (including religion); Moral code (including altruism); Social support (including unit support); Training (physical, psychological and spiritual; Purpose and meaning (mission).

While hope represents a non-institutionalized form of *non-rational* engagement with a risky future, faith and ideology are more developed and institutionalized forms that, beyond their broader sensemaking capacities, also encourage. hope and a positive orientation towards a risky future. In contrast to hoping, which seems a more situational and spontaneous form of managing a risk situation, faith and ideology provide broader and intersubjectively shared worldviews or imaginaries. They also come with secondary resources, such as social networks, which can help in many difficult life situations and include managing and coping with crises and disasters.

Both faith and ideology do more than influence the ways of approaching risk and uncertainty. They are part of broader ethical frameworks, which tend to order the world in good and evil and therefore provide certitudes in a world of growing complexity and uncertainty, which otherwise can become overwhelming. In Wohlrab-Sahr's (1999) study on the experience of a conversion to Islam, an informant described this transition as a shift to a meaningful and ordered world, after chaos had dominated before. In this way, the order provided to the individual by a complex ethical and normative framework can be considered a tendency to *rationalize* social reality. It systematizes the way to understand and manage a world, even when there might be little evidence-based justifications for the underpinning reasoning. For example, becoming unemployed can have many reasons. However, whether unemployment is explained by individual failure, fate, or a godly trial, none of which might be correct or empirically supported, yet they have different effects on the motivation to manage the situation and provide orientation in a world that might otherwise be experienced as overwhelming. From an institutional perspective, it is precisely this interpretative process, for example, of a job loss, that we call *subjectivation.*

Due to such *subjectivations,* the affected person establishes a connection between their embodied reality and a specific form of sense-making. Of course, such a "choice" of interpretative pattern is rarely done reflexively but results from an involuntary or habitualized "decision."

Even when not rationalized scientifically, faith provides many resources, such as rituals and interpretations, which allow people to engage and cope with risk and uncertainty. While these might provide meaning and confidence in the face of challenges, they are particularly valuable under conditions of uncertainty and the need to perform well, as we have already argued in Chapter 3. Because of the value of (religious or magical) rituals for helping to focus on a task and providing self-confidence and calming down in the face of high risk and pressure, one can apply them based on their subjective experience to achieve better outcomes even when, from a rational perspective, they provide wrong explanations. An assessment, which is at least partly supported scientifically (Damisch et al., 2010) and therefore comes with tendencies of *rationalization* when used strategically to improve performance. Thus, for example, religious forms of reasoning should not be devalued in unison, since they are both approaches that can help to cope with as well as perform well in the face of high risk and uncertainty.

We already referred to Loïs Bastide (2015) in Sect. 3.2, who argued with his study on work migrants between Indonesia, Malaysia, and Singapore, that people can use their faith to manage the uncertainty of the future not by referring to a rationalized worldview but the subjectivation of experience and interpreting undesired experiences as godly trials to test one's faith. The subjective sense-making of one's experiences produces a different kind of truth that is rooted in one's everyday life without connecting it to Westernized models of rationality, but to religious sense-making. It is thus efficient in mobilizing one's resources to cope with an uncertain and risky future based on practical wisdom. It is interesting how the informants in Bastide's study connect religion systematically to the world. Rather than being *irrational* as scholars may suggest from the perspective of *modern orthodoxy*, faith can help manage reasonably high risk and uncertainty. This is usually not a purely individualized strategy. Religious frameworks provide opportunities for integrating individual experiences into a broader framework. Additionally, when this approach may not be effective, institutional support is available in case of doubt or when advice is needed. If not fellow believers, then authority figures in powerful roles within a faith community can help by giving support, such as comfort and guidance. There is, however, a tension between the provision of a stable interpretative framework and the need to adapt to changing challenges of people's lives. The struggles of the catholic church to adapt to the changed realities of gender equality and acceptance of same sex intimate relationships are only an indication of the tensions that might occur within such frameworks and the lived reality of people. Therefore, faith is not only a resource to respond to risk and uncertainty. It is a framework that might also be defended against challenges. Such challenges are redefined as a threat to the worldview and normative framework, which holds a social group together. They are not defined by the reality of a threat or rational ways of managing a danger, but by prior socio-cultural values (Douglas, 1992; Douglas & Wildavsky, 1982).

Similarly to religion, ideologies come with secondary effects through the institutionalization in political parties, charitable foundations, youth organizations, and other attached organizations. They provide much more than a system of meaning, but a whole network of relevant people and activities shaping one's life and a valued identity. Independent of whether evidence-based or not, such frameworks of meaning help people to (subjectively) manage risk and uncertainty and order an in principle uncertain world and their place in it. In this way, there is indeed an extensive range of interpretive ideologies about the world from lifestyle groups (e.g., rejecting modern medicine and favoring homeopathy) to subcultural milieus of right-wing extremism (e.g., QAnon), which may provide systems of meaning and support to their followers as well as valued identities confirmed by others.

Ideologies usually seek to find at least metaphorical scientific support or evidence to give their claims weight. Whole streams of empirical research refer to broader theoretical frameworks to interpret observable reality. But it is contested whether, for example, Marxism or Liberalism is more suitable to describe empirically observable economic dynamics and their effects on people's lives. Indeed, these come with different ways of framing the world, selecting different risks and uncertainties as problematic, and providing different solutions. Seen through the lens of cultural theory (Douglas, 1985, 1990), these can be interpreted as different cultural frameworks. Even when the risks are real, the selection, understanding, and responses are framed by worldviews that are not determined by the risks per se but by the value system one cherishes. These value systems are rationalized through the provision of knowledge, but one's perspective on risk depends on one's socio-cultural positioning. They are only conclusive within people's socio-cultural perspective. Cultural theorists suggest that irreconcilable worldviews (i.e., Hierarchy, Individualism, Egalitarianism, Fatalism) are complementary and require solutions that do not challenge their integrity (Thompson, 2008).[4] Nevertheless, worldviews might still differ in the opportunities they have to connect to empirical evidence.

The COVID-19 debate in Germany can, in some respects, serve as an example for how difficult it is to manage different *non-rational* modes of reasoning that rationalize their responses to the crisis, which are rooted in the values they prioritize. The German government was firmly committed to a top-down, science-based approach, which, from the cultural perspective of Mary Douglas, follows the type of *Hierarchy*. Scientific knowledge was mobilized to support government responses, aiming to vaccinate at least 80–90 percent of the population to achieve herd immunity, thereby protecting vulnerable individuals who could not be vaccinated. The respective, mainly top-down, evidence-based campaigns to increase vaccination rates were rationalized by scientific evidence considered authoritative. However, there was little acknowledgment of the uncertainty involved in every vaccination while potential side effects were deemed negligible. In the face of the imminent uncertainty, liberals quickly insisted on their worldview of *Individualism*, that it should be up to everyone individually whether to vaccinate or not. Indeed, they could have argued about the possible side effects of vaccines but emphasized that it should be a personal decision whether to take the risk of vaccination or the risk of becoming infected. Additionally,

[4] Cultural theory does not focus on the socio-structural reasons for differences in worldviews even when considering systematic differences between cultures of the center community (hierarchy, individualism) and at the margins (egalitarianism, fatalism).

from the perspective of cultural theory, at the margins of society, *Egalitarians* such as the "Querdenker"[5] ("lateral thinkers") reject scientific knowledge sources and refer to self-made explanatory frameworks or theories instead. Even when the combination of facts and conclusions into broader conspiracy theories seemed to many people somewhat illogical or beyond formal standards of reasoning, they often still followed at least metaphorically an argumentative structure and thereby a modernist rationality. However, according to Michael Thompson, socio-culturally based risk conflicts can only be managed successfully when solutions acknowledge all cultures (Thompson, 2008). Thus, when risk conflicts primarily involve value conflicts, rationalizing cultural contradictions does not necessarily mean finding an objective space beyond culture, but rather finding solutions that relate in some way to the concerns of different socio-cultural milieus.

In this way, there are two key concerns for *non-rational* reasoning. One is about empirically weak or lacking support for *non-rational* standpoints. The other is about the social constructs that make sense of the world but are not empirically justified themselves. They might thereby help to cope with and, at the same time, invisibilize relevant aspects of risk and uncertainty. To the extent that such *non-rational* modes cannot be justified by scientific and rule-based empirical evidence, the social mechanisms are crucial. From the perspective of New Phenomenology, we consider embodied practices particularly successful for such purposes since they do not need objectified empirical evidence but a subjectively experienced feeling of truth, for example, based on shared social constructions of a community (e.g., faith group) and one's experience of growing up in or into such a group with its worldviews (this can include the stigmatization of and prejudice against specific social groups such as women, migrants, the greens, or atheists). We have already referred to *rituals* that are not merely an irrational procedure to foster hope. Instead, they are a shared reassurance and practice that helps focus on

[5] *Querdenker* or literally "lateral thinkers" refers in contemporary Germany to a protest movement that arose during the COVID-19 pandemic. While the word once had a positive meaning of unconventional or creative thinking, it is now widely associated with opponents of public health measures, conspiracy theorists, and far-right actors.

a difficult task or coping with risk and uncertainty, such as in the historical example of the Trobriand islanders provided by Malinowski (1925), who conducted rituals before the dangerous fishing in the open ocean, but not when fishing in the protected lagoon. Also, collective prayer can have positive emotional effects on the people involved, helping them gain strength to manage challenging tasks or even face death, as seen in the context of embarking on a boat migration journey across the ocean. Singing together in the church is part of community building and a form of reassurance that is institutionalized in many religions. It provides positive embodied effects for the believers in terms of bonding, health, and well-being (Pearce et al., 2015), but also for managing the risks and uncertainties of one's life. Indeed, the practiced routine or ritual of praying (e.g., the rosary) in the face of an important decision or a risky situation might be both a way of focusing on a task and a coping strategy. The boundaries between religiously interpreting the empirical world and the rituals used to navigate the secularized world may be blurring. It is in our view still essential to distinguish these two, since for both the embodied effects help the *non-rational* framework to be continued and the worldly practice to be performed well.

Theory and research on mass psychology (Moscovici, 1985) have explored the impact that large groups have on individuals. A large group of people in a stadium during a soccer game, at a concert in a great hall, attending a political speech, marching, and singing together for freedom, and much more have effects that go beyond the individual. These can result in protests turning militant, mass hysteria developing, or just a feeling of power and excitement spreading when the team one supports wins the game. In New Phenomenology, such phenomena are interpreted as a situational sensation of a shared and potentially collective embodiment (Griffero, 2021; Schmitz, 2003, p. 40; 2016, pp. 162ff.) and are well investigated at least with regard to sport events (Gugutzer, 2020; Gugutzer & Böttcher, 2012). The atmosphere of a large military parade and the marching of soldiers are expressions of strength and power that are not only meant to impress the enemy but to increase feelings of strength and power among the soldiers themselves (Fessler & Holbrook, 2014). These are powerful means to help soldiers feel more confident or assertive when facing the risks and uncertainties of a military mission.

Thus, whether masses are manipulated to convince them to follow an ideology or sing for their own courage to bring down a government, embodied experiences are powerful when engaging with and managing risk and uncertainty. Such technologies as singing speed up community building processes with strangers but have also long-term positive effects for bonding into a (faith) community (Pearce et al., 2015). Rituals work in all kinds of contexts on the micro-level as well as the institutional level. They are part of the production of socially significant events, which can provide confidence, recognition, feelings of belonging, and a range of other benefits. Another example is the development of a neo-tribal risk culture among Canadian tree planters, as described by Kevin Walby and Dale Spencer (2018).

As we have argued, all reflexive modes require some grounding in the subjective experience to become meaningful. In this respect, there is no difference between *rational* and *non-rational* modes. *Rational* modes tend to emphasize empirical facts and models of causality, but in the same way depend on *subjectivation* and, for example, democratic rituals of open debate, scientific rituals of knowledge production, and symbolic rituals to express experts' authority. For the *non-rational modes*, gaining interpretative relevance results primarily from belonging to a specific faith group or ideological milieu, which is more important than rule-based empirical evidence. Beyond biographical aspects, the interpretative relevance derives in any case from a sense of belonging when others share similar views. The perception of risk and the perception of the ability to manage risk and uncertainty are then primarily dependent on the embodied feeling of power to be able to manage risk and uncertainty rather than abstract causality. Indeed, the effects of such embodied feelings of strength can be systematically influenced and change the objective ability to manage risk. Therefore, the recent focus on resilience in disaster studies (Norris et al., 2008; Paton & Johnston, 2017) combines the knowledge about risk with the need for coping with unexpected challenges. This is the case for training individuals to be more resilient as well as for communities to enhance their preparedness and responses to disasters.

The contribution of embodied techniques to increase feelings of power and strength has also been proven as one central element for totalitarian regimes to find support in a population. In 1967, a schoolteacher at Cubberley High School in Palo Alto, California, who was frustrated by college students who did not understand how Germans had become willful followers of a totalitarian Nazi Regime going to war and killing millions of Jews, conducted a five-day experiment, known as "The Wave." The study demonstrated how a shift into a totalitarian mindset, such as in Nazi Germany, could still take place today, even in the US (Lipsett, 2008). Core elements included discipline, rituals, and uniformity, which provided the students with positive feelings of power and confidence. It was a demonstration of how such embodied technologies can be used for both good and bad purposes, and they are applied strategically all over the world to this day.

An important question remains to be discussed in the following sections. How and when do people, based on their everyday life modes of reasoning, turn to *rational* or *non-rational* modes?

## 8.3 Rationalization and Enchantment of Life-World's In-Between Reasoning

As we have argued so far, *rational* and *non-rational* modes of reasoning require subjectivation to become effective in everyday life. We have considered these everyday life modes as representing an independent rationale of reasoning that Zinn (2008, 2016) called *in-between* and systematically differs from what we tentatively described as *rational* and *non-rational* ones. The *in-between* modes are underpinned by a specific kind of embodied or tacit knowledge, which is experience-based and intuitively and/or emotionally available (compare also: Brown, 2022, pp. 91–95). These *in-between* modes, representing an embodied experience of the life-world, might be reflected upon in two different ways. Attempts can be made to connect them to empirical evidence, thereby *rationalizing one's trust, intuition, or emotions,* or they can become *enchanted* and reflected upon as empirically independent truths. As will

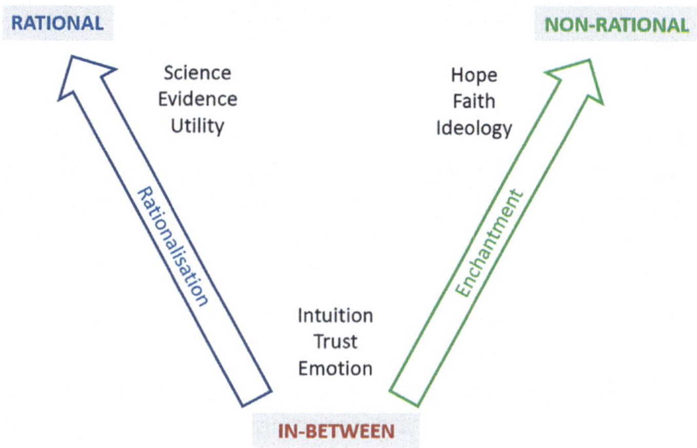


**Fig. 8.3** Rationalization and Enchantment of In-Between Modes

be shown in the following, both tendencies are empirically observable (Fig. 8.3).

As we have argued earlier (compare Sect. 4.1), from the perspective of in-between modes of reasoning, for example, trusting is neither entirely rational nor irrational but refers to subjective knowledge and practices of everyday life and constitutes an independent logic of reasoning (e.g., Frederiksen, 2016). However, the debate about the character of trust falls into two opposing positions among scholars, who view trust as *rational* (Coleman, 1990), in contrast to those who see trust as at least partly *non-rational* (Luhmann, 1979, 1988), and others who emphasize the *emotional* basis of trust (Barbalet, 2009). The conceptual debates attempted to generalize and subordinate various forms of trusting within specific, broader theoretical frameworks, albeit at the cost of neglecting essential aspects of the social practice of trusting. With our framework, these different perspectives can be integrated and made sense of as trust being an *in-between* mode of reasoning, which comes with different empirically observable tendencies of *rationalizing* and *enchanting* trust. This approach seems more fruitful to us, as it aligns with observable practices of trusting.

Debates about trust intensified with the observation of decreasing trust in modern Western societies, which has puzzled many scholars.

To make sense of this development, Anthony Giddens (1990) asserted that trust has shifted from earlier *unconditional trust* to *conditional trust*. People have become increasingly critical and are no longer prepared to trust modern institutions and their representatives unconditionally. Instead, they would carefully evaluate who and which institution to trust. Consequently, trust depends on people's experiences and reflexive evaluation of a risk as well as the information source and one's social relationship to this source (e.g., science, WHO). In this way, trust becomes, in Giddens' perspective, *conditional—a* process we describe as a tendency of *rationalization.*

A good example of the dynamics of trust is the COVID-19 crisis. A well-perceived performance of a government was generally rewarded by increasing levels of trust in responsible political leaders, such as the PM Jacinda Ardern in New Zealand (McClure, 2021). Even though trust in experts is usually higher during a crisis (Johansson et al., 2021), not all governments profited similarly. For example, trust in the regional government of Hong Kong remained relatively low in the early months of the COVID-19 crisis, compared to the gains made by governments in other countries at the same time (Chan, 2021; Sibley et al., 2020). *Conditional trust*, as defined by Giddens, could therefore be described with the help of our scheme as people's attempt to rationalize their trust-seeking for reliable evidence of trustworthiness. In the case of Hong Kong, many people who distrusted the regional government turned to advice from other countries or international organizations, such as the WHO, to inform their decisions about how to prepare and respond to COVID-19. They might have critically evaluated the trustworthiness of the regional government, but concluded that the government's slow response to the virus was due to ideological means. They might have suspected that the delayed response was due to Xi, the president of mainland China, visiting Hong Kong. Nevertheless, over time, responses developed and followed international advice. Consequently, trust increased, but it was still influenced by the experience of the opposition crackdown and the need to obey mainland China, which prevented many Hong Kong residents from placing their trust in the regional government. Other residents who did not distrust the government did not require a critical assessment and might have put their faith in the regional government's performance, even when it clearly deviated from the responses of other Asian countries, which were much more proactive. In this way, they might have followed what Giddens called *unconditional trust*, or displayed a tendency to be *enchanted* by China's commitment to population health.[6] In the case of Hong Kong people's trust, it has undoubtedly been influenced by their stance on the reunification of Hong Kong under Mainland China's rule, making it a good example of how broader social contexts shape responses to a specific challenge, such as a pandemic.

There may be good reasons why people trust an institution or its representatives based on accumulated experiences. However, there might also be valid reasons why people want to trust. For example, Patrick Brown (2009) described such engagement with trust as the "will to trust." He suggested, following Schütz, to distinguish different levels of knowledge, from abstract to affective/intuitive (Brown, 2022). In a study with terminal cancer patients, he found that patients preferred trusting medical experts about opportunities to extend their life expectancy when participating in a new cancer treatment trial. Having built a trusting relationship with a doctor over time can support the willingness to follow the doctor's advice. The personal relationship, rather than abstract knowledge or the reality of cancer trials, allows a terminal cancer patient to put trust in a doctor as a knowledgeable advisor and a representative of a powerful health institution to participate in such trials (Brown, 2009, pp. 396ff.). From our model, the concrete, embodied experience and exchange of knowledge and advice give individual decision-makers a better sense of their judgment in a desperate situation. Therefore, they tend to trust the known expert rather than putting hope or faith in an abstract system. In this way, trust becomes somewhat enchanted, as there is little evidence that the trials (especially when one is in the placebo group) offer a direct benefit to the patient. At the same time, it might be emotionally more comforting to trust another person than to rely on hope or faith, which remain more distanced from embodied everyday experience and are often drawn upon only when all other possibilities

[6] We do not want to overgeneralize these explanations. The question of what modes people turn to is an empirical one. Even when, on average, our explanations might be correct, people may have critically assessed the regional government's performance and have come to different conclusions based on the knowledge available to them.

have been exhausted. As the proverb says, "hope dies last". However, institutional representatives may not be the best independent advisors for patients in need, since they could have a conflict of interest if they profit professionally from medical trials (Brown et al., 2015).

Using our conceptual framework enables us to interpret empirical evidence by distinguishing between two tendencies of trust: *rationalized* trust, in the sense of a critical and reflexive form of trusting, and *enchanted* trust, as an unconditionally assumed form of trust. This framework also enables us to examine how various factors influence people's engagement in one approach or the other, and to what extent such forms of reflexive reasoning might be institutionally encouraged by open information policies or exaggerated by the alleged potential of expertise and science. There are further *in-between* rationales, each comes with specific characteristics, but they seem to be entangled with each other. For example, *trust* (Barbalet, 2009) as well as *intuition* (Atanasiu, 2021; Dancy, 2014) have been interpreted as being closely connected to *emotions*.

As we have argued, emotions understood as forms of embodied affectedness are not necessarily irrational but can serve as advisors in decision-making. Many interview studies feature informants describing how they "listen" to or are guided by their feelings when making decisions (Heinz et al., 1998; Zinn, 2001). This often occurs when the decision-making situation involves some uncertainty. Feeling good about a decision becomes a key aspect of the process, allowing the non-reflexive embodied sphere to play a role. In a study of middle-aged Germans making biographical decisions, one informant used the metaphor of a traffic light. Sometimes he goes when the light is green. Sometimes he goes when the light is red. It all depends on how he feels about it. He also compares a rational approach to an emotional one: "I can think: how do I benefit from this or that for my future, but I can also try out: how do I feel about it, and that's what usually works out best for me" (Zinn, 2004, p. 214). Even in hindsight, he emphasizes that the enchantment of emotions is an independent decision-making factor, not something reflexively managed or controlled. As he suggests, emotions often work best, but not always. He sees no reason to rationally explore when they work best and when they don't. Instead, he elevates emotions as a broad source of decision-making, even when outcomes are unfavorable.

Similarly, in a study on soldiers' management of risk and uncertainty, one informant explained that he always listened to his emotions. When something felt wrong, he acted on it and took a risk (Zinn, 2012). However, later in the interview, he also developed a quite different narrative of rationally managing his emotions. When he faced his own anxieties, whether in the form of personal challenges or existential threats, he had to find ways to manage his feelings and learn to rationalize them. He turned them, for example, into aggression to perform well (Zinn, 2012). While in the first example, emotions in the face of risk became an independent source of decision-making and were accompanied by a tendency towards *enchantment*, in the second example of the soldier, emotions became a resource to be reflected upon, utilized, and managed *rationally*.[7]

Another domain where emotions play a central role in decision-making is marriage and romantic love. Indeed, in a *culture of divorce* (Hackstaff, 1999), romantic love is under pressure and probably not good guidance for biographical decision-making. However, a popular culture industry still supports the idea of *romantic love* and lifelong relationships (Koontz et al., 2017). Research on middle-aged adults in Germany suggested that the concept of romantic love still guides some couples' decisions, often at the expense of prioritizing financial independence and protection in the event of divorce (Zinn, 2004, p. 209). However, when emotions seem difficult to control, the study of Jane Lewis and Sophie Sarre (2006) found that many young British couples tried to separate finances from emotions. They considered this necessary to secure financial control and independence for emotions and love to unfold freely. The rational arrangement and backup might even be a prerequisite for these women to enjoy their relationship fully.

In contrast to cases where people rely heavily on emotions as the primary source for risky decision-making, many studies indicate an increasing tendency to combine emotions with rationality or manage

[7] Indeed, there were many examples of soldiers who followed the modern orthodoxy of separating and controlling emotions rather than using them (Zinn, 2012).

conditions rationally, thereby allowing emotions to unfold without negative side effects, such as financial loss. Cultural notions of romantic love remain pervasive in modern societies, supporting enchanted understandings of love, while numerous studies demonstrate attempts to rationalize emotions or rationally manage them. With the publication of the psychologist Daniel Goleman's book on Emotional Intelligence (1995), the reflexive management of emotions has become a key topic, moving emotions from the realm of irrationality to a necessary and crucial resource for rationally shaping one's life. Studies on the framing effect (Tversky & Kahneman, 1987) showed that the decisions of people change significantly if they are emotionally addressed. Such an approach seems reasonable, enabling subjects to reflect on their embodied affection while finding solutions for evolving problems.

In recent decades, the importance of intuition for effective decision-making under conditions of limited knowledge, high complexity, and time pressure has become increasingly recognized across many social areas of professional decision-making such as management (Malewska, 2019; Thanos, 2023) and healthcare (Van den Brink et al., 2019; Wilson et al., 2023).

In the domain of healthcare, the pressure to provide infallible evidence-based services is high, where mistakes can easily end in significant harm and death. But it is specifically in high-risk domains such as Emergency Care, where time is scarce for making evidence-based decisions and intuitive decision-making is essential for saving lives. In such contexts, recognizing and training intuition are crucial for improving services (Wilson et al., 2023). At the same time, in more routine situations, such as the first assessment of patients and the first diagnosis to be further explored, there is a need to match abstract knowledge to specific patients' symptoms, requiring some degree of intuitive knowledge as well. Due to the diverse tasks in healthcare, doctors, nurses, and specialists exhibit varying levels of acceptance and utilization of intuition. Besides personal differences, the use of intuition is influenced by the complexity of the situation, the availability of knowledge, and the need to make decisions under time pressure (Van den Brink et al., 2019, p. 5; Wilson et al., 2023, p. 8).

There are differences in the use of intuition in professional practice, but nurses and doctors mainly agree on the need to check for evidence confirming intuitive judgments. They are not only aware of the limits of rationality but also the limits of intuition and the danger of overconfidence, as well as the need to be sensitive to deviations from the average and exceptional cases (Van den Brink et al., 2019). However, there are also requirements to justify decisions in case things go wrong; therefore, ideal type formalized procedures have a value also in protecting the reality of intuitive practice. There are clear trends to *rationalize* practices in healthcare by allowing *intuitive* practices to be conducted. At the same time, strong interests remain to *rationalize* intuition or make sure that "skilled intuition" or what could be called "well-informed guesswork" improves outcomes and to prevent the harm of overconfidence and routine decision-making (Van den Brink et al., 2019; Velanovich, 2023, pp. 37–42). Listening to emotions or gut feelings, discussing patients with others, and consulting more experienced doctors or nurses are among the approaches that aim to rationalize the use of intuition. The 10,000-hour rule of intensive practice to achieve mastery of complex skills, even when having become under scrutiny, is an attempt to *rationalize* intuitive practices (Velanovich, 2023, p. 40).

The danger of professional overconfidence is a general concern in intuitive decision-making, and an open discursive professional culture is one approach to prevent the *enchantment* of expertise in individuals, fostering instead a discursive professional culture. Part of it is the need to accumulate individual experience as well as gain from the experience of a medical team. In this way, the combination of evidence-based and intuition-based approaches is particularly important. Good intuitive decisions are only possible when there is a reasonable basis of expertise available. Therefore, young doctors and nurses tend to have a more analytical approach, while more experienced professionals tend to use their intuition more often. Altogether, intuition is mainly used in a rationalized way and systematically backed up (Van den Brink et al., 2019, p. 7).

At least since the 2000s there has been a growing interest in intuition in economic decision-making. For example, Karin Knorr-Cetina and Urs Bruegger (2000, p. 146) investigated the strategies of traders at computer-based financial markets and highlight that "their body and the screen world melting together in what appears to be a total immersion in the action in which they are taking part." The velocity of market movements, as Knorr-Cetina (2012, p. 129) adds, requires "the disappearance of self-reflexivity" and urges the traders to act intuitively (with regards to non-reflexive acting at financial markets compare as well Zaloon, 2006, p. 138).

In a similar perspective, Maleska emphasized a trend in recent management scholarship (Malewska, 2019). The overload of information and the volatility and unpredictability of markets would require an intuitive assessment and strategic decision-making that goes beyond the reliance on proven evidence. In this context, intuition "*means understanding, learning, or acquiring knowledge without rational inference. Intuition is not a denial of logical thinking, but it involves the use of rules other than logical inference in the process of thinking*" (Malewska, 2019). Again, while there are domains in management where intuition is less critical, strategic management for an uncertain future is often crucial, but at the same time, the most challenging activity. While rationality and intuition have frequently been researched separately to determine the more successful approach, it has become clear that a combination of intuition and rationality yield better outcomes, regardless of how they are combined. Most important for our argument is that both the complete *enchantment* of intuition and a complete focus on rationality, excluding the everyday life embodied experience, come with suboptimal outcomes. However, according to Ioannis Thanos, a rationalized approach to engaging with everyday life suggests that intuitive knowledge produces better outcomes (Thanos, 2023). It is worth noting that the studies we found in recent reviews do not explicitly include the *non-rational* aspects of the broader frameworks that guide management outcomes.

There is a connection between concerns about overconfidence in healthcare and management contexts, on the one hand, and concerns in disaster studies, on the other, regarding whether institutionalized decision-making culture might detach from reality. An ongoing shift from a relatively safe procedure to symbolic safety that Diane Vaughan called "normalization of deviance" (Vaughan, 1996) is considered the primary reason for *man-made disasters* (Turner & Pidgeon, 1997). With intuition being rooted in tacit knowledge, it might be influenced not only by experience but also by social forces, such as institutional pressure for cost savings. For example, Vaughan (1996) argued for the case of the Challenger disaster, external financial pressure contributed to a shift in the safety environment and weakening of safety standards. The understanding of safety became increasingly detached from reality. Instead, the notion of safety became more and more symbolic and *enchanted*, and as a result increased the likelihood of a major disaster.

There are different reasons why intuitive practices become *enchanted* and embedded in institutional contexts. This can be cost pressure, which encourages expert electricians to prove their skills by showing their ability to ignore safety standards for a competitive advantage. This can be railway maintenance workers in Sweden ignoring safety regulations in the belief that they are doing an excellent job for the company, securing train punctuality (Sanne, 2008), or miners in Canada who want to prove their outstanding value for a company by taking higher risks than others (Hall, 2016, 2021). It is often the combination of the desire to perform well on a job and the opportunity to do so. However, the examples from healthcare also show both the importance of intuitive practices and the techniques to prevent them from becoming enchanted, leading to overconfidence and possible disaster. However, overconfidence can also become embedded in an *enchanted* culture of an occupational or social milieu driven by a valued self-identity.

Steven Lyng (1990) observed overconfidence or an exaggerated sense of control in the social milieus of high-risk leisure sports. In his research on *edgework*, he characterized *edgeworkers* as people who cherish leisure-time risk-taking as a value in itself, including getting as close as possible to the edge of possible harm without crossing the line. However, Lyng stated that edgeworkers would regularly see conditions as controllable that are, in fact, chance-determined. However, they suggest that they can manage them based on their innate abilities, which are exclusive to real edgeworkers. In this way, the shared personal experiences of successfully exploring the edge might have contributed to an enchanted culture that blurs the realities of risk and the limits of control. When people connect subjective experiences to such a collective interpretation of a practice or situation, they might become enchanted themselves. This can contribute to increasing confidence, but at the same time, can also lead to crossing the line and exposure to heightened risk.

Some examples illustrate this point through near misses, in which edgeworkers intuitively manage a high-risk situation through reflexive action, thereby preventing serious injury or death. When somebody fails and dies, however, the person becomes re-evaluated in the milieu as lacking proper edgework skills in the first place (Lyng, 1990, p. 859). Attributing the failure of these persons one-dimensionally to their lack of intuitive skills overestimates intuition and neglects other relevant causes of the respective accidents. In this way, the edgework culture enchants individuals' abilities to explore the edge. At the same time, this interpretation protects and upholds the enchanted edgework culture against other possible interpretations.

These different examples show that when facing everyday challenges, pursuing one's wishes and dreams, or dealing with a tedious work routine, many are willing to take risks. Relying on their intuitive, experience-based knowledge often helps improve decision-making in professional settings, especially when it is part of individual or organizational practices of "skilled intuition." However, these practices might become enchanted. Such enchantment can be embedded in, for example, the culture of a social milieu, a professional identity, or an organizational corporate identity. Such cases can not only motivate people or provide them with a valued identity or meaning about their world, but can also foster exaggerated ideas of invulnerability and control. Since risk is a likelihood of an undesired event or disaster, it might not cause immediate harm when crossing the line from relative safety to heightened risk. Instead, it can work well for a long time before a disaster happens. It is therefore often difficult to determine whether one has started to follow a disaster-prone trajectory.

In summary, empirical research on trust, emotions, and intuition shows how these *in-between* modes are connected to tendencies to *rationalize* and *enchant* them, depending on social pressures and subjective desires. In between modes, when they cannot be controlled, as in the case of love, the possible negative side effects can be rationally controlled. The uncertainties in intuitive professional practices can be tamed by checking afterward their reliability. Indeed, in-between practices can shift away from tacit knowledge practices to *enchanted* practices, which increases the possibility of undesired outcomes and disaster.

## 8.4 When Does One Turn to One or the Other Mode?

With *New Phenomenology*, we shifted the perspective from primacy of cognition to primacy of embodied sensations. We related these senses to the *in-between* modes of trust, intuition, and emotions and located them in the personal situation of the affected subject. Whether these modes are utilized or one turns to *rational* or *non-rational* modes is an empirical question. The advantage of the neo-phenomenological term "situation" is that it describes the wholeness of a concretely acting person and its circumstances. This involves factors such as the concrete shared situation and its atmosphere, the biographical experiences one brings to it, including habitual patterns, as well as reflexive expectations towards the future, socio-culturally available resources and norms, institutional (working) conditions, factors which are to different degrees shaped by intersecting socio-structural forces (Giritli Nygren et al., 2020). While social class, gender, ethnicity, and other forces intersect in people's risk experiences (Finucane et al., 2000b; Olofsson & Rashid, 2011), it is an empirical question how these combine and manifest in social and individual responses (compare also Sect. 6.3). For example, vaccination resistance is observable in many social groups and driven by different rationales. When people take risks at work to make ends meet, this tells us little about the modes of reasoning they follow and the knowledge they base their decisions on.

From the body of research, we introduced to illustrate different modes of reasoning, some general tendencies can be derived. These are neither deterministic nor exhaustive. What seems clear to us is the need for *rational* patterns to refer to *non-rational* imaginaries (enchantment) and being rooted in the emotional and intuitive sensing of one's life-world (*in-between*). Similarly, what we addressed as *non-rational* forms of reasoning, such as hope, faith, and ideology, require some connection to the world to be useful. Indeed, they provide resources to cope with issues that cannot be understood or managed *rationally*, but must be accepted or dealt with emotionally, and require a firm grounding in the life-world as well. Turning the perspective, the modes rooted in the everyday embodied sensing require some reflection, which connects to both evidence and (positive) visions of the future. In summary, *rationalization*, *enchantment*, and *subjectivation* tendencies are observable in all modes of reasoning, and there are typical difficulties that emerge when these modes become disconnected from each other. As a result, our typology provides an analytical framework for identifying and further exploring how different aspects relate to each other and how *rationalization* and *enchantment* intersect with *subjectivation*, combining in specific ways. These are observable in people's ways of engaging with risk and uncertainty.

There are good indications that the tendency to use one or the other mode results from one's culturally and structurally influenced biographical experiences, which are shaped by the milieu(s) one is growing up in and the responses to the expectations one is confronted with. During the life course, people are positioned and become exposed to different (social and physical) conditions that connect to such experiences. This includes others with whom one connects and interacts, such as family members, classmates, coworkers, or friends, within the family, at school, at work, or during leisure activities. Some social institutions, such as political parties, unions, or the church, have a strong basis in most countries. To the degree one engages with such institutions, these not only shape the sense-making processes but also the ways of reasoning, whether analytically or metaphorically, whether primarily based on their embodied senses or with a stronger focus on cognitive reflexivity. Finally, the atmosphere of a collectively shared situation can be highly influential for dealing with risk and uncertainty. For example, the atmosphere of being subjectively threatened during the pandemic's onset was a kind of embodied mass-experience that involuntarily shaped people's behavior. Though such atmospheres are bodily perceived and hence are subjective, they are not necessarily individual experiences. This is crucial for engaging with and responding to risk and uncertainty, as well as identifying solutions to concrete issues.

One's position in the social world and the connections to different social spheres shape experiences. This includes exposure to arguments, normality assumptions and practices, valuations, and many more. Higher mobility and availability of information have opened more opportunities for experiences, which are relatively far from one's earlier life, opening possibilities and the need for reflection. But they can also be a force that encourages us to stick even closer to the knowledge generated earlier and to reject reconsidering risks and uncertainties, and how to handle them. There is no doubt that one's social position more generally influences the way risk and uncertainty are understood and which resources one turns to, whether to experts, public, or social media, mainstream, niche, or conspiracy theories. In Sect. 8.5, we will examine in more detail the problems that arise when people's embodied experiences cannot refer to an accepted body of institutionalized knowledge or when such embodied forms of knowledge are devalued altogether, issues that have been central to feminist and postcolonial critique (Anderson, 2002; Haraway, 1988; Harding, 1989, 1991; Murphy, 2006; Smith, 1999).

From the perspective of neo-phenomenological epistemology, the variety of *situations* (involuntary embeddedness), and *constellations* (available interpretative patterns of sense-making) one becomes engaged in and confronted with seems potentially unrestricted. What of course subjectively continues is the mentioned aspects of social, cultural, political, and economic imprinting that proceeds as a continuous personal situation throughout all this. However, the tools and resources available open opportunities to engage with risks and uncertainties in different ways, depending on this personal situation. Indeed, not all modes work well in all contexts and under all conditions. Despite different tendencies to refer to one or the other mode when engaging with risk and uncertainty, these are particularly powerful under specific conditions. To prevent any misunderstandings, all characterizations are always relational. Examples highlight tendencies of responses and mechanisms, but what is considered as complex, or overwhelming, for example, is a subjective experience within specific contexts. What is, for some, an exciting uncertainty of an open and risky horizon might, for others, be considered overwhelming and triggering anxieties. Therefore, responses to situations of perceived threat are not fully determined but remain relational.

Situations can trigger the application of highly different constellations (compare our explanations regarding interpretative relevance). They are sensed in one or the other way, thereby presenting typical challenges that people have learned to respond to in specific ways. This must be kept in mind when considering the following tendencies, which are overgeneralized ideal types open to precisely the mentioned variations to be further explored empirically.

When there is good knowledge that allows a *rational* approach to risk and uncertainty, to pray rather than using available resources seems irrational from one perspective, since it can be suboptimal in terms of outcomes, when avoidable harm arises. Conversely, when faced with an overly complex and unstable situation involving many unknowns, attempting to calculate or model them may be too resource-intensive, or even impossible, leading to unreliable and misleading results. In such cases, turning to intuitive knowledge or consulting trustworthy institutions or others might be more promising. However, we turn to such resources more routinely, not only in situations of lacking knowledge. It is often less a reflexive act but an intuitive judgment, whether turning to reflexive modes or staying within the in-between modes of reasoning. These tendencies are biographically learned and are connected to and stabilized by the milieu or institutions in which one grew up. In this way, turning to specific modes might be an intuitive, habitual exercise, which has a positive or negative relationship with emotions. One might overcome anxieties when following rational considerations, following trusted others or charismatic leaders. More often than not, it is crucial that we not only reflect on but also feel good about our decisions. Feeling good about a decision will also relate to how we experience ourselves as social beings. This includes how we think others may see us and relate to our social identity.

In the realm of risk, basic desires and anxieties related to life and death issues are important bodily drivers when engaging with risk and uncertainty. The desire to survive in the face of a deadly illness and the wish to protect our loved ones are strong motivators. When exposed to the threat of murder by a terrorist, as in the case of the Hamas terror attack on Israel in 2023, some parents tried to protect their children with their bodies.

Many refugees from Africa or elsewhere flee their country because the living conditions are so daunting or even threatening that everything else seems better. In a desperate situation when life is at stake, risking one's life becomes relative. Dreams, myths, and hope might help to manage what seems necessary but difficult to bear otherwise. In this way, all modes might complement rather than mutually exclude. Turning to the non-rational, might be crucial in such situations to manage the systematic tensions between rational desperation and emotional pressure in high-risk situations.

Another example are responses to disasters, such as a terror attack, when there is a need to make sense of the attack as well as the future, and to reduce the possibility that terror can strike again. In terms of New Phenomenology, the situationally occurring event with its overwhelming suddenness must be transformed into a (*rational* or even *non-rational*) constellation to gain distance and to regain agency. The necessity of constructing such constellational interpretation patterns is even higher in cases in which the respective event is accompanied by the bodily experience of existential threat (compare Chapter 7). The need to come to terms with a personal loss and to frame the future has been addressed by politicians such as the US President George W. Bush after the 9/11 Terror attack when enchanting the world with imaginaries such as a "war on terror" and the "axis of evil." Defining the situation as a war helped to justify political projects such as the invasion of Iraq and preparing for further sacrifices, including the loss of lives of soldiers as well as civilians. This was possible with little evidence for Iraq producing weapons of mass destruction, that has been the justification for starting the war in the first place. The now-famous narrative of the "unknown unknowns" provided by Donald Rumsfeld, at the time United States Secretary of Defense, gave a good indication of the rationale when evidence is replaced by the *imaginative extension of one's horizon* that might have some roots in intuitive guesswork but is largely detached from evidence.

In 2011, Norway also experienced a terror attack. It took place in Oslo and on Utøya island by a right-wing perpetrator, who killed 77 people. The need for a narrative to provide solace to the families of the victims, as well as giving directions for national responses, was crucial for the National Memorial Address for the Bombing Victims of Norway by the

Prime Minister Jens Stoltenberg. He also imagined a collective but rather than turning to an external threat to be destroyed he did not frame the attack as a threat for the integrity of the country but a threat against Norwegian values ("*We are a small country, but a proud people. We are still shocked by what has happened, but we will never give up our values*"). In this way, he avoided the danger of a response producing more harm than good when trying to prevent terrorist attacks at all costs. Instead, he emphasized "*Our response is more democracy, more openness, and more humanity. But never naivety.*"[8] With quoting the Labor Youth League girl interviewed by CNN he also addressed the significance of the emotional response "*If one man can create that much hate, you can only imagine how much love we as a togetherness can create.*"

There are various reasons why respective politicians put forward these narratives. Such narratives share a commonality in producing an imaginary in the face of an existential threat, providing opportunities to identify with a broader "fate community" and, simultaneously, to make sense of individual situations involving loss and sacrifice. Since the 9/11 attack was considered external, the protection against external enemies seemed a more obvious narrative than in the case of a right-wing attack from within. Here, the protection against the threat from within could have also been directed against misled members of society, with a focus on control and punishment. However, the danger to these values was prioritized on the political agenda, where achieving complete safety is not feasible. Thus, the proposed response was to strive even harder for collective values and "love." In this way, responses were a result of their personal situation, shaped by the socio-cultural contexts each politician came from and lived by. These responses seem self-evident solutions to problems, which meet as much the situation as the imagination that provides people's lives with meaning.

Another example illustrates how life-world experiences and institutionalized procedures for managing the risks of untested medical treatments can come into conflict, leading to shifts in institutional arrangements. For instance, at the time when there was not yet a cure for HIV infected people, tremendous efforts were undertaken to develop

---

[8] *Source* https://www.americanrhetoric.com/speeches/jensstoltenbergbombingmemorial.htm.

efficient treatment. In the situation when many were dying with Aids, infected people (and their relatives) asked for the possibility to attend trials of untested medicine and thereby challenged institutional procedures in place to protect the patients. As Allesandro Blasimme (2022) has argued, there is an ethical social commitment to the sufferer to provide as much help as possible and to allow terminally ill patients to take risks rather than follow the institutional procedures of risk minimization and aversion. It is then not the *enchantment* of science as a positive pull factor, but as a last resort in the face of personally experienced suffering and devastation. Blasimme (2022), who explored the various ways of how regenerative medicine and unproven therapies have contributed to an enchantment of science, suggested that "*we should remain attentive to the ways in which suffering seeks alternative forms of moral articulation*", which is "*centered on the hope to the cured, rather than on the risk to be harmed*" (ibid., p. 110). In this way, he suggested that in the face of the subjective experience of suffering and desperation, scientific progress should shift from pure evidence-based and reduction of risk to hope or from the realm of rationality to enchantment. This example shows the complexity of the argument. The shift would be justified not by the unproven promises of science but by the subjective reality of suffering and desperation, which would morally justify *enchantment*. This also suggests that the concrete situation one is in might significantly shape one's responses to risk and uncertainty, shifting from risk aversion to risk-taking and from following institutional guidance to challenging institutionalized procedures. In this way, the reality of risk (or a threat) may influence people's responses and subsequently institutional regulations.

In her path-breaking work, Mary-Jo del Vecchio Good (1990, 2001, pp. 402–403) has introduced the concept of the "*biotechnical embrace* to describe the powerful attraction of the new technologies—an attraction rooted in both clinicians' professional commitments and patients' hopes for cure or life prolongation. The embrace is produced and sustained by the culture and political economy of hope that surrounds biomedical research and clinical practice." Her work demonstrates that the *enchantment* of science through hope is supported and complemented by other social forces, including economic interests, biomedical research, and clinical practices, as well as the desires of patients. Since medical research is driven not only by need and scientific curiosity but also by financial and political rationales, it generates hope for some while others are excluded (Masters & Nutt, 2017; Shearman et al., 2022).

What seems more important to us than any attempts to develop deterministic hypotheses is the insight that people follow patterns that are learned but can also change under specific conditions, and that institutional arrangements that have evolved can also change when individual and collective experiences and attitudes change. These processes are necessarily connected not only to the development within the realms of abstract social domains or in response to specific historical events, but also, and most importantly, to responses to subjective and embodied experiences in everyday life. Changing life experiences can prompt or lead to institutional changes, while institutional changes can, in turn, lead to altered experiences. However, when considering the various powerful social forces at work, shaping institutional conditions such as professional, economic, scientific, political, and religious interests, the situation becomes more complex.

From a risk studies perspective, advice for managing risk and uncertainty must therefore connect to people's non-rational constructs, their knowledge of authoritative expertise, as well as their everyday experience of risk and uncertainty, to be successful. Such advice also has to consider the various players in the game, which shape the institutional conditions one responds to. This raises an important question. What happens when one or the other mode is neglected or detached from others in the societal debates and responses to risk and uncertainty?

## 8.5 The Disconnection of Modes

The above review of research addressing the tendencies between the ideal type modes *rationalization*, *enchantment* and *subjectivation* has already indicated some effects when modes are to some degree disconnected from each other. Without engaging in overgeneralized claims, it seems to us that at least some balance or connection of all the modes helps with reasonable decision-making. Fully detached modes are difficult to imagine. For example, a faith or ideology that is empirically fully detached from social reality would not serve people well in solving everyday life problems, such as during a pandemic. Therefore, even when enchanting the world, large religions of the world adapt to social reality. They are powerful because they serve not only as coping mechanisms but also as practical tools for engaging with the world. Most people relate to them in a practical way, interpreting them to justify their intuitive decisions and activities (Zinn, 2004),[9] resulting in complex patterns of reasoning (Kasstan, 2021). However, in this section, we reflect on and search for empirical evidence when people or institutions primarily adopt one or the other mode, and a form of reasoning becomes ideal-typically detached from the other modes. These considerations give some indication of what to expect and the difficulties resulting from such detachments. In the following, we summarize when the *rational* (Sect. 8.5.1) and *non-rational* (Sect. 8.5.2) forms of reflexive reasoning become detached from each other and the embodied reasoning of the life-world before turning to the *in-between* (Sect. 8.5.3) modes when embodied reasoning becomes detached from reflexive considerations.

### 8.5.1 Detaching the Rational

The *rational* modes come with the promise to overcome ideologies and magic as well as everyday whims and caprices, and thereby have been considered one central force of the modernization process. Purpose-based decision-making was part of the abstraction and specialization of the economic system and supported a formalized decision-making rationale of objective or subjective utility maximization (Renn, 1992). Such strategies emphasize the advantage of having a debate based on facts rather than irreconcilable ideologies or insubstantial ideas or desires. The debates about the possibility of value-free research are now history and have not to be repeated here (Adorno et al., 1976; Black, 2013). The

[9] In a study on biographical certainty constructions, Zinn (2004) found an example in which an informant justifies becoming unfaithful with his partner as a strategy to safe their marriage and meeting his sexual needs.

crucial question for our approach is what happens when rational modes of reasoning become detached from a world that is socially structured by hope, ideology, and religion? When the socio-cultural conditions of navigating risk and uncertainty are excluded from the decision-making process, various groups are still affected differently (Brown & Zinn, 2021; Giritli Nygren et al., 2020, 2025). In our view, it is rather fruitless to exclude *non-rational* modes of reasoning since these are all part of the debates about risk. Not considering the different value systems or hope for a better life means cutting off decisions from the complexities of the social world. As a result, such decisions are likely to alienate people because the value systems are the very basis of people's way of coping with the risks and uncertainties of their lives. These values are the means that hold a social unit together and are therefore at the core of its selection and sense-making of risk (Douglas & Wildavsky, 1982). A purely "evidence-based" way of reasoning is likely to affect the most vulnerable and marginalized social groups the most. This is because the evidence provided about or for these groups is usually weakest, since they are often not listened to (Dobson, 2014; Bickford, 1996). Disconnecting the *rational* from the *non-rational* could therefore come with unexpected and uncontrolled consequences for social groups when these are neglected or excluded from the debate.[10] As a result, they might experience disadvantages and politics as being authoritarian and ignorant of their needs. When these groups grow, they can become problematic for democratic societies, as they typically turn against institutions from which they are alienated.

Considering that coping with risk and uncertainty depends to a large degree on hope in its different institutionalized forms, the power of *enchantment* would be lost when risk management would only utilize rational means. Then the rational means of risk management would lack the motivational powers that hopes and desires for a better world provide in the face of often overwhelming risk and uncertainty. The need to confidently manage risky challenges might benefit from insights from real options. Being cut off from non-rational resources and facing the

[10] This can also be extended to the environment or species which do not have a social advocate therefore respective interests being silenced.

reality of risk merely rationally might be rather discouraging, decreasing people's motivation and confidence to respond to risk. We have already mentioned many examples of the need to hope, such as that it is not me who is the one getting killed in a military mission, who is among the percentage of smokers dying with cancer, not being part of the small percentage of people catching a superbug in the hospital, or not being among the people being killed while driving or cycling. Partly it is poor luck (Goffman, 1969). Still, life is less stressful and more enjoyable when we *enchant* the future by unjustified assumptions of control, magical belief, or routinely hope that we will survive the risks we (have to) take daily.

The debate and rise of the concept of resilience (Chandler, 2014; O'Malley, 2012; Paton & Johnston, 2017) have demonstrated that, in the face of high risk, uncertainty, and non-knowledge, non-rational modes are crucial for complementing evidence-based approaches with rationales that can reasonably manage ignorance.

When *rational* reasoning is detached from *non-rational* reasoning, there is the problem of a lack of self-reflection on the *non-rational* conditions of *rationality*. This is about the danger of underestimating the blind spots of an alleged rational mode. There is a need to reflect on the explicit or implicit values that influence decisions about risks and how these values shape the evaluation of what is considered a realistic assumption. For example, when the possibility of terrorists using passenger planes as weapons was considered before the attack of 9/11, it was excluded as a scenario from further consideration as it was evaluated as being too unrealistic. In this way, the failure to acknowledge the normative framework of the terrorists resulted in security risks. However, since there is a need to exclude possibilities of further consideration when resources are limited, Anne Heyerdahl has argued that security risk management in Norway is shifting from the focus on prescriptive rules to organizational practices and values (Heyerdahl, 2023). Protection against security risks reaches its limits when other societal values, such as freedom, equality, and protection against state surveillance, are at risk (Heyerdahl, 2022, 2023).

Turning to the detachment of *rational* from *in-between* modes, further challenges become apparent. When rational reasoning in the face of risk is detached from the everyday life modes of sensing related to trust, intuition, and emotions, there is the danger that abstract evaluation of risks neglects what they mean in everyday life. For example, the experience of living close to a nuclear power station might cause anxieties about an invisible threat and foster suspicion that something might be wrong. Such concerns and suspicions can be heightened when feeling unwell or when a child develops an illness such as cancer. Additionally, in cases of wind power plants, such suspicions developed and led to protests about the potential negative impact on well-being when wind power plants are built near houses. While these concerns might be unjustified, if they are correct, they are only confirmed later when empirical data can prove the causes of harm. As the earlier example of Brian Wynne's study on pesticides has shown, neglecting local knowledge can cause preventable harm and suffering. When not taking the realm of everyday life seriously, this often results in negative feelings of frustration, alienation, and distrust, as well as possible resistance, even when the concerns triggered by the life-world's intuitive knowledge may be unreasonable or unjustified. The rich scholarship in intersectional and decolonial critical studies has long addressed the power/knowledge relations shaping the social world, which is indeed in a similar way relevant for risk studies, where specific forms of knowledge are sidelined, devalued, and invisibilized, such as that of women or indigenous people (Haraway, 1988; Murphy, 2006; Tuhiwai Smith, 1999).

Another example of how reliance on formalized systems of risk management can cause unexpected harm when detached from people's embodied sensing is Chile's response to the 2010 Tsunami. In the international news, the comparatively low number of casualties for such a devastating earthquake has been celebrated. In contrast, for Chile and its experts, it was considered a failure due to the malfunctioning of the Tsunami warning system. Most people who died relied on the warning system because they lacked local knowledge or ignored their own senses. Thus, a large number of casualties were prevented not by the warning system but by people's distrust in the system. Many inhabitants of the affected regions followed their own intuitive assessment of the situation rather than the official counterfactual announcement that a tsunami would not happen. The lessons from the experienced possibility of system failure resulted in a re-evaluation of the tsunami response system, giving more weight to encouraging individual sensing in case of system failure (Gil, 2023).

Social psychological studies, such as the famous Milgram experiment (Milgram, 1963, 1974), showed that people can expose others to serious harm even when directly confronted with the suffering of others as long as they believe that it is for a good purpose. The experiment aimed to find out whether it could be true that Eichmann and other Nazis were mainly following orders. For this purpose, Milgram conducted a series of experiments in 1961 during which study participants were instructed to administer electric shocks to another person, the "learner," when making mistakes in learning exercises. Repeating errors would result in even higher electroshocks up to a level of 450 volts. The "experimenter" appeared as an authoritative scientist who asked the "learner" questions, while the learner was an actor playing the experience of electroshocks. The "teacher" was a person who volunteered in the session but was the study subject. All participants ($n = 40$) were exposed by the "teacher" to 300-volt shocks, and still 65 percent to the maximum of 450-volt. But some participants had concerns when listening to the bodily suffering of the people they punished with alleged electroshocks. Only a minimal number stopped the experiment. However, most participants had few concerns and were able to do what they were asked for, remaining detached from the sounds of suffering and people's requests to stop. The results showed that most people had been prepared to detach reflexive rationality from the intuitive and emotional reasoning, which allowed them to apply electroshocks up to deadly levels. Taken to the realm of risk research, when people are framed and considered a threat and the embodied sphere of in-between modes is excluded, severe measures might even resort to solutions with inhumane effects, such as the deportation of migrants to allegedly safe but dangerous countries of origin.

### 8.5.2 Detaching the Non-Rational

We have argued that the devaluation of the *non-rational* modes as being merely "irrational" neglects that these have indeed valuable functions when handling high-risk situations. Magic, hope, religion, and ideologies still play their role when coping with or approaching high-risk situations confidently and therefore can contribute to better outcomes. The presented examples, such as work migrants handling exploitative working conditions (Bastide, 2015), students managing tests in college or university (Rudski & Edwards, 2007), and religious conversion providing meaning and control in an overwhelming biographical situation (Wohlrab-Sahr, 1999), all illustrated how these *non-rational* modes supported the navigation of risk and uncertainty. In these examples, the *non-rational* helped provide direction and enabled people to manage dangerous situations, at least in part, with some evidence.

When these practices become increasingly detached from empirical reality, such as the large body of conspiracy theories, non-rational modes might still have positive individual outcomes, for example, in terms of group identity and attaching meaning to a complex and confusing world. However, because they focus on problems or solutions that lack empirical foundations, they cannot be debated rationally, posing serious problems for modern risk management. Similarly, Niklas Luhmann (1989) once suggested that, for environmental concerns, modern rationality has difficulties approaching the protesters' argument "I am afraid." There is little rational argument against emotions when these are not related to an objectively manifest risk but are subjectively experienced. To the degree forms of reflexive sense-making (derived from subjective experience of threat) are detached from an empirical base, they are not approachable by rational knowledge and reasoning. Instead, the trustworthiness of the information source or the judgment of a charismatic leader replaces critical engagement with the risk itself. For example, a uniform presentation of the possible responses to COVID-19 might cause suspicion where alternative viewpoints are discriminated against or stigmatized (Harambam, 2023).

In this perspective, faith in expert systems[11] differs little from faith in orthodox belief systems and ideologies to the degree these are detached from empirical reality. In such ideal type cases, for example, vaccination is a question of faith or hope, not evidence. Examples of believers changing their response in the face of risk, such as vaccinating against COVID-19, are driven by decisions of their charismatic leaders and how rational arguments can be redefined and embedded within a religious system. For example, vaccination as such might be acceptable for Muslims as long as there are no ingredients from swine (Kasstan, 2021). Another example is the Iranian leaders who encouraged their religious followers to visit holy shrines, still considered a place of healing, in the early days of the COVID-19 crisis. However, with the virus spreading, they finally changed their policy and applied stricter measures, including closing holy shrines for visitors, to reduce and slow down the spread of the virus. But some of the more orthodox believers protested against such a measure, contradicting their faith (Gambrell, 2020). Therefore, it is essential to keep in mind that the unrealistic idea of fully detaching the non-rational from the other modes of reasoning is only an ideal-type thought experiment, while the reality is much more complex (Kasstan, 2021).

For example, faith might be considered an advantage when managing the risks and suffering during high-risk work migration (Bastide, 2015). But it can also become a problem, from a rationalist point of view, when it becomes entirely detached from objectifiable experience. This means that subjectively experienced suffering would not be a possible source of change when it is considered a godly trial to be borne rather than an opportunity for change. Fully detached from empirical experience, there is little opportunity for shifting the framework of sense-making and integrating empirical strategies in faith-based navigation of risk and uncertainty. Thus, leaving the possible psychological mechanism aside, COVID-19 deniers dying in the hospital sometimes did not change their mind about the reality of the illness (Graziosi, 2022). Belief systems, such as conspiracy theories or religious attitudes, can dominate experience,

[11] When the US government decided in 1976 to vaccinate the population against a spreading swine flu with known harmful effects, one might wonder to what extent overconfidence in science informed the decision (Fisher, 2020).

even when embodied suffering (and death) might offer opportunities to consider alternative interpretations. The interpretative filter can prevent the use of personal illness experience as a reason for change. In terms of our model, even the experience of a situation of serious threat, in some cases, may not guarantee that an adequate[12] form of sense-making gains interpretative relevance. This raises the crucial question of how, in times of crisis, societies can respond to people who follow conspiracy theories and are detached from both commonly accepted knowledge and the experience of risk and disaster by reinterpreting them through their ideological lens. Such a closed system of sense-making, in which either evidence or embodied experience can hardly challenge, seems impossible to change.

The power of such detached belief systems has been demonstrated by Donald Trump's rise as a politician and to the presidency. The debate over the size of the crowds attending Donald Trump's inauguration ceremonies compared with those attending Barack Obama's was an interesting attempt to manipulate social reality (Swaine, 2018). The White House Press Secretary at the time, Sean Spicer, had claimed that the attendance number at Donald Trump's inauguration was larger than Obama's in inauguration crowd. In an Interview, Counselor to the President Kellyanne Conway suggested that Sean Spicer had not lied, as the interviewing journalist claimed, but instead presented "alternative facts." Indeed, spin and fake news have been around for quite some time, but with the advent of social media, the spread of fake news has intensified and become more widespread and influential. A body of research attributes people's misinformed responses to risks, such as COVID-19, to the power of social media to spread disinformation over the internet and the lack of skills among many people to manage the infodemic (Cooke, 2017). However, there have also been experts who provided behavioral advice and treatment suggestions. Still, some of Donald Trump's supporters preferred to follow some of Trump's questionable suggestions for unproven COVID-19 treatments such as hydroxychloroquine and chloroquine-containing drugs. In such cases, evidence was replaced

[12] Following our model, "adequate" here means to prevent the affected subject from serious harm.

by hope and ideology with considerable success (Niburski & Niburski, 2020). Still, this approach resulted in harmful consequences, such as an 11% increased mortality for users of hydroxychloroquine (Vargas, 2024).

When the non-rational modes are not only fully detached from the rational but also from the subjective embodied experiences, they become a closed system that cannot be altered by harm or disaster. This is even then the case when there is evidence for abstract risk knowledge explaining harm or disaster. Instead, changes must occur within the framework and through the acknowledged authority, respected as a rightful (charismatic) leader who provides reinterpretations and innovations. The question remains under which conditions such systems can change, or how people can leave them in favor of other modes of reflexive reasoning.

This finally leads to the question of what happens when the embodied, intuitive experiences of the life-world become entirely detached from the (*rational* and *non-rational*) reflexive modes.

### 8.5.3 Detaching the In-Between

As we have argued, supported by examples from empirical research, *in-between* modes are a valuable resource for navigating risk and uncertainty. *Trust*, *intuition*, and *emotions* are often intertwined, relating to tacit, subjectively experienced knowledge that provides people with additional resources to manage decision-making situations under uncertainty. Such modes can also be fostered by institutional arrangements when opportunities are given for embodied knowledge to guide professional practice (e.g., in healthcare). In our neo-phenomenological model, we assumed that reflexive knowledge and embodied knowledge are connected in a circular process of "emancipating" or distancing from the immediate sensing and "regressing" or falling back on such experiences (compare Chapter 6). The crucial question of this section is, what does it mean when this connection is interrupted, when the *in-between* modes of reasoning are not connected to the reflexive modes but remain an embodied reality largely disconnected from reflexive considerations?

For example, *intuitive* reasoning, as has been argued in natural decision-making research (Kahneman & Klein, 2009; Klein, 1998) as well as in studies in healthcare (Van den Brink et al., 2019; Wilson et al., 2023) and management (Malewska, 2019; Malewska & Sajdak, 2014; Thanos, 2023), rests to a large part on long-term experience sedimented in embodied knowledge. This research highlighted the value of such knowledge for managing dangerous situations such as a fire crew captain assessing a high-risk situation when trying to extinguish a fire, or nurses in a hospital when intuitively assessing whether a premature infant develops a sepsis (Klein, 1998, pp. 39 f.). When knowledge is limited, or too complex and time pressure high intuition is crucial. However, in most professional contexts, experts have emphasized the importance of reflexive post-evaluation of decisions to confirm their intuition (Van den Brink et al., 2019). Thus, when there is no empirical evidence to check on their efficiency or when the empirical outcomes become detached from the intuitive performance, overconfidence or *enchantment* might be the result. Where the empirical evidence for an evaluation of intuitive judgments is missing, it becomes suboptimal or even dangerous, as the example of Martin Kosla's study on industrial electricians has shown (Kosla, 2015). One informant suggested that all his colleagues who had intuitively neglected the use of protective gear are already dead. They ignored the dangers of asbestos based on their intuitive knowledge and, because of the long-term carcinogenic quality of asbestos, developed cancer. This suggests that intuition requires feedback to learn and interpret signs and will be less valuable when such signs do not exist and therefore cannot be sensed until it is too late.

The example of the high-risk leisure sport, or edgework, has already indicated that, according to Lyng, there is a tendency to believe in one's innate capacity to *intuitively* respond to risky situations successfully. However, when this belief lacks critical reflection, the tacit experience of being able to manage all kinds of situations successfully holds only as long as no major accident happens. In this way, the lack of critical reflection can lead to edgeworkers overestimating their intuitive skills, which sediment in their felt bodies over time.

*Intuitive* knowledge might also play a role in facemask-wearing in many Asian countries. As Mitsutoshi Horii and Adam Burgess have argued (Burgess & Horii, 2012; Horii, 2014), in Japan, facemask-wearing has become a *risk ritual* that serves cultural needs to maintain control in situations such as a pandemic. The protection might have become detached from the medical and protective rationality it once originated from; however, it can still be a valuable resource against new viruses before evidence of its effectiveness has been scientifically established. It does not matter whether wearing face masks has become a question of lifestyle or an expression of concerns about others' or one's health, when it is habitually embedded in a country's culture and people's everyday life.

In the early days of the COVID-19 pandemic, the German public responded intuitively, when buying face masks, at a time when it was still unclear how the illness was transmitted. Instead, people based their response on generalized medical expert knowledge that in the contexts of infectious diseases face masks are commonly applied. A knowledge that might have been acquired as much through expert sources as popular media. However, at this stage, experts still advised against the wearing of facemasks, while they were already sold out at pharmacies in Germany. Intuitive knowledge, even when empirical evidence is lacking, can lead to a precautionary practice that can be beneficial, even when disconnected from proven empirical evidence or broader ideologies or national cultures.

Similar to intuition, *trust* is based on a couple of sensible characteristics. But as we have argued, the experience of trustworthiness requires some intuitive proof or at least no disappointment to be maintained. If trustworthiness is not experience-based, there is a danger of unconditional trust, unreflectively falling for charismatic leaders such as Donald Trump, who advised using questionable medicine to protect against COVID-19 (Vargas, 2024), or becoming a reflex to changing situations and their "atmospheres."

More broadly, learning to interpret emotional states and place them in context is essential. Anxieties can guide reasonable responses to risk and uncertainty. However, it is crucial to know when to shift from emotional reactions to reflexive modes, or when to contain emotions and when to let them guide actions. The ability to switch to reflexive reasoning may also be a form of tacit knowledge learned over time and throughout one's life. In-between modes are therefore crucial for the kind of reflexive responses one chooses, as we have already discussed in Chapter 6. When detached, this means without reflexive reasoning, responses tend to be driven by situational forces and the surrounding atmosphere; they are like a leaf caught in the wind, lacking reflexive distancing from embodied sensing. In this way, when following traditional thinkers like Arnold Gehlen (1988), institutional contexts would shape continuity in intuition, emotions, and trust. Consequently, under volatile social conditions or when detached, a stable and reasonable response to risk and uncertainty may be achievable neither individually nor collectively.

However, we could also think about the stabilization of reasonable responses to or engagement with risk as a result of learned experiences that have been sedimented in people's experiences over time. But if there is no reflexive guidance, changes could mainly be thought of as a drift in habitual responses. It remains an open question, though, to what extent habitual engagement with risk and uncertainty can change without a conscious reflection on them. This refers to the extent to which this would be a habitual drift that occurs at the level of embodied sensing experiences or requires a reflexive engagement with knowledge. Indeed, we can assume both are happening (Zinn, 2024).

## 8.6 Concluding Comments

This chapter began by examining the interactions between different types of reasoning risk and uncertainty, as well as the observable institutional forces that shape them. The primary objective was to demonstrate that, although the *modern orthodoxy* is dominant and influential in various social domains, such as health studies, risk analysis, and economics, the reality is far more complex and nuanced. We suggest that the concept of a triangle of *rational*, *non-rational*, and *in-between* modes of reasoning is useful for gaining a deeper understanding and mapping these intricate dynamics.

The triangle helped us to argue that even the realm of *rationality* not only shows tendencies to *enchant* its orthodoxy but might be dependent on such *enchantments* to deal with the uncertainties that cannot be managed within the orthodoxy itself. Needless to say, scientific advancement would not have been possible without the desires, dreams, and *enchantment* of science. Such *enchantment* on the institutional level also accompanies the confidence and hope on the micro-level when facing challenges in everyday life or when making sense of challenges for humanity.

Indeed, the *rational* modes of navigating risks and uncertainties of the future do not only refer to hope when knowledge and other resources are limited. *Non-rational* imaginaries are crucial for giving direction to the management of risk and uncertainty by involving values and belief systems, which are difficult or impossible to justify rationally when no longer based on evidence-based reasoning. Again, systems such as those Max Weber already argued for, using the example of religion, have become increasingly systematized and formalized, or one might say, *rationalized*. When engaging in the sphere of risk and uncertainty, reinterpreting and approaching facts in a way that helps people cope with them, even when not rationally justifiable, is a reasonable way to manage them. This means that *non-rational* views of the world might be reasonable under certain conditions, as they evidently improve outcomes when engaging with a world that may be shaped by forces these rational modes do not consider or fail to systematize. But because the imaginaries of the world are efficient in shaping people's attitudes and performance, they cause better outcomes than entirely *rational* or fact-based modes could have produced. In this way, from a rationalist perspective, we are confronted with a somewhat contradictory insight that it is indeed *rational* to be to some degree "irrational" or better to say *non-rational*, and being *non-rational* helps to produce quite evidently better outcomes for the reality of collective as well as individual existence. This insight helps to understand why people sometimes follow *rational* and, at other times, *non-rational* but reasonable (!) modes of reasoning. One or the other promises better outcomes under specific conditions.

Even when we have focused on the epistemological foundations rather than the social power mechanisms, our insights are also important for understanding the continuation of social power imbalances and exploitative social mechanisms, as well as the conflicts that arise from them. *Non-rational* justification of inequalities, such as their non-empirical naturalization (e.g., gender differences and dichotomies) or the invisibilization of social groups' experiences, have also utilized (alleged) *rational* knowledge and prevented the articulation of the *non-rational* underpinnings. The devaluation of specific forms of knowledge in the name of enlightenment and modern rationality is at the core of feminism and postcolonial critique and crucial for the continuation of exploitative mechanisms in an unequal world. Reconnecting the lived experience to reflexive forms of knowledge remains crucial for any reasonable approach to navigating risk and uncertainty for the many rather than the few.

This leads to what we might have known all along. What is necessary may not always feel good, and rational choices are not always the best when they do not feel good, as this approach ignores our embodied expertise. Neo-phenomenologically, taking a decision can be seen as such a dialogue between the embodied facts of the personal situation on the one hand, and the results of the reflexive systematization of what the current situation confronts us with on the other.

# 9

# Conclusions—A New Phenomenology of Risk and Uncertainty

We started our book, *A New Phenomenology of Risk and Uncertainty*, with insights from risk studies and modernization theory. The focus on rationality and the rationalization process neglects important dimensions of people's decision-making in the face of risk. Chapters 2, 3, and 4 reviewed examples from the growing body of research to highlight the different rationales people utilize when engaging with risk and uncertainty. Not only *rational* but *non-rational* modes of reasoning, such as hope, magic, faith, and ideology, as well as what Zinn (2008, 2016) called in-between modes of reasoning, such as trust, intuition, and emotion, are widespread and can be reasonably applied when engaging with risk and uncertainty. We asserted that these three ideal types (*rational*, *non-rational*, *in-between*) span a triangle of complementary modes of reasoning, which laypeople as well as experts routinely use. We suggest that the *in-between* modes are much more common in everyday decision-making than pure *rationality* or *non-rational* modes. Nevertheless, it seemed relatively uncommon for people to turn only to one of these modes, they typically combine all of them. . For example, in the relatively banal everyday life experience of buying a car, one can assess test reports of an automobile, turn to personal experience with a car



J. O. Zinn and M. Schulz, *A New Phenomenology of Risk and Uncertainty*, Critical Studies in Risk and Uncertainty, https://doi.org/10.1007/978-981-95-7405-6_9

dealer, put faith in the producer of a specific brand, and indeed, one can also enjoy the prospect of being the owner of a car that fits one's identity. In a less banal situation, such as the Covid-19 crisis, the decision to vaccinate seems more complicated, as uncertainty entails more serious outcomes, including the threat of severe illness or vaccine side effects. Trying to understand the science behind the vaccine and its production process might reassure some people to turn to it. Other aspects are whether a trustworthy company is producing the vaccine, or significant others' stance towards vaccination. Vaccination decisions are shaped by broader experiences, which might prereflexively lead one to choose the subjectively more bearable option. Feelings might relate to worrying about family members or the responses from one's social network. Thus, for some, relying on authorities might be the solution, while for others, relying on one's own strengths might be preferable when authorities are generally distrusted.

Not all the elements involved in risky decision-making appear *rational*, but all are important in one way or another for making *reasonable* decisions. Following the insights from our book, *reasonable* means firstly, to improve the outcome of a risky situation in a way that reduces the relative harm (this includes the loss of expected gain) or at least to keep the ability to act under challenging circumstances, and secondly, that a respective path of activities coincides with the subjectively felt certainties and conditions of individual daily life.

To further explore the relationships and dynamics among the various modes in Chapters 5, 6, and 7, we examined the epistemological differences underlying the diverse rationales of reasoning. We turned to New Phenomenology to make explicit the difference between reflexive forms of knowledge underpinning *rational* and *non-rational* modes of reasoning, in contrast to tacit forms of embodied knowledge of the *in-between* modes. This approach allowed us, on the one hand, to address the involuntary givenness of the felt body with epistemological clarity and, on the other hand, to provide a differentiated analytical tool for investigating concrete subjective actions due to the neo-phenomenological understanding of *situations*. The concept of the habitus, as introduced by Pierre Bourdieu (1979b), is a good example for further elaborating this perspective along socio-economic dimensions.

Bourdieu's model of incorporated cultural capital, which develops and changes throughout the life course, exemplifies the embodied forms of knowledge that shape people's responses to their socio-material contexts. Similarly, neo-phenomenological epistemology helps us better understand how and under what circumstances various forms of knowledge gain interpretative relevance, and, based on this, empirically analyze people's engagement with risk and uncertainty as it is observable in present-day societies.

In this perspective, people are always embedded in various overlapping situational circumstances and reflexively respond to the states of their felt body to which they are involuntarily exposed. Their knowledge might be shaped by intersecting structural and cultural forces, such as social class, race, gender, or disability, as well as by the biographical accumulation of such experiences. At the same time, their felt body responds to the atmosphere of a shared situation, and as an embodied human being more generally. We used this starting point of the *personal situation* to make sense of the dynamics between the different modes. From this perspective, there is an ongoing circular process of reflexively distancing oneself from embodied forms of knowledge while also reconnecting reflexive forms of knowledge to embodied experiences to make sense of them. Regarding risk and uncertainty, climate change can serve as an example. Only when abstract climate change models are connected to everyday embodied consciousness do we fully understand their practical implications. Otherwise, they remain relatively meaningless numbers. This is because, phenomenologically, the concept of risk can be traced back to the subjective experience of a felt threat, as we argued in Chapter 7, along with epistemological and empirical considerations. Indeed, one's experience of the climate is mediated by the information we are exposed to from different sources (e.g., social media, popular science) and by more or less trustworthy people (e.g., friends, scientists, celebrities), which makes the process of subjective meaning-making rather complex.

Nevertheless, we suggested that any form of abstract knowledge regarding risk must be brought back to the involuntary, subjective experience of daily life to shape the sense-making and practices of a concrete person. We termed this process as *subjectivation*. This is the case for *non-rational* modes such as religious faith, which require some connection to the subjective reality of faith shared with others. This could, for example, be achieved through collective rituals such as singing and prayer in the church, which provide emotional and practical support for managing one's life. However, our investigation showed that *rational* modes of sense-making are, in any case, reliant on this subjectivation to gain interpretative relevance for people as well. But here the focus is on empirical confirmation rather than the coping mechanism.[1] Consequently, inspired by the early writings of Alfred Schütz and in line with neo-phenomenological epistemology, we suggested that this connection cannot be substantiated rationally and therefore creates a gap that renders rationality susceptible to enchanting tendencies and can lead to unreasonable consequences.

Among others, we used the example of the unfortunate COVID-19 deniers who died in hospital to clarify the difficult connection between embodied experience and reflexive sense-making. Some of the deniers were devastated about their unforgivable credulity, taking the experienced reality of the illness as an opportunity to revise their views (Kitching, 2021). Others, however, still denied the existence of COVID-19 and continued to adhere to conspiracy theories (Graziosi, 2022). The distinction between *echo chambers* and *epistemic bubbles* might help clarify the difference. Thi Nguyen (2020) suggested that *epistemic bubbles* are characterized by the lack of dissenting information, which could challenge one's views. In contrast, *echo chambers* are an epistemic structure in which relevant voices are excluded, devalued, or even reinterpreted to support one's worldview. Such a closed and protected belief system is difficult, if not impossible, to change. Thus, subjective, embodied experiences can become a corrective for reflexive knowledge sources, or reflexive knowledge sources can shape the interpretation of people's embodied experiences so fundamentally that these can no longer serve as a source of change.

---

[1] Similarly, Bruno Latour when examining the development of science, has argued that rationalization relies on a connection to the subjective sphere. In his laboratory studies he found that in the early days subjective witnesses of an experiment were necessary as proof for the acknowledgement of the results before laboratory procedures became institutionalized and trusted (Latour, 1993).

Indeed, the scientific sphere of rational reasoning can also turn into an *epistemic bubble* or even an *echo chamber* when critical reflection is absent, as the Milgram (1963, 1974) experiment once demonstrated (compare Sect. 8.5.1). Unconditional trust in science and its institutional representatives can lead to a dangerous form of *enchantment*. In the study, participants were even prepared to conduct deadly electric shocks to others for the sake of scientific progress. Thus, even if this might be a drastic example, it could be argued that the suggestion of many politicians to follow the science in the face of the COVID-19 pandemic (Stevens, 2020) was based on a misunderstanding of what science can deliver and could even lead to authoritarian forms of governing if not publicly discussed and politically guided.[2]

To further advance such arguments about the dangers of narrow modes of reasoning, we revisited broader debates about the modern rationalization process (compare Sect. 2.6 and Chapter 8), as outlined by Max Weber (1930). We suggested distinguishing between the institutional processes of *rationalization* and *enchantment* in contrast to the *subjective* experience of these processes when one becomes *enchanted* or *alienated*. In this way, we introduced an analytical tool to highlight possible tensions between reflexive and non-reflexive experiences of the world. The institutional perspective also allowed us to elaborate on the debate about the relationship between the historical processes of *rationalization* and *enchantment*. While many scholars viewed these developments as mutually exclusive, we followed George Ritzer's suggestion that they might be systematically related, as when, for example, *enchantment* is the result of *rationalization* processes, as in the case of the *cathedrals of consumption* (Ritzer, 2005). However, Ritzer's focus on a theory of consumption overlooked the broader point we stressed in Chapter 8, that *rationalization, enchantment,* and *subjectivation* are entangled in complex dynamics. We highlighted this point with examples of the large variety of institutionalization processes that combine different elements of knowledge and reasoning with various social practices. The most important insight was that a balance between the different modes must

[2] Indeed, the hasty vaccination campaign against the swine flu in 1976 in the US was a warning sign for unconditional trust in science, claiming many lives unnecessarily (Fisher, 2020).

be found. This is often not a straightforward process, and the reason why all the dimensions are usually involved in good decision-making. For example, scientific, purpose-based knowledge can become enchanted when people's hope is mobilized to participate in clinical trials of new cancer treatments or to invest in freezing cord blood to have stem cells available for the treatment of future illnesses. Such *enchantments* can be highly desirable for advancing scientific knowledge. However, when possible side effects or other costs are not reflected on or purposefully concealed, the enchantment of science can legitimize and/or invisibilize harm.

Another example of enchanting tendencies regarding scientific and technological progress is the hope currently associated with so-called *artificial intelligence* (AI) in the context of complex decision-making beyond human biases (Lee, 2018; Logg et al., 2019; Miller, 2018). The often-proclaimed promise of AI is that it is based purely on objective data and, therefore, considered a rational approach to solving societal problems (for example, Kahneman, Sibony, & Sunstein, 2021). Supporters of this technology argue that algorithmic decision-making, due to its impersonality, may help facilitate fair decisions by excluding human subjects from procedures—an old promise of numerically based rationalization (Porter, 1995, pp. 73ff.). However, a wide range of studies on *algorithmic bias* exist, which show that this assumption is misleading (Kordzadeh & Ghasemaghaei, 2022). Contrary to the original idea of solving societal problems in a *rational* and non-discriminatory manner, algorithmic decision-making can become an impersonal tool of objectified power that, in the end, may reinforce discrimination and is even more difficult to challenge. The problem of discrimination in such cases is merely brought to another dimension, driven by the hope of overcoming exactly what is reproduced and technologically exacerbated. In such situations, the *enchantment* of pure rationality provokes unreasonable outcomes, a process that can be understood as a dialectical tipping point. This implies that the means introduced to overcome a specific form of domination—namely, domination through discriminatory categorization—become a powerful means of that very categorization. Similarly, Max Horkheimer and Theodor W. Adorno argued in "Dialectics of Enlightenment" (1947, 2002 [1947]) that forms of Western Enlightenment would create specific means of emancipation that may turn into instruments that reinforce the very domination they promised to overcome. This is a classic example, among the large body of critical scholarship, that raised concerns about the adverse effects of *rationalization* becoming detached from humanist ideals of enlightenment and potentially leading to disaster. In the context of our book, what has been criticized in these approaches is that the process of objectifying rationalization has gone so far that even human beings are merely apprehended as things or numbers, rather than as embodied and self-conscious entities. Zygmunt Bauman famously argued for the connection between modern rationalization and the Holocaust (Bauman, 1989, 1991), while Hannah Arendt analyzed Eichmann's reasoning for the conduct of rationalized mass murder of Jews in Nazi Germany (Arendt, 2006). Indeed, the dehumanization of the Other and their subjective, embodied experience were central to the rationalization and enchantment of ideological frameworks in which the ends justified the means.

Turning back to risk studies, and in a more positive light, we suggested that *non-rational* modes, such as hope, faith, and ideology, are also essential resources for engaging in high-risk activities efficiently. But what can help to stay calm and act reasonably in the face of risk can become counterproductive as well, when, for example, faith or ideology do not complement but fully replace available evidence, as we have seen in the above examples of COVID-19 avoidance or the faith of some scholars in AI detached from empirical observations. These are already examples of the adverse effects that can occur when different forms of reasoning become largely disconnected (compare Sect. 8.5).

Altogether, we argued for a perspective on navigating risk and uncertainty that considers each mode requiring the other.[3] Such a perspective would help prevent exaggeration in either direction and keep avenues for critique and change open. Thereby, approaches could be prevented,

[3] Support for our position can also be found in other disciplines such as psychiatric research. The philosopher and psychiatrist Thomas Fuchs stresses that a decoupled rationality tends to become pathologic and can lead into an alienated relation to oneself and the world, a "nightmare of alienation" in which "the world gets 'on the other side' and freezes in empty existence, in dead facticity" (Fuchs, 2008, p. 272). Similarly to this argument, we suggested that a non-pathological handling of rationality should be rooted in the sphere of bodily sensations to avoid alienation and serious individual and collective harm.

such as when the ends justify the means or when the means become fully detached and unfold an idiosyncratic dynamic. The assumption is that as long as people's voices are not silenced and/or dehumanized, our approach can help to prevent the worst.

The underlying problem that can provoke a reversal of *rationality*, resulting in unreasonable outcomes, can be summarized as follows: *Rationality*, as a scientific enterprise of knowledge production as well as a purpose-oriented, systematic activity, is a kind of strictly formalized procedure that applies adequate and signifies efficient means for an end. Given that such ends cannot be found rationally, pure rationality tends to detach from reason in the sense that the respective goals of individual or collective action may be sidelined, neglected, or rendered invisible. This is because any goal requires a standpoint from which one can derive an end, and such standpoints may differ enormously from one person to another, depending on their social position, which is characterized by intersecting social forces (Giritli Nygren et al., 2020). However, once relieved from such normative problems, rationality does not rely on a human being. In contrast, such a detached rationality, against the background of its own standards, can be conducted (often even more effectively) by a machine, pursuing impersonally a prescribed and unscrutinized end by following formal rules of calculation. Following our argument, the problem with such detached rationality is that the underlying *enchantment* is neglected, which provokes the misleading notion that impersonality guarantees reasonableness.

Rationality presupposes defined ends, yet rationality itself provides no guidance for selecting them. Without anchoring in consciously and subjectively chosen ends, rationality remains empty and cannot become reasonable. Ulrich Pothast (1993) addressed this tension by introducing the concept of "vibrant reasonableness," distinguishing rationality—concerned with means—from reasonableness, which emerges from the personal standpoint of a *vibrantly self-sensing* subject. He, similarly to us, argued that rationality and reason lose practical value when detached from this embodied self-sensing (Pothast, 2009). His assumption that reason gains substance from the perspective of concretely affected, situationally embedded persons, resonates well with our model (Sects. 5. 4 and 6.2) and Alfred Schütz's early writings (Sect. 5.1). Both stress that meaning derives from qualitative, pathic experience. Only when actions, whether individual or collective, are normatively grounded in such embodied experiences can they be considered reasonable. Under conditions of risk and uncertainty, these pathic experiences often emerge involuntarily, as threats impose specific ends—what the late Schütz described as "thematic relevance." The end of preventing harm, for instance, arises not as a formal truth but as an embodied certainty that offers subjective orientation. While such ends are subjective in origin, they are not necessarily individual; in situations of threat, the orientation towards harm prevention may be reasonable for most, even if not universally shared.

Applying these thoughts to the field of risk studies, our findings align well with insights that suggest communicating risk must consider the diversity of the audience it addresses (Árvai & Rivers III, 2014; Heath & O'Hair, 2009). Since there cannot be a one-fits-all approach in risk communication, strategies must connect abstract risk knowledge to the subjective, embodied experiences of different audiences, rather than alienating or excluding specific social groups. Examples from the COVID-19 pandemic can illustrate two crucial issues. Firstly, vaccination hesitancy or rejection of expert recommendations to vaccinate during the pandemic might result less from a lack of comprehension of the concept of vaccination but from other reasons connected to one's experiences and life situation. This relates to our insight that due to the subjectivity of one's experiences, it is not reasonable to expect a homogeneous form of choosing specific means independent from the subjective life situation. It is therefore challenging for experts, politicians, or other risk communicators to find effective ways to reach diverse audiences. This is not merely about connecting to different social milieus but to people's various experiences of intersecting socio-structural inequalities.

Secondly, in crises, the *enchantment* of expert knowledge must be considered cautiously, as listening to people's concerns may reveal important knowledge that is easily ignored or purposefully excluded (Otway & Wynne, 1989). There are indeed good examples, such as vaccines being introduced and applied too quickly, which have caused harmful side effects and fatalities (Fisher, 2020), suggesting that we should be cautious when judging people for being more hesitant. More generally, as the work of Brian Wynne has shown, local and practical knowledge remain crucial, as evidenced by a growing body of intersectional and decolonial critical studies. Different kinds of knowledge should not be ignored in favor of laboratory knowledge, as this would prevent valuable societal knowledge sources from being considered in the face of risk (Wynne, 1996). Therefore, socially navigating risk requires skills not only in *communicating* with the public but also in *listening* to the public and critically reflecting on one's own knowledge base and intuitive prejudices (Bassel, 2017; Bickford, 1996; Dobson, 2014). If people, for example, do not experience a situation as highly risky or do derive the "wrong" consequences shaped by their culturally and structurally formed life experiences, overloading them with impersonal, objectified, and highly abstract data or even forcing them into the "right" mode by legal requirements, might trigger resistance and forceful counter responses rather than compliance.

As our investigation suggests, understanding societal debates about risk requires taking into account the two central spheres of human orientation. These are the bodily sensations on the one hand, and language-based (and numerically elaborated) systematizations on the other. These should neither be detached from each other, nor should one side be prioritized by disregarding the other. In our view, reasonable sense-making, especially in situations of risk, is the result of an interaction between pathic sensations and symbol-mediated insights, shaped by the personal situation of the concretely affected entity. However, if rational modes become detached from the subjective life-world and situational embeddedness, a political measure based on good intentions and scientific knowledge can turn into a paternalistic, or even authoritarian, exercise of power. Among other aspects, these findings highlight the importance of better understanding the interaction of embodied and symbol-mediated forms of sense-making and the resulting patterns of subjective orientation in the social management and communication of risk. These issues become more complicated to the degree that many risks in modern society are invisible and difficult to comprehend.

In summary, the key insight and argument for societal and individual engagement with risky decision-making is the need to reflect on and acknowledge the different kinds of knowledge and reasoning involved in all decision-making. This is not merely a philosophical reflection; as we have argued, it underpins engagement with risk and uncertainty in many social domains, such as environmental protection. For example, when producing lists of endangered species, it is essential to be aware of the *non-rational* assumptions underlying these lists, or the epistemic limits of rationalizing the environment in general. Species that are less visible or, for other cultural reasons, might not be considered, such as fungi (Burgman, 2005). Habitats, which are possibly more environmentally productive and valuable, such as the mudflat, but less "beautiful" than the tropical rain forest, might be easily overlooked in the research that concerns protecting and securing the natural environment (Lebreton et al., 2019). Such cases may serve as good examples of the epistemological insight of New Phenomenology, which suggests that our human experience, with all its embedded situational circumstances, cannot be exhaustively systematized by reflexive thinking—even if the respective techniques may be as elaborated as possible. Therefore, our approach helps keep us aware of these limits, as well as the *enchantments* of nature we engage with as human beings (Rogers, 2015), even when trying to be as rational as possible.

In conclusion, the book's overall insight is a plea for decision-making strategies that utilize the strengths of different forms of reasoning and underlying knowledge, while also addressing their deficits and dangers to prevent adverse effects from developing. In this way, it is an approach considering all modes as part and parcel of human decision-making and thereby comes closer to Aristotle's notion of *phronesis* (Aristotle, 1926) and Pothast's suggestion of *vibrant reasonableness* (Pothast, 1993) than modern concepts of *rationality* (Flyvbjerg et al., 2012). Anthropologically, the developed model refers to a broader understanding of what human beings are and how their relation to themselves and to the surrounding circumstances to which they are exposed is characterized. Therefore, the conceptual suggestions we developed throughout the book, in conversation with empirical studies and theoretical frameworks, do not provide easy answers for managing and communicating risk and uncertainty. Instead, it emphasizes the need for further research on both theoretical and methodological questions. Nevertheless, what it provides is insight into the relevance and importance of the different aspects of reasoning and knowledge in the face of risk and uncertainty. In democratic societies, it is open to debate what the right balance between various forms of reasoning is, whether in everyday life or on an institutional level. Additionally, solutions will vary from group to group, individual to individual, and from one social context to another. There is no one-fits-all approach. Instead, the framework helps consider the different aspects that must be taken into account to prevent unreasonable exaggeration of either dimension.

Every engagement with risk and uncertainty is a balancing act between what we reflexively and non-reflexively know, what we intuitively assume, and what ought to be. This is indeed shaped by the unequal conditions in functionally differentiated and unequal societies. Decent and legitimate decision-making in the face of risk relies on all these forms of reasoning and underpinning knowledge, as well as their reflexive and non-reflexive, practical negotiation.

# References

Adorno, T. W. (1966). *Negative Dialektik*. Suhrkamp.

Adorno, T. W., Albert, H., Dahrendorf, R., Habermas, J., Pilot, H., & Popper, K. R. (1976). *The positivist dispute in German sociology*. Heinemann.

Alaszewski, A. (2015). Anthropology and risk: Insights into uncertainty, danger and blame from other cultures—A review essay. *Health, Risk & Society, 17*(3–4), 205–225. https://doi.org/10.1080/13698575.2015.1070120

Alaszewski, A., & Wilkinson, I. (2014). The paradox of hope for working age adults recovering from stroke. *Health: An Interdisciplinary Journal for the Social Study of Health, Illness and Medicine, 19*(2), 172–187. https://doi.org/10.1177/1363459314555242

Albas, D., & Albas, C. (1989). Modern magic: The case of examinations. *The Sociological Quarterly, 30*(4), 603–613. https://doi.org/10.1111/j.1533-8525.1989.tb01537.x

Albers, C. (2023). 'The air is a little too dangerous': How children navigate between rules and risks in times of COVID-19. *Health, Risk & Society, 25*(7–8), 285–303. https://doi.org/10.1080/13698575.2023.2254104

Allen, J. (2006). Playing with Hope and despair: Bourdieu and the habitus of horse betting. In J. F. Cosgrave (Ed.), *The sociology of risk and gambling reader* (pp. 185–205). Routledge.

Anderson, W. (2002). *The cultivation of whiteness: Science, health, and racial Destiny in Australia*. Basic Books.


J. O. Zinn and M. Schulz, *A New Phenomenology of Risk and Uncertainty*, Critical Studies in Risk and Uncertainty, https://doi.org/10.1007/978-981-95-7405-6

Andiloro, A. (2023). *Something in the air—A phenomenology of videogame atmosphere* (PhD-Thesis). Swinburne University of Technology.

Andrade, C. (2018). Internal, external, and ecological validity in research design, conduct, and evaluation. *Indian Journal of Psychological Medicine, 40*(5), 498–499. https://doi.org/10.4103/ijpsym.Ijpsym_334_18

Ardissone, A. (2024). "In such a dark period, the only light": Patients' motivations and strategies to seek care from an online health community during the COVID-19 pandemic. *SSM—Qualitative Research in Health, 5*, 100425. https://doi.org/10.1016/j.ssmqr.2024.100425

Arendt, H. (2006). *Eichmann in Jerusalem: A report on the banality of evil.* Penguin Books.

Aristotle. (1926). *The Nicomachean ethics* (H. Rackham, Trans.). William Heinemann.

Arnoldi, J. (2009). *Risk.* Polity Press.

Árvai, J., & Rivers, L., III (Eds.). (2014). *Effective risk communication.* Earthscan.

Asad, T. (1993). *Genealogies of religion: Discipline and reasons of power in Christianity and Islam.* Johns Hopkins University Press.

Asad, T. (2003). *Formations of the secular: Christianity, Islam, modernity.* Stanford University Press.

Assmann, A. (2013). *Ist die Zeit aus den Fugen? Über den Aufstieg und Fall des Zeitregimes der Moderne.* Carl Hanser.

Atanasiu, R. (2021). Reason, emotions, intuition. In R. Atanasiu (Ed.), *Critical thinking for managers: Structured decision-making and persuasion in business* (pp. 41–47). Springer.

Atman, C. J., Bostrom, A., Fischhoff, B., & Morgan, M. G. (1994). Designing risk communications: Completing and correcting mental models of hazardous processes, Part I. *Risk Analysis, 14*(5), 779–788. https://doi.org/10.1111/j.1539-6924.1994.tb00289.x

AWSD (Aid Worker Security Database). (2023). *Number of victims by incident type (1997–2021).* https://aidworkersecurity.org/incidents/report/victims

Bach, M. (2004). *Jenseits des rationalen Handelns: Zur Soziologie Vilfredo Paretos.* Springer.

Baker, M. (2016). 1500 scientists lift the lid on reproducibility. *Nature, 533*(7604), 452–454. https://doi.org/10.1038/533452a

Balog-Way, D. H. P., & McComas, K. A. (2020). COVID-19: Reflections on trust, tradeoffs, and preparedness. *Journal of Risk Research, 23*(7–8), 838–848. https://doi.org/10.1080/13669877.2020.1758192

Banks, S. (2008). Critical commentary: Social work ethics. *British Journal of Social Work, 38*(6), 1238–1249. https://doi.org/10.1093/bjsw/bcn099

Barbalet, J. (2009). A characterization of trust, and its consequences. *Theory and Society, 38*(4), 367–382. https://doi.org/10.1007/s11186-009-9087-3

Bassel, L. (2017). *The politics of listening: Possibilities and challenges for democratic life*. Palgrave Pivot.

Bastide, L. (2015). Faith and uncertainty: Migrants' journeys between Indonesia, Malaysia and Singapore. *Health, Risk & Society, 17*(3–4), 226–245. https://doi.org/10.1080/13698575.2015.1071786

Bauman, Z. (1989). *Modernity and the holocaust*. Cornell University Press.

Bauman, Z. (1991). *Modernity and ambivalence*. Cornell University Press.

Bauman, Z. (1993). *Postmodern ethics*. Blackwell.

Beck, U. (1992). *Risk society: Towards a new modernity*. Sage.

Beck, U. (2009). *World at risk*. Polity Press.

Beck, U. (2016). *The metamorphosis of the world*. Polity Press.

Beck, U., & Beck-Gernsheim, E. (2002). *Individualization: Institutionalized individualism and its social and political consequences*. Sage.

Beckert, J. (2016). *Imagined futures: Fictional expectations and capitalist dynamics*. Harvard University Press.

Beckert, J., & Lutter, M. (2009). The inequality of fair play: Lottery gambling and social stratification in Germany. *European Sociological Review, 25*(4), 475–488. https://doi.org/10.1093/esr/jcn063

Beckert, J., & Lutter, M. (2012). Why the poor play the lottery: Sociological approaches to explaining class-based lottery play. *Sociology, 47*(6), 1152–1170. https://doi.org/10.1177/0038038512457854

Bennett, J. (2001). *The enchantment of modern life: Attachments, crossings, and ethics*. Princeton University Press.

Berger, P. L. (1967). *The sacred canopy: Elements of a sociological theory of religion*. Doubleday.

Berger, P. L., & Luckmann, T. (1967). *The social construction of reality: A treatise in the sociology of knowledge*. Allen Lane.

Bergson, H. (1911 [1907]). *Creative evolution* (A. Mitchell, Trans.). Henry Holt and Company. (Original: L'Évolution créatrice).

Berning, M., & Hardon, A. (2016). Educated guesses and other ways to address the pharmacological uncertainty of designer drugs: An exploratory study of experimentation through an online drug forum. *Contemporary Drug Problems, 43*(3), 277–292. https://doi.org/10.1177/0091450916662164

Bernstein, P. L. (1996). *Against the gods: The remarkable story of risk*. Wiley.

Bickford, S. (1996). *Dissonance, democracy: Listening, conflict and citizenship*. Cornell University Press.

Bikker, A. P., Macdonald, S., Robb, K. A., Conway, E., Browne, S., Campbell, C., Weller, D., Steele, R. J. C., & Macleod, U. (2019). Perceived colorectal cancer candidacy and the role of candidacy in colorectal cancer screening. *Health, Risk & Society, 21*(7–8), 352–372. https://doi.org/10.1080/13698575.2019.1680816

Bishop, E. C., & Willis, K. (2014). "Without hope everything would be doom and gloom": Young people talk about the importance of hope in their lives. *Journal of Youth Studies, 17*(6), 778–793. https://doi.org/10.1080/13676261.2013.878788

Black, D. (2013). On the almost inconceivable misunderstandings concerning the subject of value-free social science. *The British Journal of Sociology, 64*(4), 763–780. https://doi.org/10.1111/1468-4446.12034

Blasimme, A. (2022). Regenerative medicine, unproven therapies and the framing of clinical risk. In B. Świtek, A. Abramson, & H. Swee (Eds.), *Extraordinary risks, ordinary lives: Logics of precariousness in everyday contexts* (pp. 91–117). Springer.

Bloch, E. (1959). *Das Prinzip Hoffnung*. Suhrkamp.

Bloch, E. (1986). *The principle of hope*. Basil Blackwell.

Böhme, G. (2013). *Atmosphären: Essays zur neuen Ästhetik* (7th ed.). Suhrkamp.

Böhme, G. (2016). *Ästhetischer Kapitalismus*. Suhrkamp.

Bonß, W. (1995). *Vom Risiko: Unsicherheit und Ungewissheit in der Moderne* (1st ed.). Hamburger Edition.

Bonß, W. (2015). Karriere und sozialwissenschaftliche Potentiale des Resilienzbegriffs. In M. Endreß & A. Maurer (Eds.), *Resilienz im Sozialen* (pp. 15–31). Springer.

Bonß, W., & Zinn, J. O. (2005). Erwartbarkeit, Glück und Vertrauen: Zum Wandel biographischer Sicherheitskonstruktionen in der Moderne. *Soziale Welt, 56*(2/3), 79–98. https://doi.org/10.2307/40878492

Bourdieu, P. (1979a). *La distinction: Critique sociale du jugement*. Éditions de Minuit.

Bourdieu, P. (1979b). *Outline of a theory of practice*. Cambridge University Press.

Bourdieu, P. (1986). The forms of capital. In J. Richardson (Ed.), *Handbook of theory and research for the sociology of education* (pp. 241–258). Greenwood.

Boyne, R. (2003). *Risk*. Open University Press.

Breakwell, G. M. (2001). Mental models and social representations of hazards: The significance of identity processes. *Journal of Risk Research, 4*(4), 341–351. https://doi.org/10.1080/13669870110062730

Bredewold, F., & van der Weele, S. (2025). Navigating uncertainty: Taking methodological cues from relatives and care professionals for researching the perspectives of people with profound intellectual and multiple disabilities. *Journal of Intellectual & Developmental Disability, 50*(2), 139–150. https://doi.org/10.3109/13668250.2024.2408553

Brown, N. (2003). Hope against hype: Accountability in biopasts, presents and futures. *Science Studies, 16*(2), 3–21.

Brown, N. (2005). Shifting tenses: Reconnecting regimes of truth and hope. *Configurations, 13*(3), 331–355.

Brown, N., & Rappert, B. (2000). *Contested futures: A sociology of prospective techno-science*. Ashgate.

Brown, P. (2009). The phenomenology of trust: A Schutzian analysis of the social construction of knowledge by gynae-oncology patients. *Health, Risk & Society, 11*(5), 391–407. https://doi.org/10.1080/13698570903180455

Brown, P. (2020). Studying COVID-19 in light of critical approaches to risk and uncertainty: Research pathways, conceptual tools, and some magic from Mary Douglas. *Health, Risk & Society, 22*(1), 1–14. https://doi.org/10.1080/13698575.2020.1745508

Brown, P. (2022). *On vulnerability: A critical introduction.* Routledge.

Brown, P., de Graaf, S., & Hillen, M. (2014). The inherent tensions and ambiguities of hope: Towards a post-formal analysis of experiences of advanced-cancer patients. *Health, 19*(2), 207–225. https://doi.org/10.1177/1363459314555241

Brown, P., de Graaf, S., Hillen, M., Smets, E., & van Laarhoven, H. (2015). The interweaving of pharmaceutical and medical expectations as dynamics of micro-pharmaceuticalisation: Advanced-stage cancer patients' hope in medicines alongside trust in professionals. *Social Science & Medicine, 131*, 313–321. https://doi.org/10.1016/j.socscimed.2014.10.053

Brown, P., Moerman, G., & Bröer, C. (2019). Interviews as a means of exploring risk lifeworlds: Excavating the roots of everyday meanings, experiences and practices. In A. Olofsson & J. O. Zinn (Eds.), *Researching risk and uncertainty: Methodologies, methods and research strategies* (pp. 205–230). Springer.

Brown, P., Scrivener, A., & Calnan, M. (2024). The co-construction and emotion management of hope within psychosis services. *Frontiers in Sociology, 8*, 1270539. https://doi.org/10.3389/fsoc.2023.1270539

Brown, P., & Vickerstaff, S. (2011). Health subjectivities and labour market participation: Pessimism and older workers' attitudes and narratives around retirement in the UK. *Research on Aging, 33*(5), 529–550.

Brown, P., & Zinn, J. O. (2021). COVID-19, pandemic risk and inequality: Emerging social science insights at 24 months. *Health, Risk & Society, 23*(7–8), 273–288. https://doi.org/10.1080/13698575.2021.2002367

Bryant, J., & Ellard, J. (2015). Hope as a form of agency in the future thinking of disenfranchised young people. *Journal of Youth Studies, 18*(4), 485–499. https://doi.org/10.1080/13676261.2014.992310

Buhrmann, H. G., & Zaugg, M. K. (1981). Superstitions among basketball players: An investigation of various forms of superstitious belief and behavior among competitive basketballers at the junior high school to university level. *Journal of Sport Behavior, 4*(4), 163.

Burch, M., & Furman, K. (2019). Objectivity in science and law: A shared rescue strategy. *International Journal of Law and Psychiatry, 64*, 60–70. https://doi.org/10.1016/j.ijlp.2019.02.004

Burger, J. M., & Lynn, A. L. (2005). Superstitious behavior among American and Japanese professional baseball players. *Basic and Applied Social Psychology, 27*(1), 71–76. https://doi.org/10.1207/s15324834basp2701_7

Burger, W. (2008). Wozu braucht man in der Medizin Philosophie? Die Bedeutung der Neuen Phänomenologie von Hermann Schmitz für die Medizin. In M. Großheim (Ed.), *Neue Phänomenologie zwischen Praxis und Theorie: Festschrift für Hermann Schmitz* (pp. 141–150). Albert.

Burgess, A., & Horii, M. (2012). Risk, ritual and health responsibilisation: Japan's "safety blanket" of surgical face mask-wearing. *Sociology of Health & Illness, 34*(8), 1184–1198. https://doi.org/10.1111/j.1467-9566.2012.01466.x

Burgman, M. (2005). *Risks and decisions for conservation and environmental management*. Cambridge University Press.

Calestani, M., Roderick, P., Tonkin-Crine, S., Pruthi, R., Ravanan, R., & Leydon, G. M. (2024). Managing uncertainty in multidisciplinary renal team meetings: Decision-making processes and complex challenges in kidney transplant listing. *Health, Risk & Society, 26*(1–2), 53–74. https://doi.org/10.1080/13698575.2023.2236487

Campbell, C. (1996). Half-belief and the paradox of ritual instrumental activism: A theory of modern superstition. *The British Journal of Sociology, 47*(1), 151–166. https://doi.org/10.2307/591121

Castoriadis, C. (1987). *The imaginary institution of society*. Polity Press.

Chan, R. K. (2021). Tackling COVID-19 risk in Hong Kong: Examining distrust, compliance and risk management. *Current Sociology, 69*(4), 547–565. https://doi.org/10.1177/0011392121990026

Chandler, D. (2014). *Resilience: The governance of complexity*. Routledge.

Chiu, Y.-C., & Yu, S.-H. (2019). Everyday strategies for handling food safety concerns: A qualitative study of distrust, contradictions, and helplessness among Taiwanese women. *Health, Risk & Society, 21*(7–8), 319–334. https://doi.org/10.1080/13698575.2019.1685658

Clancy, G., Boardman, F., & Rees, S. (2022). Exploring trust in (bio)medical and experiential knowledge of birth: The perspectives of pregnant women, new mothers and maternity care providers. *Midwifery, 107*, 103272. https://doi.org/10.1016/j.midw.2022.103272

Clark, T., Edgley, A., & Kerry, R. (2025). Making healthcare decisions on behalf of people in a disorder of consciousness. A "risk-making" theory of decisional practices. *AJOB Neuroscience, 16*(3), 129–145. https://doi.org/10.1080/21507740.2025.2464112

Coleman, J. S. (1990). *Foundations of social theory*. Belknap Press of Harvard University Press.

Cook, J. (2016). Young adults' hopes for the long-term future: From re-enchantment with technology to faith in humanity. *Journal of Youth Studies*. https://doi.org/10.1080/13676261.2015.1083959

Cook, J. (2017). *Imagined futures: Hope, risk and uncertainty*. Springer.

Cooke, N. A. (2017). Posttruth, truthiness, and alternative facts. *The Library Quarterly: Information, Community, Policy, 87*(3), 211–221.

Cottingham, M. D., & Fisher, J. A. (2016). Risk and emotion among healthy volunteers in clinical trials. *Social Psychology Quarterly, 79*(3), 222–242. https://doi.org/10.1177/0190272516657655

Covello, V. T., Sandman, P. M., & Slovic, P. (1988). *Risk communication, risk statistics, and risk comparisons*. Chemical Manufacturers Association.

Crosby, A. W. (1997). *The measure of reality: Quantification and western society 1250–1600*. Cambridge University Press.

Damasio, A. (1996). *Descartes' error: Emotion, reason and the human brain*. Macmillan Press Ltd.

Damisch, L., Stoberock, B., & Mussweiler, T. (2010). Keep your fingers crossed! How superstition improves performance. *Psychological Science, 21*(7), 1014–1020. https://doi.org/10.1177/0956797610372631

Dancy, J. (2014). Intuition and emotion. *Ethics, 124*(4), 787–812. https://doi.org/10.1086/675879

Danzer, G. (1993). Philosophische Fragen im Bereich psychosomatischer Medizin. In M. Großheim (Ed.), *Rehabilitierung des Subjektiven. Festschrift für Hermann Schmitz* (pp. 209–223). Bouvier.

de Graaf, S. (2016). The construction and use of hope within health-settings: Recent developments in qualitative research and ethnographic studies. *Sociology Compass, 10*(7), 603–612. https://doi.org/10.1111/soc4.12380

Dean, M. (1999). *Governmentality: Power and rule in modern society*. Sage.

del Vecchio Good, M.-J. (2001). The biotechnical embrace. *Culture, Medicine and Psychiatry, 25*(4), 395–410.

del Vecchio Good, M.-J., Good, B. J., Schaffer, C., & Lind, S. E. (1990). American oncology and the discourse on hope. *Culture, Medicine and Psychiatry, 14*(1), 59–79.

Denu, M. K. I., Montrond, A., Piltch-Loeb, R., Bonetti, M., Toffolutti, V., Testa, M. A., & Savoia, E. (2022). Freedom of choice to vaccinate and COVID-19 vaccine hesitancy in Italy. *Vaccines (Basel), 10*(11). https://doi.org/10.3390/vaccines10111973

Descartes, R. (1644). *Principia Philosophiæ*. Ludovicum Elzevirios.

Destutt de Tracy, A. L. C. (1801). *Éléments d' idéologie*. Didot.

Dobson, A. (2014). *Listening for democracy. Recognition, representation, reconciliation*. Oxford University Press.

Douglas, M. (1985). *Risk acceptability according to the social sciences* (Vol. 11). Russell Sage Foundation.

Douglas, M. (1990). Risk as a forensic resource. *Daedalus, 119*(4), 1–16.

Douglas, M. (1992). *Risk and blame: Essays in cultural theory*. Routledge.

Douglas, M. (2003 [1970]).*Natural symbols. Explorations in cosmology*. Routledge.

Douglas, M., & Wildavsky, A. B. (1982). *Risk and culture: An essay on the selection of technical and environmental dangers*. University of California Press.

Dufourmantelle, A. (2011). *Éloge du risque*. Payot & Rivages.

Egger, E.-M., Jones, S., Justino, P., Manhique, I., & Santos, R. (2023). Africa's lockdown dilemma: High poverty and low trust. *Journal of International Development, 35*(7), 1648–1666. https://doi.org/10.1002/jid.3745

Eller, J. (2010). What is atheism? In P. Zuckerman (Ed.), *Atheism and secularity* (Vol. 12–13). Praeger.

Elster, J. (1998). Emotions and economic theory. *Journal of Economic Literature, XXXVI*, 47–74.

Endreß, M. (2009). Trust and modernity. In G. Möllering, R. Bachmann, & A. Zaheer (Eds.), *Handbook of trust research* (pp. 24–39). Edward Elgar.

Endreß, M. (2012). Trust and modernity. In R. Zucker & R. Bachmann (Eds.), *Handbook of advances in trust research* (pp. 492–506). Edward Elgar.

Endreß, M. (2014). Structures of belonging, types of social capital, and modes of trust. In D. Thomä, C. Henning, & H. B. Schmid (Eds.), *Social capital, social identities: From ownership to belonging* (pp. 55–74). De Gruyter.

Endrissat, N., Islam, G., & Noppeney, C. (2015). Enchanting work: New spirits of service work in an organic supermarket. *Organization Studies, 36*(11), 1555–1576. https://doi.org/10.1177/0170840615593588

Esposito, E. (2018). The time of money in finance and US society. *Finance and Society, 4*(1), 15–25. https://doi.org/10.2218/finsoc.v4i1.2738

Estrin, D. (2021, April 22). How Israel persuaded reluctant ultra-orthodox jews to get vaccinated against COVID-19. *npr*. https://www.npr.org/2021/04/22/988812635/how-israel-persuaded-reluctant-ultra-orthodox-jews-to-get-vaccinated-against-cov

Evers, A., & Nowotny, H. (1987). *Über den Umgang mit Unsicherheit. Die Entdeckung der Gestaltbarkeit der Gesellschaft*. Suhrkamp.

Ewald, F. (1986). *L'Etat providence*. B. Grasset.

Fama, E. F. (1970). Efficient capital markets: A review of theory and empirical work. *The Journal of Finance, 25*(2), 383–417.

Fessler, D. M. T., & Holbrook, C. (2014). Marching into battle: Synchronized walking diminishes the conceptualized formidability of an antagonist in men. *Biology Letters, 10*(8), 20140592. https://doi.org/10.1098/rsbl.2014.0592

Fichte, J. G. (2000). *Die Bestimmung des Menschen*. Meiner.

Finucane, M. L., Alhakami, A., Slovic, P., & Johnson, S. M. (2000a). The affect heuristic in judgments of risks and benefits. *Journal of Behavioral Decision Making, 13*, 1–17.

Finucane, M. L., Slovic, P., Mertz, C. K., Flynn, J., & Satterfield, T. A. (2000b). Gender, race, and perceived risk: The 'white male' effect. *Health, Risk & Society, 2*(2), 159–172.

Fischhoff, B. (1995). Risk perception and communication unplugged: Twenty years of process. *Risk Analysis, 15*(2), 137–145. https://doi.org/10.1111/j.1539-6924.1995.tb00308.x

Fischhoff, B., & Kadvany, J. D. (2011). *Risk: A very short introduction*. Oxford University Press.

Fisher, I. (1930). *The theory of interest: As determined by impatience to spend income and opportunity to invest it*. The Macmillan Company.

Fisher, R. (2020, September 22). The fiasco of the 1976 'swine flu affair'. *BBC, Future*. http://www.bbc.com/future/article/20200918-the-fiasco-of-the-us-swine-flu-affair-of-1976
Flyvbjerg, B., Landman, T., & Scharm, S. (Eds.). (2012). *Real social science—Applied phronesis*. Cambridge University Press.
Foucault, M. (1965). *On madness and civilization: A history of insanity in the age of reason*. Vintage Books.
Fraser, D. (1981). *The evolution of the British welfare state*. Macmillan.
Frederiksen, M. (2016). Divided uncertainty: A phenomenology of trust, risk and confidence. In S. Jagd & L. Fuglsang (Eds.), *Trust, organizations and social interaction. Studying trust as process within and between organizations* (pp. 43–67). Edward Elgar.
Freud, S. (1930). Das Unbehaben in der Kultur.
Fuchs, T. (2000). *Leib, Raum, Person. Entwurf einer phänomenologischen Anthropologie*. Klett-Cotta.
Fuchs, T. (2008). *Leib und Lebenswelt: neue philosophisch-psychiatrische Essays* (Vol. 51). Graue Edition.
Fuchs, T. (2011). The brain—A mediating organ. *Journal of Consciousness Studies, 18*(7–8), 196–221.
Fuchs, T. (2017). *Ecology of the brain: The phenomenology and biology of the embodied mind*. Oxford University Press.
Füredi, F. (1997). *Culture of fear: Risk-taking and the morality of low expectation*. Cassell.
Gadamer, H.-G. (1996). *The enigma of health: The art of healing in a scientific age*. Stanford University Press.
Gambrell, J. (2020, March 17). Shiite hardliners in Iran storm 2 shrines that were closed to stop Coronavirus spread. *Times* . https://web.archive.org/web/20200317140841/https://time.com/5804546/iran-shiite-storm-coronavirus/
Ganßmann, H. (2007). Doppelte Kontingenz und wirtschaftliches Handeln. In J. Beckert et al. (Eds.), *Märkte als soziale Strukturen* (pp. 63–79).
Gee, S., & Skovdal, M. (2017). The role of risk perception in willingness to respond to the 2014–2016 West African Ebola outbreak: A qualitative study of international health care workers. *Global Health Research and Policy, 2*(1), 21. https://doi.org/10.1186/s41256-017-0042-y
Gehlen, A. (1980). *Man in the age of technology*. Columbia University Press.
Gehlen, A. (1988). *Man, his nature and place in the world*. Columbia University Press.
Giddens, A. (1990). *The consequences of modernity*. Stanford University Press.

Giddens, A. (1994a). *Beyond left and right: The future of radical politics*. Stanford University Press.

Giddens, A. (1994b). Risk, trust, reflexivity. In U. Beck, A. Giddens, & S. Lash (Eds.), *Reflexive modernization: Politics, tradition and aesthetics in the modern social order* (pp. 184–197). Polity Press.

Giddens, A. (1999). Lecture 2: Risk—Hong Kong. *Reith Lectures 1999. Runaway World*: BBC-Radio 4.

Giddens, A. (2000). *Runaway world. How globalization is reshaping our lives*. Routledge.

Gigerenzer, G. (2006). Out of the frying pan into the fire: Behavioral reactions to terrorist attacks. *Risk Analysis, 26*(2), 347–351.

Gigerenzer, G. (2007). *Gut feelings*. Viking.

Gigerenzer, G., & Todd, P. M. (2001). In G. Gigerenzer, P. M. Todd et al. (Eds.), *Fast and frugal heuristics: The adaptive toolbox* (pp. 3–34). Oxford University Press.

Gil, M. (2023). *Risk transfer in sociotechnical systems*. XX World Congress of Sociology.

Giritli Nygren, K., Olofsson, A., Bowleg, L., Curran, D., Hannah Moffat, K., Mitchell, C.,... & Zinn, J. O. et al. (2024). Thoughts about intersectionality and risk. Interviews with key scholars. *Journal of Risk Research, 27*(9), 1070–1082.

Giritli Nygren, K., Olofsson, A., & Öhman, S. (2020). *A framework of intersectional risk theory in the age of ambivalence*. Palgrave Macmillan.

Glaser, B. G., & Strauss, A. L. (1968). *Time for dying*. Aldine.

Goffman, E. (1969). *Where the action is. Three essays*. Allen Lane. The Penguin Press.

Goleman, D. (1995). *Emotional intelligence. Why it can mater more than IQ*. Bantam.

Goncharov, I. (1915 [1859]). *Oblomov* (C. J. Hogarth, Trans.). George Allen & Unwin LTD.

Graziosi, G. (2022, January 7). Prominent QAnon conspiracy theorist dies from Covid after saying only 'idiots' get vaccinated. *Idependent* (online). *https://www.independent.co.uk/news/world/americas/cirsten-weldon-qanon-conspiracy-covid-b1989036.html*

Griffero, T. (2021). *The atmospheric "we". Moods and collective feelings*. Mimesis International.

Griffiths, M. D. (1993). Fruit machine gambling: The importance of structural characteristics. *Journal of Gambling Studies, 9*, 387–399.

Groos, H. (2011). *Ein schöner Tag zum sterben. Als Bundeswehrärztin in Afghanistan.* S. Fischer.

Gross, M. (2022). Technological fixes. Nonknowledge transfer and the risk of ignorance. In L. Pellizzoni, E. Leonardi, & V. Asara (Eds.), *Handbook of critical environmental politics* (pp. 308–317). Edward Elgar.

Großheim, M. (2002). Erkennen oder Entscheiden. Der Begriff der »Situation« zwischen theoretischer und praktischer Philosophie. *Internationales Jahrbuch für Hermeneutik, 1*, 279–300.

Guenther, L. (2021). Six senses of critique for critical phenomenology. *Puncta, 4*(2), 5–23.

Gugutzer, R. (2020). Beyond Husserl and Schütz. Hermann Schmitz and Neophenomenological sociology. *Journal for the Theory of Social Behaviour, 50*(2), 184–202. https://doi.org/10.1111/jtsb.12240

Gugutzer, R., & Böttcher, M. (Eds.). (2012). *Körper, Sport und Religion: Zur Soziologie religiöser Verkörperungen.* Springer VS.

Habermas, J. (1984). *The theory of communicative action.* Polity.

Hacking, I. (1975). *The emergence of probability.* Cambridge University Press.

Hackstaff, C. (1999). *Marriage in a culture of divorce.* Temple University Press.

Hall, A. (2016). Trust, uncertainty and the reporting of workplaces hazards and injuries. *Health, Risk & Society, 18*(7–8), 427–448. https://doi.org/10.1080/13698575.2016.1264576

Hall, A. (2021). *The subjectivities and politics of occupational risk. Mines, farms and auto factories.* Routledge.

Hall, K. T. (2022). *Placebos.* MIT Press.

Harambam, J. (2023). Distrusting consensus: How a uniform Coroan pandemic narrative fostered suspicion and conspiracy theories. *Journal of Digital Social Research, 5*(3), 109–139.

Haraway, D. (1988). Situated knowledges: The science question in feminism and the privilege of partial perspective. *Feminist Studies, 14*(3), 575–599.

Haraway, D. (1991). *Simians, cyborgs and women: The reinvention of nature.* Free Association Books.

Harding, S. (1991). *Whose science? Whose knowledge? Thinking from women's lives* (p. 1991). Cornell University Press.

Harding, S. (1998). *Is science multicultural? Postcolonialisms, feminisms, and epistemologies.* Indiana University Press.

Hayenhjelm, M. (2006). Out of the ashes: Hope and vulnerability as explanatory factors in individual risk taking. *Journal of Risk Research, 9*(3), 189–204. https://doi.org/10.1080/13669870500419537

He, J., Liu, H., Sing, T. F., Song, C., & Wong, W.-K. (2019). Superstition, conspicuous spending, and housing market: Evidence from Singapore. *Management Science, 66*(2), 783–804. https://doi.org/10.1287/mnsc.2018.3198

Heath, R. L., & O'Hair, H. D. (Eds.). (2009). *Handbook of risk and crisis communication*. Routledge.

Hegewald, S., & Schraff, D. (2022). Who rallies around the flag? Evidence from panel data during the COVID-19 pandemic. *Journal of Elections, Public Opinion and Parties*, 1–22. https://doi.org/10.1080/17457289.2022.2120886

Heidegger, M. (1967 [1927]). *Sein und Zeit*. Max Niemeyer.

Heidegger, M. (1977 [orig. 1954]). The question concerning technology. In *The question concerning technology: And other essays* (pp. 3–35). Harper & Row.

Heidegger, M. (1995). *The fundamental concepts of metaphysics. World, finitude, solitude*. Indiana University Press.

Heilbron, J. L. (1990). Introductory article. In T. Fraengsmyr, J. L. Heilbron, & R. E. Rider (Eds.), *The quantifying Spirit in the eighteenth century* (pp. 1–23). University of California Press.

Heinz, W. R. (2000). Selbstsozialisation im Lebenslauf. Umrisse einer Theorie biographischen Handelns. In M. H. Erika (Ed.), *Biographische Sozialisation* (pp. 165–186). De Gruyter Oldenbourg.

Heinz, W. R., Kelle, U., Witzel, A., & Zinn, J. O. (1998). Vocational training and career development in Germany: Results from a longitudinal study. *International Journal of Behavioral Development, 22*(1), 77–101.

Henslin, J. (1967). Craps and magic. *The American Journal of Sociology, 73*, 316–330.

Hernández-Carretero, M., & Carling, J. (2012). Beyond "kamikaze migrants": Risk taking in West African boat migration to Europe. *Human Organization, 71*(4), 407–416. https://doi.org/10.17730/humo.71.4.n52709742v2637t1

Heyerdahl, A. (2022). Risk assessment without the risk? A controversy about security and risk in Norway. *Journal of Risk Research, 25*(2), 252–267. https://doi.org/10.1080/13669877.2021.1936610

Heyerdahl, A. (2023). From prescriptive rules to responsible organisations—Making sense of risk in protective security management—A study from Norway. *European Security, 32*(1), 147–169. https://doi.org/10.1080/09662839.2022.2070006

Hirschman, A. O. (1977). *The passion and the interests. Political arguments for before its triumph*. Princeton University Press.

Hirwani, P. (2022, January 23). Jacinda Ardern cancels wedding amid new Covid restrictions in New Zealand. *Independent*. http://www.independent.co.uk/news/world/australasia/jacinda-ardern-new-zealand-covid-b1998812.html

Hochschild, A. R. (1983). *The managed heart. Commercialization of human feeling*. The University of California Press.

Hoerning, E. M., & Alheit, P. (1995). Biographical socialisation. *Current Sociology, 43*, 101–114.

Homans, G. (1941). Anxiety and magic. *American Anthropologist, 43*, 164–172.

Hope, W. (2011). Global financial crisis|time, communication and financial collapse. *International Journal of Communication, 4*.

Hope, W. (2020). Time and global. In K. Goetz (Ed.), *The Oxford handbook of time and politics*. Oxford University Press.

Horii, M. (2014). Why do the Japanese Wear masks? *Electronic journal of contemporary. Japanese Studies, 14*(2), art. 8.

Horkheimer, M., & Adorno, T. W. (1947). *Dialektik der Aufklärung. Philosophische Fragmente*. Querido.

Horkheimer, M., & Adorno, T. W. (2002 [1947]). *Dialectic of enlightenment* (E. Jephcott, Trans.). Stanford University Press.

Horlick-Jones, T. (2005). Informal logics of risk: Contingency and modes of practical reasoning. *Journal of Risk Research, 8*(3), 253–272. https://doi.org/10.1080/1366987042000270735

Hunt, E. (2021). Words matter: How New Zealand's clear messaging helped beat Covid. *The Guardian* (26 Feb 2021).

Husserl, E. (1970). *The crisis of European sciences and transcendental phenomenology*. Northwestern University Press.

Husserl, E. (1976 [1913]). *Ideen zu einer reinen Phänomenologie und phänomenologischen Philosophie, Buch 1, Aus Husserliana Gesammelte Werke, Band 3*. Kluwer.

Husserl, E. (2012). *Ideas. General introduction to phenomenology*. Routledge.

Jackson, S., Demain, S., O'Malley, F., & Kunkel, D. (2025). The yin and yang of safety and risk: A content analysis and critical narrative synthesis exploring the conceptualisation of risk in the stroke rehabilitation literature. *Health, Risk & Society, 27*(5–6), 276–314.

Jahoda, G. (1969). *The psychology of superstition*. The Penguin Press.

Jarvis, P. (1980). Towards a sociological understanding of superstition. *Social Compass, 27*(2–3), 285–295. https://doi.org/10.1177/003776868002700209

Jasanoff, S., & Kim, S.-H. (2015). *Dreamscapes of modernity: Sociotechnical imaginaries and the fabrication of Power*. University of Chicago Press.

Jauch, L. (2021). Power and academia, an endless story. *Elephant in the Lab*. https://doi.org/10.5281/zenodo.4467761

Joelsson, T. (2019). 'So that we don't spoil them': Understanding children's everyday mobility through parents' affective practices. *Children's Geographies, 17*(5), 591–602.

Johansson, B., Hopmann, D. N., & Shehata, A. (2021). When the rally-around-the-flag effect disappears, or: When the COVID-19 pandemic becomes "normalized". *Journal of Elections, Public Opinion and Parties, 31*(sup1), 321–334. https://doi.org/10.1080/17457289.2021.1924742

Kahneman, D., & Klein, G. (2009). Conditions for intuitive expertise: A failure to disagree. *American Psychologist, 64*(6), 515–526. https://doi.org/10.1037/a0016755

Kahneman, D., Sibony, O., & Sunstein, K. R. (2021). *Noise. A flaw in human judgment*. Little, Brown Spark.

Kasperson, R. (2014). Four questions for risk communication. *Journal of Risk Research, 17*(10), 1233–1239. https://doi.org/10.1080/13669877.2014.900207

Kasstan, B. (2021). "If a rabbi did say 'you have to vaccinate,' we wouldn't": Unveiling the secular logics of religious exemption and opposition to vaccination. *Social Science & Medicine, 280*, 114052. https://doi.org/10.1016/j.socscimed.2021.114052

Keynes, J. M. (1936). *The general theory of employment interest and money*. McMillan.

Kinsella, E. A., & Pitman, A. (Eds.). (2012). *Phronesis as professional knowledge: Practical wisdom in the professions*. Sense Publishers.

Kiriscioglu, E., & Ustubici, A. (2025). "At least, at the border, I am killing myself by my own will": Migration aspirations and risk perceptions among Syrian and afghan communities. *Journal of Immigrant & Refugee Studies, 23*(2), 292–306.

Kiriscioglu, E., & Van Heelsum, A. (2024). Stuck in a whirlpool? The role of hope and despair in dealing with risks during afghan migration journeys. *Journal of Refugee Studies, feae055*.

Kitching, C. (2021, January 6). COVID-19 denier catches virus and admits he was wrong in warning from hospital. *Mirror* (online) https://www.mirror.co.uk/news/us-news/COVID-19-denier-catches-virus-23270542

Klein, G. A. (1998). *Sources of power: How people make decisions*. MIT Press.

Knight, F. H. (1921). *Risk, uncertainty, and profit*. Houghton Mifflin Co.

Knorr-Cetina, K. (2012). What is a financial market? Global markets as microinstitutional and post-traditional social forms. In K. Knorr-Cetina & A. Preda (Eds.), *The Oxford handbook of the sociology of finance* (pp. 115–134). Oxford University Press.

Knorr-Cetina, K., & Bruegger, U. (2000). The market as an object of attachment: Exploring postsocial relations in financial markets. *The Canadian Journal of Sociology/Cahiers canadiens de sociologie, 25*(2), 141–168.

Knorr-Cetina, K., & Preda, A. (2007). The Temporalization of financial markets: From network to flow. *Theory, Culture & Society, 24*(7–8), 116–138.

Knorr-Cetina, K. D. (1999). *Epistemic cultures: How the sciences make knowledge*. Harvard University Press.

Koontz, A., Norman, L., & Okorie, S. (2017). Realistic love: Contemporary college women's negotiations of princess culture and the "reality" of romantic relationships. *Journal of Social and Personal Relationships, 36*(2), 535–555. https://doi.org/10.1177/0265407517735694

Kordzadeh, N., & Ghasemaghaei, M. (2022). Algorithmic bias: Review, synthesis, and future research directions. *European Journal of Information Systems, 31*(3), 388–409. https://doi.org/10.1080/0960085X.2021.1927212

Koselleck, R. (1985). *Futures past: On the semantics of historical times*. MIT Press.

Koselleck, R. (1988). *Critique and crisis: Enlightenment and the pathogenesis of modern society*. MIT Press.

Kosla, M. T. (2015). The safety dance: Men without [hard] hats. *Health, Risk & Society, 17*(5–6), 388–403. https://doi.org/10.1080/13698575.2015.1116499

Kosny, A. A., & Eaking, J. M. (2008). The hazards of helping: Work, mission adn risk in non-profit social service organisations. *Health, Risk & Society, 10*(2), 149–166.

Kreps, S. E., & Kriner, D. L. (2020). Model uncertainty, political contestation, and public trust in science: Evidence from the COVID-19 pandemic. *Science Advances, 6*(43), eabd4563. https://doi.org/10.1126/sciadv.abd4563

Krieken, R. V. (Ed.). (2014). *Sociology: An introduction to sociology Scs110* (custom ed.). Pearson.

Krimsky, S. (2007). Risk communication in the internet age: The rise of disorganized skepticism. *Environmental Hazards, 7*, 157–164.

Krohn, W., & Krücken, G. (1993). *Riskante Technologien: Reflexion und Regulation*. Suhrkamp.

Lagerspetz, O. (1998). *Trust. The tacit demand*. Kluwer Academic.

Langenohl, A. (2018). Sources of financial synchronism: Arbitrage theory and the promise of risk-free profit. *Finance and Society, 4*(1), 26–40. https://doi.org/10.2218/finsoc.v4i1.2737

Langewitz, W. (2008). Der Ertrag der Neuen Phänomenologie für die Psychosomatische Medizin. In M. Großheim (Ed.), *Neue Phänomenologie zwischen Praxis und Theorie. Festschrift für Hermann Schmitz* (pp. 126–141). Alber.

Larsen, T. S., Halberg, N., Jensen, P. S., & Christensen, K. (2023). Emotional risk work during the pandemic: Healthcare professionals' perceptions from a COVID-19 ward. *Health, Risk & Society, 25*(3–4), 110–128.

Lash, S. (2002). Foreword: Individualization in a non-linear mode. In U. Beck & E. Beck-Gernsheim (Eds.), *Individualization*. Sage.

Latour, B. (1993). *We have never been modern*. Harvard University Press.

Latour, B., & Woolgar, S. (1979). *Laboratory life: The social construction of scientific facts*. Sage Publications.

Lebreton, B., Rivaud, A., Picot, L., Prévost, B., Barillé, L., Sauzeau, T.,... & Lavaud, J. (2019). From ecological relevance of the ecosystem services concept to its socio-political use. The case study of intertidal bare mudflats in the Marennes-Oléron Bay, France. *Ocean & Coastal Management,* 172, 41–54. https://doi.org/10.1016/j.ocecoaman.2019.01.024

Lee, M. K. (2018). Understanding perception of algorithmic decisions: Fairness, trust, and emotion in response to algorithmic management. *Big Data & Society, 5*(1), 2053951718756684. https://doi.org/10.1177/2053951718756684

Lewis, J., & Sarre, S. (2006). Risk and intimate relationships. In P. Taylor-Gooby & J. O. Zinn (Eds.), *Risk in social science* (pp. 140–159). Oxford University Press.

Leyshon, A., & Thrift, N. (2007). The capitalization of almost everything. The future of finance and. *Theory Culture Society, 24*(7–8), 97–115.

Linder, S. B. (1971). *Das Linder-Axiom. Oder: Warum wir keine Zeit mehr haben*. Bertelsmann.

Lipsett, A. (2008, September 16). Like history in the first person. *The Guardian* (online).

Loewenstein, G. F., Weber, E. U., Hsee, C. K., & Welch, N. (2001). Risks as feelings. *Psychological Bulletin, 127*(2), 267–286.

Löfstedt, R. E. (2005). *Risk management in post-trust societies*. Palgrave Macmillan.

Logg, J. M., Minson, J. A., & Moore, D. A. (2019). Algorithm appreciation: People prefer algorithmic to human judgment. *Organizational Behavior and*

*Human Decision Processes, 151*, 90–103. https://doi.org/10.1016/j.obhdp.2018.12.005

Løgstrup, K. E. (1997). *The ethical demand*. Notre Dame Press.

Luhmann, N. (1979). *Trust and Power*. Wiley.

Luhmann, N. (1984). *Soziale Systeme: Grundriss einer allgemeinen Theorie* (1st ed.). Suhrkamp.

Luhmann, N. (1985). *A sociological theory of law*. Routledge, Taylor and Francis.

Luhmann, N. (1988). In D. Gambetta (Ed.), *Familiarity, confidence, trust: Problems and alternatives* (pp. 94–107). Blackwell.

Luhmann, N. (1989). *Ecological communication*. Polity Press.

Luhmann, N. (1993). *Risk: A sociological theory*. A. de Gruyter.

Luhmann, N. (1995). *Social systems*. Stanford University Press.

Lupton, D. (1999). *Risk*. Routledge.

Lupton, D. (2013a). *Risk* (2nd ed.). Routledge.

Lupton, D. (2013b). Risk and emotion: Towards an alternative theoretical perspective. *Health, Risk & Society, 15*(8), 634–647. https://doi.org/10.1080/13698575.2013.848847

Lupton, D., & Tulloch, J. (2002). 'Life would be pretty dull without risk': Voluntary risk-taking and its pleasures. *Health, Risk & Society, 4*(2), 113–124.

Lutter, M. (2010). *Märkte für Träume: Die Soziologie des Lottospiels* (Vol. 72). Campus.

Lyng, S. (1990). Edgework: A social psychological analysis of voluntary risk taking. *The American Journal of Sociology, 95*(4), 851–886. https://doi.org/10.1086/229379

Lyng, S. (2005a). *Edgework. The sociology of risk-taking*. Routledge.

Lyng, S. (2005b). In S. Lyng (Ed.), *Sociology at the edge: Social theory and voluntary risk taking* (pp. 17–49). Routledge.

Lyng, S. (2008). In J. Zinn (Ed.), *Edgework, risk, and uncertainty* (pp. 106–137). Blackwell.

Lyotard, J.-F. (1979). *La Condition postmoderne*. Minuit.

Lyotard, J.-F. (1984). *The postmodern condition: A report on knowledge*. University of Minnesota Press.

MacGregor, S. (2006). *Beyond mothering earth: Ecological citizenship and the politics of care*. UBC Press.

Magri, E., & McQueen, P. (2023). *Critical phenomenology—An introduction*. Polity Press.

Malewska, K. (2019). Intuition in decision-making—A review of empirical research in the area of magagement. In Š. Hittmár (Ed.), *Theory of management 8: The selected problems for the development support of management Knowledge Base* (pp. 165–170). University of Zilina.

Malewska, K., & Sajdak, M. (2014). The intuitive manager and the concept of strategic leadership. *Management, 18*(2), 44–58. https://doi.org/10.2478/manment-2014-0041

Malinowski, B. (1925). Magic, science and religion. In B. Malinowski (Ed.), *Magic, science and religion and other essays* (pp. 17–92).

Manca, T. (2018). Fear, rationality, and risky others: A qualitative analysis of physicians' and nurses' accounts of popular vaccine narratives. *Technology in Society, 55*, 119–125.

Manch, T. (2020). Coronavirus: New Zealand likely to follow Taiwan in advising cancellation of crowded gatherings. *Stuff*. Retrieved March 15, 2020, from www.stuff.co.nz/national/health/coronavirus/120294477/coronavirus-new-zealand-likely-to-follow-taiwan-in-advising-cancellation-of-crowded-gatherings

Mannheim, K. (2015 [1929]). *Ideologie und Utopie (Mit einer Einleitung von Jürgen Kaube)* (9th ed.). Vittorio Klostermann.

March, J. G. (1988). In R. Bell & Tversky (Eds.), *Bounded rationality, ambiguity, and the engineering of choice* (pp. 33–57). Cambridge University Press.

Marcuse, H. (1971). *One-dimensional man: Studies in the ideology of advanced industrial society*. Beacon Press.

Marx, K. (1867). *Das Kapital. Kritik der politischen Oekonomie*. Otto Meisner.

Masci, P. (2011). The history of insurance: Risk, uncertainty and entrepreneurship. *Journal of the Washington Institute of China Studies, 5*(3), 25–68.

Masters, A., & Nutt, D. (2017). A plutocratic proposal: An ethical way for rich patients to pay for a place on a clinical trial. *Journal of Medical Ethics, 43*(11), 730–736. https://doi.org/10.1136/medethics-2016-104050

Mattingly, C. (2006). Hoping, willing, and narrative re-envisioning. *The Hedgehog Review, 8*(3), 21–35.

Mayhew, H. (1861). *London labor and the London poor* (Vol. II). Dover Publications.

McClure, T. (2021, August 30). Even as New Zealand battles Covid, trust in government bucks global trend. *The Guardian* (online).

McEnery, T. (2019). *Corpus linguistics*. Edinburgh University Press.

McGuire, D., Cunningham, J. E. A., Reynolds, K., & Matthews-Smith, G. (2020). Beating the virus: An examination of the crisis communication approach taken by New Zealand prime minister Jacinda Ardern during the COVID-19 pandemic. *Human Resource Development International, 23*(4), 361–379. https://doi.org/10.1080/13678868.2020.1779543

Mead, G. H. (1934). *Mind, self society from the standpoint of a social behaviorist*. The University of Chicago Press.

Mellini, L., & Poglia Mileti, F. (2022). 'If you know the person, there are no risks': 'In-between' strategies for reducing HIV sexual risk among young sub-Saharan migrants living in Switzerland. *Health, Risk & Society, 24*(7–8), 277–296. https://doi.org/10.1080/13698575.2022.2105309

Mellor, P. A., & Shilling, C. (2010). Body pedagogics and the religious habitus: A new direction for the sociological study of religion. *Religion, 40*(1), 27–38.

Mellor, P. A., & Shilling, C. (2014). Re-conceptualising the religious habitus: Reflexivity and embodied subjectivity in global modernity. *Culture and Religion, 15*(3), 275–297.

Merleau-Ponty, M. (2002 [1945]). *Phenomenology of perception*. Routledge.

Merton, R. K. (1938). Science, technology and Society in Seventeenth Century England. *Osiris, 4*, 360–632.

Merton, R. K. (1973 [1942]). The normative structure of science. In R. K. Merton (Ed.), *The sociology of science: Theoretical and empirical investigations* (pp. 267–278). University of Chicago Press.

Mignolo, W. D. (2009). Epistemic disobedience, independent thought and Decolonial freedom. *Theory, Culture & Society, 26*(7–8), 159–181.

Milgram, S. (1963). Behavioral study of obedience. *The Journal of Abnormal and Social Psychology, 67*(4), 371–378. https://doi.org/10.1037/h0040525

Milgram, S. (1974). *Obedience to authority: An experimental view*. Tavistock Publications.

Miller, A. P. (2018). Want less-biased decisions? Use algorithms. *Harvard Business Review, 26*(26). https://hbr.org/2018/07/want-less-biased-decisions-use-algorithms

Mishra, A. K. (1996). Organizational responses to crisis: The centrality of trust. In R. Kramer & T. Tyler (Eds.), *Trust in Organizations: Frontiers of theory and research* (pp. 261–287). Sage.

Moldzio, A. (2006). Zur schizophrenen Entfremdung auf der Grundlage der Neuen Phänomenologie. In D. Schmoll & A. Kuhlmann (Eds.), *Symptom und Phänomen*. Karl Alber.

Möllering, G. (2006). *Trust: Reason, routine, reflexivity*. Elsevier.

Montgomery, K. (2006). *How doctors think: Clinical judgment and the practice of medicine*. Oxford University Press.

Morgan, M. G., Fischhoff, B., Bostrom, A., & Atman, C. J. (2002). *Risk communication. A mental models approach*. Cambridge University Press.

Morgan, T., Pilimatalawwe, D., Morgan, K., Duschinsky, R., Gott, M., & Wiles, J. (2024). 'Assessing my risk and that of my whānau is my right': A longitudinal media analysis of risk and COVID-19 pandemic in New Zealand news media. *Health, Risk & Society, 26*(5–6), 282–300.

Moscovici, S. (1985). *The age of the crowd: A historical treatise on mass psychology*. Cambridge University Press.

Müller, H.-P. (2011). Rationalität, Rationalisierung, Rationalismus. Von Weber zu Bourdieu? In A. Maurer & U. Schimank (Eds.), *Die Rationalität des Sozialen* (pp. 43–64). Springer.

Muriwai, E., Turner, N., Palmer, S. C., Huria, T., Stanley, J., & Signal, L. (2024). Supporting whānau during COVID-19 pandemic in Aotearoa New Zealand: A systems thinking case study. *BMC Health Services Research, 24*, 843. https://doi.org/10.1186/s12913-024-11164-z

Murphy, M. (2006). *Sick building syndrome and the problem of uncertainty: Environmental politics, Technoscience, and women workers*. Duke University Press.

Nansen, F. (1926, November 3). *The spirit of adventure*. Speech at St. Andrews University.

Negt, O. (1988). Der Kampf um die Arbeitszeit ist der Kampf um die Lebenszeit. In R. Zoll (Ed.), *Zerstörung und Wiederaneignung von Zeit* (pp. 531–543). Suhrkamp.

Nguyen, C. T. (2020). Echo chambers and epistemic bubbles. *Episteme, 17*(2), 141–161. https://doi.org/10.1017/epi.2018.32

Niburski, K., & Niburski, O. (2020). Impact of trump's promotion of unproven COVID-19 treatments and subsequent internet trends: Observational study. *Journal of Medical Internet Research, 22*(11), e20044. https://doi.org/10.2196/20044

Nielsen, M., Langley, M. C., Shipton, C., & Kapitány, R. (2020). Homo neanderthalensis and the evolutionary origins of ritual in Homo sapiens. *Philosophical Transactions B, 375*(1805), 1–7.

Norris, F. H., Stevens, S. P., Pfefferbaum, B., Wyche, K. F., & Pfefferbaum, R. L. (2008). Community resilience as a metaphor, theory, set of capacities, and strategy for disaster readiness. *American Journal of Community Psychology, 41*(1), 127–150. https://doi.org/10.1007/s10464-007-9156-6

Ojala, M. (2012). Hope and climate change: The importance of hope for environmental engagement among young people. *Environmental Education Research, 18*(5), 625–642. https://doi.org/10.1080/13504622.2011.637157

Olofsson, A., & Rashid, S. (2011). The White (male) effect and risk perception: Can equality make a difference? *Risk Analysis, 31*(6), 1016–1032.
O'Malley, P. (2012). From risk to resilience. Technologies of the self in the age of catastrophes. *Carceral Notebooks, 7*, 41–68.
Otway, H., & Wynne, B. (1989). Risk communication: Paradigm and paradox. *Risk Analysis, 9*(2), 141–145.
Pareto, V. (1916). *Trattato di Sociologia Generale*. G. Barbèra.
Pareto, V. (1963). *The mind and society; a treatise on general sociology*. Constable and Company.
Parker, J., & Stanworth, H. (2005). 'Go for it!' towards a critical realist approach to volutnary risk-taking. *Health, Risk and Society, 7*(4), 319–336. https://doi.org/10.1080/13698570500390853
Parsons, T. (1980). In S. Fiddle (Ed.), *Health, uncertainty and the action structure* (pp. 145–162). Praeger.
Pascal, B. (1655). *The physical treatises of Pascal*. Octagon.
Paton, D., & Johnston, D. (2017). *Disaster resilience. An integrated approach* (2nd ed.). Charles C. Homas Publishers Ltd.
Pearce, E., Launay, J., & Dunbar, R. I. M. (2015). The ice-breaker effect: Singing mediates fast social bonding. *Royal Society Open Science, 2*(10), 150221.
Pellegrino, E. D., & Thomasma, D. C. (1993). *The virtues in medical practice*. Oxford University Press.
Peltzer, K., & Renner, W. (2003). Superstition, risk-taking and risk perception of accidents among South African taxi drivers. *Accident Analysis & Prevention, 35*(4), 619–623. https://doi.org/10.1016/S0001-4575(02)00035-0
Peou, C., & Zinn, J. (2015). Cambodian youth managing expectations and uncertainties of the life course—A typology of biographical management. *Journal of Youth Studies, 18*(6), 726–742. https://doi.org/10.1080/13676261.2014.992328
Peretti-Watel, P., Ward, J. K., Vergelys, C., Bocquier, A., Raude, J., & Verger, P. (2019). 'I think I made The right decision … I Hope I'm not wrong'. Vaccine hesitancy, commitment and trust among parents of young children. *Sociology of Health & Illness, 41*(6), 1192–1206. https://doi.org/10.1111/1467-9566.12902
Petersen, A. R. (2015). *Hope in health: The socio-politics of optimism*. Palgrave Macmillan.
Petit, P. (2003). *To reach the clouds*. Faber & Faber.

Pidgeon, N., Hood, C., Jones, D., Turner, B., & Gibson, R. (1992). *Risk perception.* In S. The Royal (Ed.), (pp. 89–134).

Pilkington, C. J., Kern, W., & Indest, D. (1994). Is safer sex necessary with a "safe" partner? Condom use and romantic feelings. *The Journal of Sex Research, 31*(3), 203–210. https://doi.org/10.1080/00224499409551753

Pixley, J. (2004). *Emotions in finance: Distrust and uncertainty in global markets.* Cambridge University Press.

Plessner, H. (2019 [1928]). *Levels of organic life and the human: An introduction to philosophical anthropology*. Fordham University Press.

Porsanger, L., & Magnussen, L. I. (2021). Risk and safety management in physical education: A study of teachers' practice perspectives. *Frontiers in Sports and Active Living, 3*, 663676.

Porter, T. M. (1995). *Trust in numbers: The pursuit of objectivity in science and public life*. Princeton University Press.

Pothast, U. (1993). Lebendige Vernünftigkeit als philosophischer Gegenstand. In M. Großheim (Ed.), *Rehabilitierung des Subjektiven. Festschrift für Hermann Schmitz* (pp. 3–23).

Pothast, U. (2009). Lebendige Vernünftigkeit. Exposition eines philosophischen Konzepts. *Rostocker Phänomenologische Manuskripte, 4*.

Power, M. (2004). Counting, control and calculation: Reflections on measuring and management. *Human Relations, 57*(6), 765–783.

Putnam, R. D. (1993). *Making democracy work. Civic traditions in modern Italy*. Princeton University Press.

Putnam, R. D. (2000). *Bowling alone: The collapse and revival of American community*. Simon Schuster.

Qiu, J. (2024). Assembled knowledges and situated choices: Women's understandings and practices concerning childbirth risks in urban China. *Health, Risk & Society, 26*(7–8), 334–349.

Reber, A. (1995). *Implicit learning and tacit knowledge: An essay on the cognitive unconscious*. Oxford University Press.

Renn, O. (1992). In S. Krimsky & D. Golding (Eds.), *Concepts of risk: A classification* (pp. 53–79). Praeger.

Renn, O. (2008). *Risk governance. Coping with uncertainty in a complex world*. Earthscan.

Renn, O., & Levine, D. (1991). Credibility and trust in risk communication. In R. E. Kasperson & P. J. M. Stallen (Eds.), *Communicating risks to the public* (pp. 175–217). Kluwer.

Reuter, S. Z. (2018). The anatomy of uncertainty: A critical interpretative phenomenological analysis of childless academic women's reproductive decision-making. *Women's Studies International Forum, 70*, 109–117.

Reynolds, B., Seeger, W., & M. (2005). Crisis and emergency risk communication as an integrative model. *Journal of Health Communication, 10*(1), 43–55.

Ritzer, G. (2005). *Enchanting a disenchanted world* (2nd ed.). Pine Forge Press.

Ritzer, G. (2013). *The McDonaldization of society*. Sage.

Rogers, J. (2015). *Eagle*. Reaktion Books.

Rohrmann, B., & Renn, O. (2000). In O. Renn & B. Rohrmann (Eds.), *Risk perception research. An introduction* (pp. 11–53). Kluwer.

Rosa, E. A., Renn, O., & McCright, A. M. (2014). *The risk society revisited*. Temple University Press.

Rosa, H. (2013). *Social acceleration: A new theory of modernity*. De Gruyter.

Rosa, H. (2019). *Resonance: A sociology of our relationship to the world*. Polity Press.

Rosenau, P. M. (1992). *Post-modernism adn the social science: Insights, inroads, and intrusions*. Princeton University Press.

Rosenthal, D., Gifford, S., & Moore, S. (1998). Safe sex or safe love: Competing discourses? *AIDS Care, 10*(1), 35–47. https://doi.org/10.1080/09540129850124569

Roth, S. (2015a). Aid work as edgework—Voluntary risk-taking and security in humanitarian assistance, development and human rights work. *Journal of Risk Research, 18*(2), 139–155. https://doi.org/10.1080/13669877.2013.875934

Roth, S. (2015b). *The paradoxes of aid work. Passionate professionals*. Routledge.

Roy, E. A. (2020a). New Zealand health minister David Clark quits over handling of COVID-19 outbreak. *The Guardian*. Retrieved July 2, 2020, from www.theguardian.com/world/2020/jul/02/new-zealand-health-minister-david-clark-quits-over-handling-of-COVID-19-outbreak

Roy, E. A. (2020b). New Zealand health minister demoted after beach visit broke lockdown rules. *The Guardian*. Retrieved April 7, 2020, from www.theguardian.com/world/2020/apr/07/new-zealand-health-minister-demoted-after-beach-visit-broke-lockdown-rules

Royal Commission of Inquiry into COVID-19 Lessons Learned. (2024). *Phase one report: Insights into Aotearoa New Zealand's COVID-19 response*. Department of Internal Affairs. Retrived September 3, 2025, from https://covid19inquiry.nz

Rückversicherung, B. (Ed.). (1987). *Gesellschaft und Unsicherheit*. Verlag für Versicherungswirtschaft.

Rudski, J. M., & Edwards, A. (2007). Malinowski goes to college: Factors influencing students' use of ritual and superstition. *The Journal of General Psychology, 134*(4), 389–403. https://doi.org/10.3200/GENP.134.4.389-404

Ruston, A., & Clayton, J. (2002). Coronary heart disease: Women's assessment of risk-a qualitative study. *Health, Risk & Society, 4*(2), 125–137.

Said, E. W. (1978). *Orientalism*. Pantheon Books.

Salamon, G. (2018). What's critical about critical phenomenology? *Puncta, 1*(1), 8–17.

Sandy, M., & Milhorance, F. (2020). Brazil's president still insists the Coronavirus is vverblown. These governors are fighting back. *Time Magazine* (April 6). https://time.com/5816243/brazil-jair-bolsonaro-coronavirus-governors/

Sanne, J. M. (2008). Framing risks in a safety-critical and hazardous job: Risk-taking as responsibility in railway maintenance. *Journal of Risk Research, 11*(5), 645–658. https://doi.org/10.1080/13669870701715550

Sawyer, A.-M., Green, D., Moran, A., & Brett, J. (2009). Should the nurse change the light globe?: Human service professionals managing risk on the frontline. *Journal of Sociology, 45*(4), 361–381. https://doi.org/10.1177/1440783309346478

Scamell, M., & Stewart, M. (2014). Time, risk and midwife practice: The vaginal examination. *Health, Risk & Society, 16*(1), 84–100. https://doi.org/10.1080/13698575.2013.874549

Schmidt, S. (2009). Shall we really do it again? The powerful concept of replication is neglected in the social sciences. *Review of General Psychology, 13*(2), 90–100. https://doi.org/10.1037/a0015108

Schmitz, H. (1980). *Neue Phänomenologie*. Bouvier Verlag.

Schmitz, H. (1992). Die entfremdete Subjektivität von Fichte zu Hegel. philpapers.org

Schmitz, H. (1994). *Neue Grundlagen der Erkenntnistheorie*. Bouvier.

Schmitz, H. (1995). *Der Leib, der Raum und die Gefühle*. Aisthesis.

Schmitz, H. (1996). *Husserl und Heidegger*. Bouvier.

Schmitz, H. (2002). Hermann Schmitz, the "New Phenomenology". *Phenomenology world-wide*. https://doi.org/10.1007/978-94-007-0473-2_52

Schmitz, H. (2003). *Was ist Neue Phänomenologie?* Bouvier.

Schmitz, H. (2005). *Situationen und Konstellationen: Wider die Ideologie totaler Vernetzung*. Verlag Karl Alber.

Schmitz, H. (2007). *Der unerschöpfliche Gegenstand. Grundzüge der Philosophie* (3rd ed.). Bouvier Verlag.
Schmitz, H. (2010a). *Bewusstsein*. Verlag Karl Alber.
Schmitz, H. (2010b). *Jenseits des Naturalismus*. Verlag Karl Alber.
Schmitz, H. (2011). *Der Leib. Ein Überblickswerk*. De Gruyter.
Schmitz, H. (2016). *Ausgrabungen zum wirklichen Leben. Eine Bilanz*. Karl Alber.
Schmitz, H. (2017a). The felt body and embodied communication. *Yearbook for eastern and western philosophy*. https://doi.org/10.1515/yewph-2017-0004
Schmitz, H. (2017b). *Zur Epigenese der Person*. Verlag Karl Alber.
Schmitz, H. (2018a). *Wozu philosophieren?* Karl Alber.
Schmitz, H. (2018b). The felt body and embodied communication *yearbook for eastern and Western. Philosophy, 2017*(2), 9–19. https://doi.org/10.1515/yewph-2017-0004
Schmitz, H. (2019a). *New phenomenology: A brief introduction*. Mimesis International.
Schmitz, H. (2019b). *System der Philosophie (10 Bände)*. Karl Alber Verlag.
Schmitz, H., Müllan, R. O., & Slaby, J. (2011). Emotions outside the box-the new phenomenology of feeling and corporeality. *Phenomenology and the Cognitive Science, 10*, 241–259. https://doi.org/10.1007/s11097-011-9195-1
Schulz, M. (2016). *Die Privatisierung der Zukunft—Zur Genese finanzmarktinduzierter Herrschaftsverhältnisse*. AVM.
Schulz, M. (2020). Haben Beatmungsgeräte einen Grenznutzen? Auf dem Weg zu einer neophänomenologischen Definition existenzieller Güter. *Zeitschrift für Praktische Philosophie, 7*(2), 253–278.
Schulz, M. (2024). Existenz und Gesellschaft. In *Eine leibphänomenologische Vergesellschaftungstheorie nach Georg Simmel und Hermann Schmitz*. Transcript.
Schulz, M., & Zinn, J. O. (2023). Rationales of risk and uncertainty and their epistemological foundation by new phenomenology. *Journal of Risk Research, 26*(3), 219–232. https://doi.org/10.1080/13669877.2022.2162105
Schütz, A. (1943). The problem of rationality in the social world. *Economica, 10*(38), 130–149.
Schütz, A. (1970). *Reflections on the problem of relevance*. Yale University Press.
Schütz, A. (1972). *The phenomenology of the social world* (G. Walsh & F. Lehnert, Trans.). Heinemann Educational.

Schütz, A. (1981). *Theorie der Lebensformen (frühe Manuskripte aus der Bergson-Periode)* (Vol. 350, 1. Aufl. ed.). Suhrkamp.
Schütz, A. (2013). *Life forms and meaning structure*. Routledge.
Schütz, A., & Luckmann, T. (1973). *The structures of the life-world* (Vol. 1) (R. M. Zaner & H. T. Engelhardt Jr., Trans.). Northwestern University Press.
Schütz, A., & Luckmann, T. (1989). *The structures of the life-world* (Vol. 2) (R. M. Zaner & D. J. Parent, Trans.). Northwestern University Press.
See, J., Cuaton, G. P., Webber, S., Opdyke, A., & Peja, P. J. (2025). Building resilience or reinforcing vulnerability? The enduring allure of hard infrastructure as adaptation. *Environment and Planning E: Nature and Space, 8*(5), 1789–1811.
Seligman, A. B. (2000). *The problem of trust*. Princeton University Press.
Shearman, K., Masters, A., Nutt, D., Bowman, S., & Draper, H. (2022). Acceptability of donor funding for clinical trials in the UK: A qualitative empirical ethics study using focus groups to elicit the views of research patient public involvement group members, research ethics committee chairs and clinical researchers. *BMJ Open, 12*(6), e055208.
Shum, M., Sun, W., & Ye, G. (2014). Superstition and "lucky" apartments: Evidence from transaction-level data. *Journal of Comparative Economics, 42*(1), 109–117. https://doi.org/10.1016/j.jce.2013.10.001
Sibley, C. G., Greaves, L. M., Satherley, N., Wilson, M. S., Overall, N. C., Lee, C. H. J.,... & Barlow, F. K. (2020). Effects of the COVID-19 pandemic and nationwide lockdown on trust, attitudes toward government, and well-being. *American Psychologist, 75*, 618–630. https://doi.org/10.1037/amp0000662
Siegrist, M. (2021). Trust and risk perception: A critical review of the literature. *Risk Analysis, 41*(3), 480–490. https://doi.org/10.1111/risa.13325
Simmel, G. (1900). *Philosophie des Geldes*. Duncker & Humblot.
Simmel, G. (1978). *The philosophy of money*. Routledge.
Simon, H. A. (1982). *Models of bounded rationality*. MIT Press.
Slovic, P. (1999). Trust, emotion, sex, politics, and science: Surveying the risk-assessment battlefield. *Risk Analysis, 19*(4), 689–701.
Slovic, P. (2000). *The perception of risk* (R. S. Revied by Cass Ed.). Earthscan Publications Ltd.
Slovic, P., Finucane, M. L., Peters, E., & MacGregor, D. G. (2002). *Risk as analysis and risk as feelings. Some thoughts about affect, reason, risk, and rationality*. Routledge.
Smith, L. T. (1999). *Decolonizing methodologies: Research and indigenous peoples*. Zed Books.

Snyder, C. R., Irving, L. M., & Anderson, J. R. (1991). Hope and health. In C. R. Snyder & D. R. Forsyth (Eds.), *Handbook of social and clinical psychology: The health perspective* (pp. 285–305). Pergamon Press.

Srivastava, R. (2023, November 21). My young cancer patient revused all treatment. After her death I found out why. *The Guardian* .

Stäheli, U. (2007). *Spektakuläre Spekulation: Das Populäre der Ökonomie* (Vol. 1). Suhrkamp.

Starr, C. (1969). Social benefit versus technological risk. In *What is our society willing to pay for safety?, 165*, 1232–1238.

Steinberg, L. (2004). Risk taking in adolescence: What changes, and why? *Annals of the New York Academy of Sciences, 1021*(1), 51–58. https://doi.org/10.1196/annals.1308.005

Steinberg, L. (2007). Risk taking in adolescence: New perspectives from brain and behavioral science. *Current Directions in Psychological Science.* https://doi.org/10.1111/j.1467-8721.2007.00475.x

Stevens, A. (2020). Governments cannot just 'follow the science' on COVID-19. *Nature Human Behaviour, 4*(6), 560–560. https://doi.org/10.1038/s41562-020-0894-x

Stolz, J. (2020). Secularization theories in the twenty-first century: Ideas, evidence, and problems. *Social Compass, 6*(2), 282–308. https://doi.org/10.1177/0037768620917320

Stouffer, S. A., Lumsdaine, A. A., Lumnsdaine, M. H., Williams, R. M., Smith, M. B., Janis, I. L.,... & Cottrell, L. S. (1949). *The American soldier: Combat and its aftermath* (Vol. II). Princeton University Press.

Strydom, P. (2002). *Risk, environment and society: Ongoing debates, current issues and future prospects.* Open University Press.

Swaine, J. (2018, September 6). Trump inauguration crowd photos were edited after he intervened. *The Guardian* . https://www.theguardian.com/world/2018/sep/06/donald-trump-inauguration-crowd-size-photos-edited

Talmont-Kaminski, K. (2013). *Religion as magical ideology. How the supernatural reflects rationality.* Routledge/Taylor and Francis.

Taylor, C. (2007). *A Secular Age.* Harvard University Press.

Te Hiringa Mahara—Mental Health and Wellbeing Commission (2023). Māori responses to COVID-19 are exemplars for crisis health and wellbeing support. *Te Hiringa Mahara.* Retrived September 3, 2025, from https://www.mhwc.govt.nz/news-and-resources/maori-responses-to-COVID-19-are-exemplars-for-crisis-health-and-wellbeing-support/

Thaler, R. H. (2016). Behavioral economics: Past, present, and future. *American Economic Review, 106*(7), 1577–1600. https://doi.org/10.1257/aer.106.7.1577

Thanos, I. C. (2023). The complementary effects of rationality and intuition on strategic decision quality. *European Management Journal, 41*(3), 366–374. https://doi.org/10.1016/j.emj.2022.03.003

Thomas, W. I., & Thomas, D. S. (1970). The child in America: Behavior problems and programs (Johnson Reprint ed.). *Johnson Reprint Corporation.* (Orig. pub. 1928 by A. A. Knopf).

Thompson, E. P. (1963). *The making of the english working class.* V. Gollancz.

Thompson, M. (2008). *Organising & Disorganising. A dynamic and non-linear theory of institutional emergence and its implications.* Triarcy Press.

Toner, J. (2024). *Risk in the Roman world.* Cambridge University Press.

Turner, B. A. (1978). *Man-made disasters* (Vol. 53). Wykeham Publications (London).

Turner, B. A., & Pidgeon, N. F. (1997). *Man-Made Disasters.* Heinemann.

Tversky, A., & Kahneman, D. (1974). Judgement under uncertainty: Heuristics and biases. *Science, 185*, 1127–1131.

Tversky, A., & Kahneman, D. (1987). Rational choice and the framing of decisions. In R. Hogarth & M. Reder (Eds.), *Rational choice: The contrast beween economics and psychology* (pp. 67–84). University of Chicago Press.

Tversky, A., & Kahneman, D. (1988). Rational choice and the framing of decisions. In D. E. Bell, H. Raiffa, & A. Tversky (Eds.), *Decision making. Decriptive, normative and prescriptive interactions* (pp. 167–192). Cambridge University Press.

U.S. Bureau of Labor Statistics. (2017). *National census of fatal occupational injuries in 2016.* https://www.bls.gov/news.release/pdf/cfoi.pdf

Van den Brink, N., Holbrechts, B., Brand, P. L. P., Stolper, E. C. F., & Van Royen, P. (2019). Role of intuitive knowledge in the diagnostic reasoning of hospital specialists: A focus group study. *BMJ Open, 9*(1), e022724. https://doi.org/10.1136/bmjopen-2018-022724

van der Molen, M., & Brown, P. (2021). Following Dutch healthcare professionals' experiences during COVID-19: Tensions in everyday practices and policies amid shifting uncertainties. *Current Sociology, 69*(4), 453–470.

Vargas, R. A. (2024). Malaria drug Trump touted as Covid cure increased chance of death—study. *The Guardian* online, (12 Jan). Retrieved from https://www.theguardian.com/world/2024/jan/12/hydroxychloroquine-covid-increase-chance-death-trump

Vaughan, D. (1996). *The challenger launch decision: Risky technology, culture, and deviance at NASA*. University of Chicago Press.

Velanovich, V. (2023). Rationality, reasoning, logic, argumentation and intuition: The bases of medical assessments and decisions. In V. Velanovich (Ed.), *Medical persuasion* (pp. 11–44). Springer.

Vickerstaff, S., Loretto, W., Billings, J. R., Brown, P. R., Mitton, L., Parkin, T., & White, P. (2008). Encouraging labour market activity among 60–64 year olds. In *Research report: Department of work and pensions*.DWP.

Vogl, J. (2014). *The specter of capital*. Stanford University Press.

Vyse, S. (1997). *Magical thinking: The psychology of superstition*. Oxford University Press.

Vyse, S. (2020). *Superstition: A very short introduction*. Oxford University Press.

Wacquant, L. D. (1996). Die Unschärfenlogik des praktischen Sinns. In P. B. Wacquant & D. Loic (Eds.), *Reflexive anthropologie*. Suhrkamp.

Walby, K., & Spencer, D. C. (2018). Tree planting as neo-tribalism: Ritual, risk boundaries, and group effervescence. *Emotion, Space and Society, 28*, 60–66. https://doi.org/10.1016/j.emospa.2018.06.006

Walls, J., Pidgeon, N., Weyman, A., & Horlick-Jones, T. (2004). Critical trust: Understanding lay perceptions of health and safety risk regulation. *Health, Risk & Society, 6*(2), 133–150.

Wardle, H., Keily, R., Astbury, G., & Reith, G. (2014). 'Risky places?': Mapping gambling machine density and socio-economic deprivation. *Journal of Gambling Studies, 30*(1), 201–212. https://doi.org/10.1007/s10899-012-9349-2

Weber, M. (1930). *The Protestant ethic and the spirit of*. G. Allen & Unwin, ltd.

Weber, M. (1948). In H. H. M. C. W. Gerth (Ed.), *Science as a vocation* (pp. 129–156). Routledge & Kegan Paul Ltd.

Weber, M. (1978). *Economy and society*.

Weber, M. (1980). *Wirtschaft und Gesellschaft: Grundriss der verstehenden Soziologie* (5th ed.). Mohr.

Weber, M., Parsons, T., & Tawney, R. H. (1930). *The Protestant ethic and the spirit of*. G. Allen & Unwin, Ltd.

Wendt, A. N. (2015). Empirisch ernüchterte Phänomenologie des Leibes—über die Fissur in der phänomenologischen Psychologie. *Psychologie und Gesellschaftskritik, 39*(4), 97–113.

Wigginton, B., & Lafrance, M. N. (2014). 'I think he is immune to all the smoke I gave him': How women account for the harm of smoking during pregnancy. *Health, Risk & Society, 16*(6), 530–546. https://doi.org/10.1080/13698575.2014.951317

Wildavsky, A. B. (1988). *Searching for safety*. Transaction Books.

Wildavsky, A. B. (1989). The secret of safety lies in danger. *Society, 27*(1), 4–5. https://doi.org/10.1007/BF02695442

Wilkinson, I. M. (2005). *Suffering: A sociological introduction*. Polity Press.

Wilson, S., Rixon, A., & Brown, C. (2023). Non-clinical intuitions and adaptive heuristics in emergency care: A scoping review. *International Emergency Nursing, 71*, 101371. https://doi.org/10.1016/j.ienj.2023.101371

Wilson, W. (1942). Miners' superstitions. *Life and Letters Today, 32*, 86–93.

Wohlrab-Sahr, M. (1999). Conversion to Islam: Between syncretism and symbolic battle. *Social Compass, 46*(3), 351–362. https://doi.org/10.1177/003776899046003010

Wohlrab-Sahr, M., & Burchardt, M. (2012). Multiple secularities: Toward a cultural sociology of secular modernities. *Comparative Sociology, 11*(6), 875–909. https://doi.org/10.1163/15691330-12341249

Wright, A. L., Sonin, K., Driscoll, J., & Wilson, J. (2020). Poverty and economic dislocation reduce compliance with COVID-19 shelter-in-place protocols. *Journal of Economic Behavior and Organization, 180*, 544–554. https://doi.org/10.1016/j.jebo.2020.10.008

Wynne, B. (1982a). In H. C. Kunreuther & E. V. Ley (Eds.), *Institutional mythologies and dual societies in the management of risk* (pp. 127–143). Springer.

Wynne, B. (1982b). *Rationality and ritual: The windscale inquiry and nuclear decisions in Britain*. British Society for the History of Science.

Wynne, B. (1989). In J. Brown (Ed.), *Frameworks of rationality in risk management: Towards the testing of naive sociology* (pp. 33–47). Belhaven Press.

Wynne, B. (1992). In S. Krimsky & D. Golding (Eds.), *Risk and social learning: Reification to engagement*. Praeger.

Wynne, B. (1996). May the sheep safely graze? A reflexive view of the expert-lay knowledge divide. In S. Lash, B. Szerszynski, & B. Wynne (Eds.), *Risk, environment and modernity: Towards a new ecology* (pp. 44–83). Sage.

Yıldırım, M., & Arslan, G. (2020). Exploring the associations between resilience, dispositional hope, preventive behaviours, subjective well-being, and psychological health among adults during early stage of COVID-19. *Current Psychology*. https://doi.org/10.1007/s12144-020-01177-2

Zaloom, C. (2006). *Out of the pits: Traders and technology from Chicago to London*. University of Chicago Press.

Zega, N. (2021). Behind NZ'S COVID response. *Otago Magazin, 53*, 10–15.

Zigon, J. (2009). Hope dies last: Two aspects of hope in contemporary Moscow. *Anthropological Theory, 9*(3), 253–271. https://doi.org/10.1177/1463499609346986

Zinn, J. O. (2001). *Zwischen Gestaltungsanspruch und Strukturvorgaben: junge Fachkräfte in den ersten Berufsjahren: Erwerbsverläufe, Handlungskontexte und biographische Gestaltungsmodi* (1st ed.). Nomos.

Zinn, J. O. (2004). Health, risk and uncertainty in the life course: A typology of biographical certainty constructions. *Social Theory & Health, 2*, 199–221.

Zinn, J. O. (2008a). Heading into the unknown: Everyday strategies for managing risk and uncertainty. *Health, Risk & Society, 10*(5), 439–450. https://doi.org/10.1080/13698570802380891

Zinn, J. O. (2008b). *Social theories of risk and uncertainty. An introduction.* Blackwell Publishing.

Zinn, J. O. (2010). The biographical management of risk and uncertainty—British veterans. *Forum Qualitative Sozialforschung/Forum: Qualitative Social Research, 11*(1, Art. 10), 116 paragraphs, http://nbn-resolving.de/urn:nbn:de:0114-fqs1001102

Zinn, J. O. (2011). The biographical management of risk and uncertainty—British veterans. *Historical Social Research/Historische Sozialforschung, 36*(3), 237–269. https://doi.org/10.12759/hsr.36.2011.3.237-269

Zinn, J. O. (2012). Soldiers, work and emotions—Perspectives from the sociology of risk and uncertainty. In TASA (Ed.), *Emerging and Enduring Inequalities: The Australian Sociological Association* (conference proceedings).

Zinn, J. O. (2016). 'In-between' and other reasonable ways to deal with risk and uncertainty: A review article. *Health, Risk & Society, 18*(7–8), 348–366. https://doi.org/10.1080/13698575.2016.1269879

Zinn, J. O. (2020). *Understanding risk-taking*. Palgrave Macmillan.

Zinn, J. O. (2024). Risk-taking and social inequality. *Journal of Sociology, 60*(2), 364–381. https://doi.org/10.1177/14407833231162865

Zinn, J. O., & Schulz, M. (2024). Rationalization, enchantment, and subjectivation—Lessons for risk communication from a new phenomenology of everyday reasoning. *Journal of Risk Research, 27*(2), 295–312. https://doi.org/10.1080/13669877.2024.2328195

# Index







J. O. Zinn and M. Schulz, *A New Phenomenology of Risk and Uncertainty*, Critical Studies in Risk and Uncertainty, https://doi.org/10.1007/978-981-95-7405-6

The manufacturer's authorised representative in the EU is Springer Nature Customer Service Centre GmbH, Europaplatz 3, 69115 Heidelberg, Germany. If you have any concerns regarding our products, please contact ProductSafety@springernature.com

Printed and bound by CPI Group (UK) Ltd, Croydon, CR0 4YY

21/09/2026

02219963-0003